Eurocommunism

Recent Titles in
Contributions in Political Science
Series Editor: Bernard K. Johnpoll

Eurocommunism
The Ideological and Political-Theoretical Foundations

Edited by George Schwab

CONTRIBUTIONS IN POLITICAL SCIENCE, NUMBER 60

Greenwood Press

WESTPORT, CONNECTICUT

Library of Congress Cataloging in Publication Data

Cuny Conference on History and Politics, 3d, 1978.
  Eurocommunism, the ideological and political-
theoretical foundations.

  (Contributions in political science ; no. 60
ISSN 0147-1066)
  Includes bibliographical references and index.
  1. Communism—Europe. 2. Communist parties—
Europe. I. Schwab, George. II. Title. III. Series.
HX238.5.C86 1978   335.43'094   80-26864
ISBN 0-313-22908-2 (lib. bdg.)

Library of Congress Catalog Card Number: 80-26864
ISBN: 0-313-22908-2
ISSN: 0147-1066

First published in 1981

Greenwood Press
A division of Congressional Information Service, Inc.
88 Post Road West, Westport, Connecticut 06881

Printed in the United States of America

10 9 8 7 6 5 4 3 2 1

In Memory of
Peter Christian Ludz
Honored Colleague, Delightful Friend

CONTENTS

viii
Contents

G. L. Ulmen

IN MEMORIAM, PETER CHRISTIAN LUDZ

Peter C. Ludz was a divided man in a divided world, and his search for an understanding and a reconciliation of these divisions give both structure and meaning to his life and work. He was, in a sense that perhaps only a German can be, a representative postwar intellectual. Not only was the postwar partition of the world between West and East the most visible and sharpest in Berlin and Germany, but the German attempt to make a complete break with the past mirrored the rootlessness felt by many intellectuals in the West after the physical and spiritual debacle of the war and the rapid socio-economic, sociotechnological, and sociopolitical transformations that it had wrought.

*This tribute was originally published in a shorter version as a "Foreword and Farewell" to Ludz's article "Hauser and Lukács," a translation of his epilogue to Arnold Hauser, *Im Gespräch mit Georg Lukács* (Munich, 1978), in *Telos* no. 41, Fall 1979.

Nazism had destroyed the old Germany. Communism had divided the new Germany. Moreover, even though these ideologies pursued to their logical conclusions would spell the end of politics, they nevertheless embodied specific political theories and practices that had far-reaching consequences for the structure of economy and society and the role of ideas and intellectuals. As a student in postwar West Berlin, Ludz interested himself in ideology and politics. At the Free University, he embraced the democratic political ideas of Americanism, which had no ideology, and at the same time found in "Western" Marxism an ideology that might overcome the gross perversion of socialism—that is, communism—that he rejected. Americanism without imperialism, Marxism without communism: These were the two wide avenues that Ludz traveled throughout his life. His attempt to straddle them was first evident in his doctoral dissertation, "The Ideological Conception of the Young Marx and Its Further Development in the Thought of Georg Lukács and Karl Mannheim" (1955).

In his student and early teaching years, Ludz concentrated his seemingly insatiable intellectual curiosity and indefatigable energy on the connections between ideology, social structure, and aesthetic theory. As Georg Lukács, in spite of his *partiinost* and occasional subservience to Soviet ideology, was the leading thinker of "Western Marxism," Ludz undertook a study of Lukács' life and work and edited two representative volumes of Lukács' writings, *Schriften zur Literatursoziologie* (1961) and *Schriften zur Ideologie und Politik* (1967), to which he wrote introductory monographs: "Marxism and Literature: A Critical Introduction to the Work of Georg Lukács" and "The Concept of 'Democratic Dictatorship' in the Political Philosophy of Georg Lukács." All the later contributions to political sociology and social science that Ludz was to make grew out of his early intellectual concerns.

For Ludz, man is not only a social and political animal; he

is also a spiritual animal, whose aesthetic dimension is at least as important as the social and political. Although, for the most part, he wrote sociological and political treatises because these spoke more directly to the present, he was intimately concerned with the more profound and important problem of the precarious situation of man as a spiritual *(geistige)* being in the postwar world. In the end, he had found no certain answer; but his search manifested itself in a wealth and variety of endeavors that are his epitaph.

Born in Stettin, Pomerania, on May 22, 1931, Ludz attended elementary and high school in Berlin and Ingolstadt (Bavaria) and in 1949 made his *Abitur* at the Humanistische Gymnasium in Berlin-Zehlendorf. From 1949 to 1956 he was educated at the universities of Mainz, Munich, Berlin, and the Sorbonne, where he studied economics, philosophy, sociology, and political science. Between 1957 and 1969 he held various positions at the Free University of Berlin, where he became professor of political science in 1967. At the same institution, he was head of the Department of East German and East European Affairs in the Research Institute for Political Science from 1960 to 1969. From 1970 to 1973 he was professor of political science and sociology at the newly-founded University of Bielefeld, and from 1973 until his death, he was professor of political science at the Geschwister-Scholl-Institut für Politische Wissenschaft at the University of Munich.

From 1968 on Ludz was guest lecturer or visiting professor at various universities outside the Federal Republic of Germany: at the University of Santiago de Chile, Harvard University, Columbia University (where he was also a senior fellow at the Research Institute on Communist Affairs), the New School for Social Research (where he was Theodor Heuss Professor at the Graduate Faculty), at several other universities in the United States, Canada, Japan, Yugoslavia, and Denmark. In 1976 Ludz was elected a member of the program committee for the XI World Congress of the International Political Science Association held in Moscow in August 1979.

Indeed, Ludz's professional activities went far beyond the academic world: He was a member of the board and director of studies of the government-sponsored Stiftung Wissenschaft und Politik in Ebenhausen (1975-1979); a member of the advisory commission to the Senate of West Berlin and co-author of the commission's report, *Studien zur Lage und Entwicklung West-Berlins* (1969); director of studies and co-author of the three volume *Materialien zum Bericht zur Lage der Nation* (1971, 1972, and 1974), published by the Ministry of Inner-German Affairs of the Federal Republic of Germany; and acting chairman of the Arbeitskreis für vergleichende Deutschlandforschung (1975-1978). During the last years of his life, Ludz's scholarly interests had begun again to prevail over his political and consulting commitments. The most obvious manifestation of this development was his advancement to the position of coeditor (together with René Koenig and Friedhelm Neidhardt) of the *Kölner Zeitschrift für Soziologie und Sozialpsychologie,* for which in earlier years he had edited two ground-breaking special issues: *Studien und Materialien zur Soziologie der DDR* (1964) and *Soziologie und Sozialgeschichte* (1972).

Throughout the world Peter Ludz was known as a specialist on East German and communist affairs—the primary subject of his more than 200 books, articles, and reviews. But even in these writings, and particularly in his classic 1968 study of the Communist party elite in East Germany, *Partei-elite im Wandel, Funktionsaufbau, Sozialstruktur und Ideologie der SED-Führung. Eine empirisch-systematische Untersuchung,* he forged a highly original methodological approach. In the introduction to the 1972 American edition, *The Changing Party Elite in East Germany,* Zbigniew Brzezinski wrote that Ludz's "pioneering" study "was

immediately recognized as a contribution of lasting importance not only to our understanding of East German politics
but to political science and political sociology itself." Less
known in the English-speaking world is that Ludz also wrote
essays on Utopia and utopians, on Montaigne, Lemettrie,
Helvetius, Holbach, Feuerbach, Marx, alienation as a concept
in the social sciences, on secret societies in the eighteenth and
nineteenth centuries, on convergence theory, anarchy and
anarchism, the history of German sociology, Kuhn's paradigm thesis, concept analysis, and so on.

Some of Ludz's most important essays on ideology and
Marxism were published in 1976 under the title *Ideologie-
begriff und Marxistische Theorie: Ansätze zu einer
immanenten Kritik.* His stated intention reflected both his
own concerns and the present state of European social
thought. Indeed, this book testifies to the attempts of one of
Europe's leading political sociologists to assimilate the major
postwar West European and American trends in sociological
and political theory into "West European Marxism" and to
relate this complex synthesis to and contrast it with the
ideological and sociological trends in postwar East European
and Soviet Marxism. In this book Ludz systematically explored, from a "metatheoretical" standpoint, certain perspectives derived from the sociology of knowledge and the critique of ideology and linked them with a historically- and
sociologically-oriented functionalism. He sought to place the
thesis of the historicosociological conditioning of theoretical
constructs on a more precise basis than prior formulations of
the sociology of knowledge and to lay concrete foundations
for historical convergences through positive research. From
this standpoint, he sought to bridge the gap between norma-
tive-prescriptive and empirical-descriptive research methods
in the social sciences.

Ludz considered these collected essays "material" for a
"metatheory" of ideology—"metatheory" understood as "the

systematic theoretical joining of the epistemological and categorical levels of the concept of ideology as well as their conversion into research programs. They were prolegomena for three planned projects: (1) a comparative study of "political secret societies" in terms of the relations between ideology, Utopia, and organization; (2) an analysis of "European Marxism" and those facets and nuances that converge toward and overlap the Marxian and post-Marxian theories of ideology in the light of East-West conflicts, the perspective of political science, and the critique of ideology; (3) the systematic consideration of aesthetics and politics, that is, an essay-like study on *Politische Theorie und Ästhetik.*

Ludz succeeded in editing and contributing to a volume on secret societies, *Geheime Gesellschaften* (1979), but his interests were also turning in a different direction—away from ideology and Marxism, in fact away from Germany and Europe—to America. With a grant from the Volkswagenwerk Foundation, in 1975 he began a project on "Political Theories in the United States" that was to encompass all the rapidly-developing trends. Preliminary work took many years, and no part of the American project was completed; but the all-encompassing conception and the collection of theoretical and empirical materials that he amassed laid a foundation that no German or European can ignore because Ludz looked to the future. It was his understanding, expressed again and again in lectures and talks, that the major developments in the social sciences were taking place in the English-speaking world and particularly in the United States.

Yet Ludz's intimate involvement with European intellectual and political life past and present continued to weigh heavily on him and found expression in other endeavors, such as writing an afterword to Arnold Hauser's *Im Gespräch mit Georg Lukács* (1978). This essay stemmed from Ludz's introduction to and conversations with Lukács' political and aesthetic antipode in the German language shortly before

Hauser's death in 1978. The published dialogue between Hauser in London and Lukács in Budapest, like an intellectual tightrope stretched across the face of Europe and the years separating the spiritual unity of their youth and the political alienation of their old age, ending with Hauser's essay on variations in Lukács' search for the *tertium datur,* and in between Hauser's discussions of the struggle against "mechanistic positivism and materialism," of the ethical impulse and problem, of Marxism as a theory of social science and history, the concept of structure, the dominant influence of sociology, the *freischwebenden Intellektuellen* (above all, Lukács, Mannheim, "the Frankfurt School," et al.), the relation of the individual to society, and the communication problem of aesthetics in an age of aggressive alienation, it is a kind of existential metaphor of the spiritual odyssey of the West in the twentieth century. Because of Ludz's strong affinity with the times and personalities of prewar and postwar Europe and his understanding of the intellectual and political issues involved, he succeeded in conveying that feeling of spiritual isolation and in indicating those political and aesthetic issues that gave form to the substance of thought and action of both Hauser and Lukács and gives form to our own.

Early in 1979, with an agenda of promised manuscripts to complete for several journals and institutions in Europe and the United States, Ludz, possessed with a new idea, put all aside to write *Mechanismen der Herrschaftssicherung. Eine sprachpolitische Analyse gesellschaftlichen Wandels in der DDR,* a book he completed in less than six months.* Returning to that manifest and multifaceted problem that had shaped his life and work—the division of Germany—he succeeded in synthesizing his wide-ranging knowledge and

*Scheduled for publication in spring 1980 by Carl Hanser Verlag, Munich.

bringing it to bear on the most fundamental problems of the postwar world.

The book can be read on several levels. On the most immediate level, it is a study of the possibilities for innovation, modernization, and change in East Germany and addresses itself to these possibilities in general in our time. In the foreword, he explained its relation to his earlier research: "As a sociologist and political scientist who has been engaged in research on the GDR and in comparative studies of the two Germanies and who was also in a position to apprehend the political dimension of his field of study, this author feels almost duty-bound to write a few words about the political and scientific aspects of this book. Since the early sixties, when I began to publish about the GDR, I have attempted to examine realistically this society and its characteristic features. Analyses in science, and particularly in the social sciences, should reveal what exists; they should seek to explain why things that exist are such and not otherwise; they should offer interpretative models that are plausible."

On another level, and with specific reference to Edward Sapir's concept that the texture of "cultural patterns" of a civilization can be detected by studying the language in which the civilization articulates itself, Ludz's book proceeds on the basis that the comprehension of these mechanisms of language facilitates insights into the history, society, and behavioral structure of a given time. On yet another level, the book can be characterized as an experiment in interdisciplinary methodology—drawing on the sociology of knowledge, the sociology of science, the critique of ideology, *Weltanschauung* analysis, historical semantics and language analysis, metaphor tests and citation tables, and, not least, the phenomenological-historical interpretation of texts that is the legacy of a specific German form of macrosociological analysis. Beyond methodology, it is concerned with the linguistic and political role of metaphors, analogies, tautologies, and "empty formulas"—with survey research employed to legitimize political power in a communist-ruled system.

On the personal and perhaps most important level, Ludz's last book can be read as the odyssey of a postwar intellectual, in particular, a German intellectual attempting to come to grips with the existential divisions of our time by drawing on all the means at his disposal. He dedicated his book "to the dreams on which our lives depend [*den Träumen, an denen wir hängen*]." This motto had less to do with the work than with its author. On September 2, 1979, in a forest near Feldafing, Germany, where he made his home, Peter Christian Ludz gave up his life. Reality could not sustain him; the dreams were not enough.

G. L. Ulmen

Berlin/Feldafing
October 3, 1979

PREFACE

The delay in the appearance of the proceedings of the third CUNY Conference on History and Politics that was held on October 5, 6, and 7, 1978, at the Graduate Center of the City University of New York was occasioned by the untimely death of Professor Peter Christian Ludz. Because of his genuine commitment to his colleagues, to the topic—"Eurocommunism: The Ideological and Political-Theoretical Foundations"—and to the Graduate Center, I, his coeditor, resolved to continue working on the volume, with the intention of dedicating the finished work to him, my friend.

I am particularly indebted to G. L. Ulmen. In addition to completing Professor Ludz's manuscript, he always responded to my requests for advice. The alacrity with which he gave his precious time is merely a small indication of his devotion to Mrs. Ludz and to her late husband. I also wish to thank Professor Bernard Brown for his consent to write the

concluding chapter that Professor Ludz had originally intended to do.

The quality of the volume reflects the provocative and
sometimes heated discussions that the subject aroused in general and the contributions made by the following discussants
in particular: Joel Colton of the Rockefeller Foundation,
Lewis J. Edinger of Columbia University, Feliks Gross of the
Graduate Center, and Robert Legvold of the Council on
Foreign Relations.

Acknowledgment is due to the president of the Graduate
Center, Harold M. Proshansky, and to the provost of the
Graduate Center, Hans J. Hillerbrand. As with previous conferences, his executive assistant, Mrs. Dorothy Weber, helped
most graciously with the numerous details that are involved
in arranging a gathering of this kind. This conference is also
indebted to Max Weiner, the former dean of university and
special programs.

Irrespective of the amount of work that went into organizing the three-day scholarly exchange, there would have
been no gathering had it not been for the generous support
we received in particular from the *Stiftung Volkswagenwerk,*
the Center for European Studies at the Graduate Center, and
the Graduate School and University Center, CUNY.

I would finally like to thank my assistant, Miss Edwina
McMahon. Without her skilled editorial assistance this volume
could not have appeared in its present form.

George Schwab, Director
CUNY Conference on
History and Politics

George Schwab

INTRODUCTION

The third Conference on History and Politics that was held at the Graduate Center of the City University of New York focused attention on Eurocommunism. This topic was in many ways a logical sequence to the first conference that was held in 1974 and dealt with detente[1] and the second gathering that was held in 1976 and dealt with the relationship between ideology and foreign policy.[2]

As is well known, the word *Eurocommunism* is of recent vintage. It was coined to describe a phenomenon that has emerged in Western Europe. Its roots, in addition to being indigenous to Western Europe, must also be traced to developments in the Soviet camp. Of critical importance in this context were: (1) Tito's break with Stalin in 1948; (2) Khrushchev's revelations about Stalin's rule made at the twentieth congress of the Communist party of the Soviet Union in 1956; and (3) the invasion of Czechoslovakia in 1968.

Had it not been for the events of 1956 and 1968, Tito's break with Stalin would, in all likelihood, have become an anachronism. Although true that the split was not accompanied by an erosion of the cohesive relationship that had existed between the Soviet Union and the communist movements in Western Europe, the break did, however, point to the possibility of more than one road leading to socialism, a possibility that assumed crucial significance in the wake of Khrushchev's revelations.

Whereas, prior to 1956, charges of purges, forced labor camps, and the violation of individual rights in the Soviet Union did not constitute topics of serious intraparty discussions among communists in Western Europe, Khrushchev's speech in 1956, in which he confirmed that purges had taken place, that forced labor camps had existed, and that individual rights had been violated, rocked the communist movements in Western Europe and raised the so-called Russian question. If the first socialist state was unable to escape committing grievous errors and, in fact, continued to err, as evidenced by the ruthless crushing of the Hungarian uprising in the same year, the possibilities of a road to socialism other than the Soviet road and of forging a model other than the Soviet model could no longer be ruled out. Even though the communist Cuban model had not yet appeared, Yugoslavia and the People's Republic of China were concrete examples that were not overlooked by the supple Palmiro Togliatti. In the wake of Khrushchev's revelations, for example, Togliatti began to speak of a "via italiana" to socialism.

Despite the momentous events of 1956, including the Polish October, and notwithstanding Togliatti, the ideological ties of the communist parties of Western Europe to the Soviet Union still did not suffer substantively. The status quo can perhaps be explained by the fact that between the two political and military giants, West European communists perceived the Soviet Union to be progressive vis-à-vis American imperialism. In addition to applauding Soviet support of liberation movements in the third world, communists in Western Europe viewed the formation of NATO in 1949, and especially the accession to it by the Federal Republic of Germany in 1955, as a manifestation of the American imperialist policy of encircling the Soviet Union. America's gradually growing involvement in Vietnam was further proof to them of United States aggression.

Despite the drag that the aforementioned developments had on any kind of meaningful ideological separation from Moscow, the events of 1948 and especially of 1956 did produce a cumulative impact that only became evident in 1968, in the wake of the Soviet-orchestrated Warsaw-Pact invasion of Czechoslovakia.

However the phenomenon of Eurocommunism may eventually be judged, 1968 is widely regarded as a watershed. Whereas Stalinist Marxists-Leninists could explain Tito's break with Stalin as a form of right revisionism and post-Stalinist Marxists-Leninists could explain Stalin's crimes as the pathological behavior of a warped personality, the crushing of Dubček's experiment, which was highly popular in Czechoslovakia and among communists in much of Western Europe, rocked rank-and-file communists. The questions that were immediately raised included: (1) What kinds of men were leading the Soviet Union? (2) How could those leaders reconcile initiating a substantively different era in the Soviet Union with crushing an experiment that aimed at forging a socialist state based on democratic and pluralist theories in which the party would, nevertheless, have retained its leading role? (3) Is the first socialist state continuing to err? To put the last question differently: To what extent is post-Stalinist Russia really post-Stalinist?

The official explanation that issued from Moscow, namely, that military occupation was justified on the ground that the indivisible socialist system had to be preserved from world imperialism and the counterrevolution (the Brezhnev Doctrine), did not allay the mistrust of many communists in Western Europe. Benefiting from a remarkable growth in the standard of living and from the seriousness with which political freedoms were safeguarded in the major West European countries, a consensus appeared to have emerged among them on the necessity of communist parties in Western Europe loosening their ideological links with the Soviet Union. It was in this overall context, namely, under the impact of a rising standard of living, the growth of political freedoms, a lessening of tensions between Washington and Moscow, and the invasion of Czechoslovakia, that Eurocommunism assumed its contours.

Because of the particular historical settings in which communist parties developed in West European countries and in view of the aforementioned occurrences that seemed to have led to a distancing between them and the Soviet Union, we cannot speak of Eurocommunism in the strict sense of the word but of a host of Eurocommunisms. To gain an understanding of the content of the general phenomenon of Eurocommunism it is first necessary to study the individual communist parties in Western Europe. What are some of the ideological and political-theoretical questions that need to be treated in order to shed light on this phenomenon?

What is immediately at stake is the question that centers on a core concept in Marxist-Leninist thought, namely, the notion of the "dictatorship of the proletariat." As is well known, this phrase has recently been dropped from Eurocommunist party programs. This central concept in the Marxist-Leninist theory of class struggle is, among other things, inextricably linked with the struggle that communist parties wage in leading the proletariat to victory. Inasmuch as this struggle involves strategy and tactics, a question that needs to be answered is: In the endeavor of Eurocommunist parties to attain governmental and state power as the first step in the "long road to socialism," is the Eurocommunist commitment to bourgeois electoral methods and to political pluralism genuine? Should the answer be in the affirmative, then the abandonment of the notion of the "dictatorship of the proletariat" as understood by Marxists-Leninists would indeed constitute a substantive shift from Marxism-Leninism.

Because the notion of the "dictatorship of the proletariat" is also inextricably linked with the transition phase between capitalism and communism, it need not detain us any longer. But in ascertaining the content of Eurocommunism, specifically the ideological and political-theoretical thrust, the question of the end product remains. Although no clear-cut theoretical constructs have yet been formulated, a picture, however blurry, may perhaps emerge by ascertaining the attitudes of individual Eurocommunist parties toward (a) the Soviet societal and state model, (b) the societal models that prevail in Eastern Europe, and (c) the societal and state models of Northern Europe.

If a consensus were to emerge that Eurocommunism is indeed something substantively new, the questions that immediately arise are: (1) What are the substantive differences between the Eurocommunist and Eurosocialist parties? (2) To what extent have Eurosocialist parties influenced Eurocommunist parties, and vice versa?

If, however, a consensus were to emerge that the proclaimed abandonment of the notion of the "dictatorship of the proletariat," and all that this implies from the perspective of strategy and tactics, is nothing more than a facade, a tactical maneuver, then classical Marxism-Leninism is well and alive, including, of course, Lenin's prescription to communist revolutionaries on the necessity of being flexible in the tactics to be utilized in their struggle for power. Were it to be established that Eurocommunism is nothing more than a tactical maneuver, with variations on a theme—a Machiavellian trick—then the immediate and practical question to confront is the appropriateness of extending to communist parties an "equal chance" to compete for governmental and state power, that is, the right to compete for power with parties that are committed to preserving the existing order of things.[3] Furthermore, should it be established that Eurocommunism is indeed nothing substantively new, would we be justified in dissociating "Euro" from communism, despite disillusionment of Eurocommunists in Western Europe with Stalinist Marxism-Leninism and the Soviet societal and state model?

Given the time limit of the conference, one could not hope to answer every conceivable question. If a learned discussion ensues, as it did in the instance of the detente gathering in 1974 and in the instance of the conference on ideology and foreign policy in 1976, the third CUNY conference will have accomplished its purpose.

Spring 1979

NOTES

1. The proceedings of this conference have been published under the title *Detente in Historical Perspective,* ed. George Schwab and Henry Friedlander (New York, 1975).

2. The proceedings of the second conference have been published under the title *Ideology and Foreign Policy: A Global Perspective,* ed. George Schwab (New York, 1978).

3. The idea of the "equal chance" was originally advanced by Carl Schmitt in 1932, in the face of the possibility of extremist parties gaining power in Weimar Germany. To safeguard the Weimar state, he argued for the necessity of withdrawing from such parties the right to compete for governmental and state power. See his *Legalität und Legitimität,* 2nd ed. (Berlin, 1968), pp. 30ff., 61. See also his recent highly provocative discussion of the legal world revolution. "Die legale Weltrevolution, Politischer Mehrwert als Prämie auf juristische Legalität und Superlegalität" in *Der Staat,* Heft 3, 1978, pp. 321-339.

Part I The Political Context

Rudi Supek

RIGHTIST REVISIONISM
AND EUROCOMMUNISM:
A YUGOSLAV MARXIST VIEW

In investigating the ideological roots of Eurocommunism, some hypotheses can be summarized:

1. Eurocommunism is only a surface manifestation or a symptom of the continuing crisis of the workers' movement in Europe; it is also a conscious attempt at overcoming that crisis insofar as it relates to the goals and the strategy of the workers' movement. Hence the causes of Eurocommunism are to be sought at a deeper level of meaning that transcends communist-party documents and the statements of party leaders.

2. The gravity of the crisis does not arise so much from the framework of national politics or from everyday working-class struggles. Instead, it stems from epochal introspection, namely, a questioning of the content of socialism. It has become impossible to separate the movement from the content of its goals. Thus the crisis is taking place on an ideologi-

*Translated by Professor Bogdan Denitch

cal plane that is shifting the movement's preoccupation with everyday socioeconomic struggle to formulating the emancipatory role of the working class in particular and the socialist movement in general.

3. If the preceding hypotheses are correct, we are dealing primarily with an ideological crisis—a crisis involving the self-consciousness of the workers' movement, that is, a crisis involving those forces that strive to transform society through conscious and practical action. The crisis relates to the ideological content of a wide and differentiated political movement of which Eurocommunism is one important element.

4. The crisis centers on the ideological lag in the contemporary workers' movement, characterized in Europe by the discrepancy between the relative inertness of mass organizations (political parties—communist and socialist—and unions) and the relative ideological avant-gardism of individuals and groups that hold progressive and revolutionary ideas but possess no organizational power. The problem is how to reestablish accord between socialist theory and political action and forge an efficient political power base for these avant-garde groups.

5. Eurocommunism means a critical orientation toward Marxist thought—a desire for its rehabilitation—and toward socialism as a concrete historical experience—an attempt to dispel the myths surrounding past revolutions. The adoption of this critical position has been conditioned primarily by the multiplicity of socialist experiences (Soviet, Chinese, Cuban, Yugoslav, and so on).

6. The end of the myth about "the leading country of socialism" and the acceptance of the principle of "finding one's own way to socialism" imply a revision in the disposition toward internationalism that characterized communist movements. Communists have been forced to recognize variation in their political and strategic tasks, yet they continue to subscribe to socialism as the single ideal. (The ideologists of

Eastern Europe, who speak of their regimes as "real socialism," continue to mystify critical inquiry into socialist goals.)

7. Eurocommunists' emphasis on democracy and human rights is, for the time being, their main defense against statism and bureaucratic monopoly that are typical of one-party East European nations. However, the question of socialist democracy and human rights is still open, making it possible for some observers to accuse Eurocommunists of advocating the adoption of social democracy.

8. Eurocommunists will probably have to emulate the European workers' movements in striving toward industrial democracy and workers' self-management. The Yugoslav system is one possible expression. Industrial democracy is the basis of socialist democracy in the real sense of that term.

"Rightist Revisionism" as Defined by Soviet Ideologists

Soviet ideologists warn that the term Eurocommunism is not well chosen because it incorrectly connotes the geographical limitation of the socialist movement. (Japanese communists, for instance, are also proponents of Eurocommunism.) As far as the term revisionism is concerned, Marxist intellectuals have even more reason to separate themselves from such a label and to protest its contemporary use. For example, the term is used by both Soviet theoreticians of Marxism-Leninism and Western non-Marxist historians and students of Marxism to refer to Marxists who demand a return to "authentic Marxism." Non-Marxists consider Soviet Marxism-Leninism a revision of Marx's original thought.[1] Such usage of the term not only associates contemporary creative Marxism with socialist reformism from Bernstein to today but also legitimizes Soviet Marxism-Leninism as "authentic" Marxist thought. Many authors in Western countries tend to equate the socialist character of the October Revolution with "communism," that is, the modern Soviet systems, and "Soviet communism" with Marxism. They consider everything that deviates from the Soviet conception of communism and Marxism a kind of revision. Revisionism by definition is that which is radically or even slightly distanced from its source—the official doctrine of the Soviet Union. Using such reasoning, superficial interpreters of the Marxist situation in contemporary Europe can hardly escape making errors.

The authentic Marxist thought of contemporary Europe stands in critical relationship to Soviet Marxism and practice. Among the critics are many who were until recently fervent defenders of Soviet Marxist practices. The change from an apologetic to a critical position in the realm of theory came about through confronting Marxist thought with Soviet practice. Authors who first expressed doubts in the 1950s were labeled rightist revisionists and conscious or unconscious agents of the bourgeoisie. But such labeling did not prevent a continuous increase in the number of "revisionists" that today include all renowned Marxists who are able to think for themselves.

We shall look at what Soviet ideologists call rightist revisionism. Official Soviet ideology differentiates between leftist revisionism (Maoism) and rightist revisionism. At the 1969 meeting of communist parties in Moscow, Brezhnev defined both brands of revisionism in the following way:

Rightist revisionism means the nullification of the position—its degradation to the point of political and ideological flirting with social democracy. In socialist countries, rightist opportunism negates the leading role of the Marxist-Leninist party. This can lead to the loss of those positions that have already been won by socialism to the capitulation to antisocialist powers. "Leftist" opportunists, who hide behind ultraleftist phrases, incite the masses into adventurist actions and provoke sectarianism in the party that weakens its ability to gather fighters against imperialism. Even though the deviations from Marxism-Leninism to the right and left can be differentiated, they ultimately have equally damaging effects: They weaken the communist parties' ability to struggle and erode the revolutionary positions of the working class and the unity of antiimperialist powers.[2]

Brezhnev's criticism of rightist revisionism referred primarily to events in Czechoslovakia and to those communist parties that had condemned the occupation of Czechoslovakia by the Warsaw Pact countries. However, his criticism was also directed at all Marxist tendencies, growing more pronounced at that time, that took an adverse stand vis-à-vis Soviet Marxism-Leninism and the Soviet model of socialism. One should keep in mind that the vanguard of Marxist thinkers who adopted a critical attitude toward the ideology and the regimes of the socialist camp enlarged significantly at that time primarily because the de-Stalinization process that, however reluctantly, had been initiated by East European communist parties after the twentieth congress of the Communist party of the U.S.S.R. had not been extended to the basic principles of Soviet (that is, Stalinist) Marxism-Leninism. The official ideology of the Soviet Union and of the nations that follow its example was still that version of Marxism-Leninism—that is, Marxism-Leninism-Stalinism—to which Stalin, Yudin, and Mitin, among others, gave final form in the thirties. The process of de-Stalinization consisted mainly of leaving out the name of the "fourth hero" of Marxism.[3]

The need to continue ideological struggle against any kind of "Titoism"—although not by means as brutal as those employed by Stalin—required the strengthening of ideological confrontation. With that goal in mind, a conference of communist parties (except the Yugoslav party) was held in Moscow in 1957 on the occasion of the fortieth anniversary of the October Revolution. It was decided that the "crisis of de-Stalinization" was over. The next task was to be the unity of the world communist movement and the struggle against rightist revisionism. It should be noted that the conference was held only one year after the notorious uprisings in

Hungary, Poland, and East Germany. "The main danger is revisionism or, in other words, rightist opportunism as an expression of bourgeois ideology that weakens the revolutionary fervor of the working class and promotes the maintenance and restoration of capitalism," said the conferees in the statement issued at the conclusion of the conference.[4]

The struggle against rightist revisionism revealed a dichotomy: Although the leaders of the Soviet Union and their faithful allies in Eastern and Southeastern Europe were prepared to compromise in the international political sphere on the desire of particular communist parties to determine their policies independently and find their "own way to socialism," there was a sharp confrontation observable in the ideological sphere. That confrontation was differentiated tactically, according to the target in question: Attacks on Marxist philosophers and intellectuals who showed independence in their work were intemperate. They were called agents of imperialism. Conversely, the tactic employed against the leaders of major European communist parties and their apparatuses was more subtle: From time to time sharp arrows were launched, followed by the firing of blanks. That tactical device has often been acknowledged for what it is, merely contrived noise made by "secondhand sources." It has always been a practice to order certain newspapers to launch attacks so that party officials can proffer the excuse that those attacks do not express "official opinion." In connection with the differentiation of attacks on "rightist revisionism," it is important to remember that dogmatic leaders compromise more readily on international rather than on domestic issues because their main concern is to preserve the legitimacy of their regimes. Thus in recent decades the progressive and voluntary isolation of the socialist camp has been revealed in such fields as the social sciences and Marxism. For example, it is much easier for an American representative of "bourgeois sociology" to communicate with Soviet Marxists than it is for a European or a Yugoslav Marxist from the praxis group to do so. (This conclusion was voiced by Alvin Gouldner, an objective observer of the development of theoretical analysis in socialist countries.)[5]

Having outlined the ambivalent situation of "rightist revisionism," let us find out whom the well-known East German ideologue, Alfred Kosing, identified as its proponents:

The group of Yugoslav philosophers and sociologists around the journal *Praxis* has had an especially active role in creating modern rightist revisionism as an international movement and in publicizing its conceptions. Among them are P. Vranički and Il Kuvačić from Zagreb and V. Korać, Lj. Tadić, G. Petrović, M. Kangra, R. Supek, D. Grlić, S. Stojanović, M. Zivotić, M. Marković from Belgrade. Regardless of some differences, this group shares a common conception, the so-called philosophy of praxis, which for many reasons became the focal point of contemporary rightist revisionism. The international success of "praxis philosophers" stems primarily from two factors: First, "praxis philosophers" offered relatively early (at the beginning of the sixties) a complete philosophical conception which pretended to be the real Marxist philosophy and which contained all the essential elements of deviation from Marxist philosophy; it was suitable for imperialism's struggle against Marxism-Leninism and the real, existing socialism. Second, this philosophy came from a socialist country and was marked by an anti-Soviet and anti-Leninist attitude which made it particularly attractive to some circles. This is why "praxis philosophy" could have a stimulating and unifying effect on the revisionist positions in both socialist and capitalist countries and why it could get sympathetic support from imperialist ideologists and institutions. In recent years the journal *Praxis,* edited by that group, developed into an open center of revisionism as did the Korčula summer schools held every year. Such a development was also helped by the formation of an international editorial board of *Praxis* in which participated almost all important revisionists and renegades as well as the bourgeois proponents of their ideas, such as: Lefèbvre, Kolakowski, Kosík, Baumann, Strinka, Lukács (who died subsequently), Axelos, Fromm, Marcuse, Habermas, and others. The fact that Ernst Fischer, Frantz Marek, and Roger Garaudy publicly expressed solidarity with *Praxis* and ardently wrote for it only makes the picture complete.[6]

Other well-known Marxists were subsequently identified as rightist revisionists, for instance, L. Lombardo-Radice, L. Goldmann, S. Mallet, P. Naville, Andras Hegedüs, Ágnes Heller, and A. Schaff—in effect, the most important Marxists in Europe. Kosing's list is expanding, even though he praised many of the so-called rightist revisionists as "real Marxists" not so long ago. Kosing seems to have forgotten that he maintained correct relations with Marxist colleagues from other socialist countries until he began to castigate them after the occupation of Czechoslovakia.

In the post-Stalinist period, annual meetings of editors of philosophical and socialist journals published in socialist countries were held. During one of the last meetings, held in Opatija (Yugoslavia), a fervent discussion ensued about the reflection theory of reality. Soviet defenders of this theory were supported by Bulgarian and East German philosophers, whereas representatives of other socialist countries (Poland, Hungary, Romania, and Czechoslovakia) upheld the paper delivered by P. Vranički (a member of the praxis group). The Polish philosophers Baumann and Morawski especially engaged themselves in defending the Yugoslav position. As a consequence, they were denounced as rightist revisionists and dismissed from Warsaw University, together with Kolakowski, Bruš, and Hirsovicéva. Strinka and Kosík, Czech philosophers who took similar positions in the Opatija discussions, experienced in 1968 the same fate as the Polish philosophers had suffered. Three years later, in 1971, the same thing happened to Lukács's students. The struggle against "rightist revisionism" culminated in the dismissal of praxist professors from the universities of Belgrade and Zagreb in 1975.[7]

Before the invasion of Czechoslovakia, representatives of official Marxism-Leninism recognized the alleged "rightist revisionists" as Marxists and engaged in polemics according to a prescribed code of behavior. Since 1968, they have issued moralistic denunciations and equivocal accusations ranging from "treason to the working class," to "agents of imperialism," and similar epithets. What is the source of such behavior? It seems to me that it stems from the need to defend not so much a certain interpretation of Marxism as a specific political system that does not tolerate dissent. A polemical statement made by Kosing validates this observation.

Together with other rightist revisionists, they [praxis philosophers] insist that the real, existing socialism in the Soviet Union, Poland, Czechoslovakia, the [German] Democratic Republic, and so on is a "bureaucratic-statist" degeneration of socialism, which does not any more [or not yet] deserve the name *socialism*. "State socialism" is just a myth, they say, because it is in fact a new class society in which the state bureaucratic class has at its disposal the means of production, which it uses according to its interest to exploit the working people.[8]

Since the normalization of relations between the Soviet Union and Yugoslavia, the once-frequent attacks on self-management as a kind of "anarcho-liberalism" have become milder, although Soviet ideologists have not changed their pronounced opinions. They have centered their attacks on the philosophical and Marxist bases of self-governing socialism, as evidenced, for example, in an important Soviet publication, *Contemporary Problems of Marxist Philosophy* (1974),[9] which echoed the official line. Although the title denotes a general Marxist theme, its authors' preoccupation with continuing the attacks can be discerned from their assertion that in Yugoslavia there are "true" Marxists-Leninists who follows Soviet *Diamat* and *Histomat* as well as "rightist revisionists" associated with the journal *Praxis.*

The authors of the introduction to this Soviet book, A. P. Shentulin and M. B. Savić, repeated views about *Praxis* that reinforce the observation that nothing has changed in Stalinist Marxism-Leninism in the last four decades. They contended that there occurred in Yugoslavia during the sixties a differentiation between "orthodox" and "authentic" Marxists, especially after the notorious discussion in Bled in 1960 when the advocates of the reflection theory lost the battle. The authors asserted that the journal *Praxis*, by ". . . including many philosophers from various countries of the world on the editorial board, . . . became a theoretical support of international revisionism and anti-Marxism. . . . In the realm of theory, the authentic Marxists carried out a number of manipulations for the purpose of throwing doubt on certain basic principles of Marxism-Leninism or in order to revise them. The crusade against these principles was organized with the slogan 'Back to Marx, back to authentic Marxism.' In fact, the slogan 'Back to Marx,' " the Soviet authors continued, "is nothing but a smoke screen whose function is to hide the fact of their decided return to bourgeois philosophy. They understand man not as a product of society, not as the totality of social relations, but as a generic anthropological essence, as a Sartreian unique man, with individuality which is absolutely unrepeatable, as a nonhistorical being, socially undetermined. . . . In this theoretical foundation of anthropological Marxism an important component is the theory of alienation. From their viewpoint, the category of alienation is not only the basic methodological principle and the theoretical basis of Marxist philosophy (Supek), but the category which most adequately expresses the essence of the anthropological, humanistic theory of Marx. It is the nucleus of his teachings (G. Petrović, M. Zivotić)."

Because the category of alienation is suitable for the analysis of a bureaucratized, statist society, the authors of the introduction hold that it is typical only for "praxists" and "abstract humanists," such as G. Lukács, E. Bloch, M. Horkheimer, H. Marcuse, J. Habermas, and other representatives of the Frankfurt School.

All the objections that Shentulin and Savić posed to "praxis philosophers" in the name of Soviet Marxism-Leninism repeated the litany of attack. Only one more will be mentioned because it is typical of the political bureaucracy and reveals its apologetic character: the attack on the concept of "the critique of everything existing." (The advocacy of that concept was the main reason why Yugoslav politicians forbade activity on the part of the group associated with the journal *Praxis*.) "Already in their introductory, programatic article the editors of *Praxis* underlined that in their work on the restoration of authentic Marxism they would follow Marx's basic principle of unsparing criticism of everything existing. According to G. Petrović, this is the universal principle of Marxist dialectics, unrestricted by either time or place. M. Kangra insists on the principle even more firmly."[10]

Obviously, the principle is uncongenial to bureaucrats in socialist countries because citizens may get the idea that they are allowed to criticize political leaders and that the activities of these leaders do not follow the "strict, objective laws of the dialectical development of society."

The Origins of "Rightist Revisionism"

Soviet and East European ideologues today avoid discussions about various models of socialism (even though they reflect historical facts) and insist that their states and societies constitute "real socialism" resulting from the "lawful development" of society. In earlier periods, however, all attempts at evaluating the Soviet model and propositions similar to Eurocommunism were condemned in the sharpest terms and were terminated by administrative fiat. We need only recall in this context the events in European Marxism after the Tito-Stalin conflict and the twentieth party congress when Khrushchev gave the famous report on "Stalin's mistakes."

To the resolution of the Cominform (1948) the Yugoslav leadership answered with demands that specific rights be respected:

1. The equality of communist parties in the world without any "leading center";

2. the economic and political equality of all socialist countries;

3. establishing one's own way to socialism in accordance with national cultural, political, and economic conditions.

Furthermore, the socialist character of Soviet statism and centralism was questioned, and a commitment was made to develop workers' self-management. Similar movements started in other socialist countries in the context of the politics of de-Stalinization.[11]

At Humboldt University in East Germany in 1956, Ernst Bloch gave some lectures that produced resounding echoes. He demanded the abandonment of the narrow tracks of *Histomat* and *Diamat* and the creation of space for Marxist anthropology, ethics, and aesthetics. The fresh and vivid spirit of the philosopher of *The Principle of Hope* protested the scholastic formality and the spiritual desert of official philosophy. "No wooden teachers distanced from life, no paper aestheticians far from art, no philosophizing far from philosophy will help us."[12] His students, especially Wolfgang Harich, who subsequently defected to the West, were even more radical. Referring to the conclusions of the twentieth party congress of the Communist party of the U.S.S.R. (1956), they demanded liberation from Stalinism, political action in the context of peaceful coexistence (which would mean agreements with the West German socialist party, the SPD); the expansion of Marxism-Leninism to include the contributions of Bukharin, Rosa Luxemburg, Trotsky, and, in part, Kautsky, and the introduction of workers' councils (which would mean abandoning the Soviet model of socialism).

The consequences of this program are known: E. Bloch's revisionism was condemned as the intrusion of bourgeois ideology into Marxism. Harich was sentenced to ten years in prison; Günther Zehn was sentenced to four years; and Richard Lorenz and Bernhard Zwerenz succeeded in escaping to West Germany. Bloch was forced to retire a year later. He soon left East Germany and lived in West Germany until his death. The emigration of eminent Marxists from the socialist camp to capitalist countries began then and is continuing today.

The tense situation of the "Polish October" of 1956 ended more peacefully because the general secretary of the party had to withdraw and Gomulka assumed that position. During those events a student newspaper, *Po Prostu,* gained national readership as a critic of the Stalinist order. Leszek Kolakowski published in it his renowned theses on "the concept of the left." That newspaper was the first to publish Rosa Luxemburg's critique of Lenin's concept of socialism. At that time Polish Marxists called themselves revisionists, although they maintained that the Stalinist version of Marxism-Leninism constitutes the real revision. Helena Eilstein wrote:

If we characterize Stalinism as dogmatic, one could get the impression that it, more than any other Marxist current in the communist movement, adheres to old Marxist theoretical traditions. The impression would be absolutely wrong. Stalinism is a definite revision of Marxist traditions that had existed before it. I think that Stalinism is in its deepest essence a revision of the Marxist concept of the dictatorship of the proletariat.[13]

The Hungarian uprising of 1956 was preceded by very lively discussions through which the Petöfi circle became widely known. Georg Lukács participated in those discussions. The "Polish October" was a signal for mass demonstrations against Stalinism and in Budapest against the Rakosi regime, in which tens of thousands of people participated. Workers and soldiers joined together in the demonstration and organized workers' councils everywhere. It is significant that whenever the working class acts spontaneously against bureaucratic regimes, it creates workers' councils as its form of government. The creation of workers' councils was characteristic of Hungary in 1956 and Czechoslovakia in 1968. The working class of Eastern Europe after the Second World War expressed the same kind of behavior as did the working class in capitalist countries after World War I. The seizure of factories and the creation of workers' councils reflect the nature of the revolutionary movements of the working class.

The German philosopher of Marxism, Karl Korsch, pointed out in the thirties that the Leninist conception of revolution does not answer "the practical needs of the international class struggle of the proletariat at the present stage of development."[14] He proposed industrial democracy and workers' self-management as the bases for socialist democracy.[15] K. Korsch and G. Lukács, along with some members of the Frankfurt School, were the most eminent Marxists who opposed Lenin's reflection theory. They were branded revisionists long before World War II.

Soon after the beginning of the process of de-Stalinization, Lukács warned that the rejection of Stalinism and the corresponding emphasis on Leninism could engender the same kind of dogmatic behavior, and he argued that it was necessary to fight such a tendency. He also expressed the need for peaceful coexistence as well as for openness and receptivity to developments in capitalist countries. "If we succeed in making attractive the appearance of socialism, it will not any more be a scarecrow for the masses."[16]

After the Hungarian uprising was suppressed, Lukács was arrested and deported to Romania, but in 1957 he returned to Budapest. Thereafter he was attacked continually as a revisionist, a bourgeois democrat, and a Hegelian; his theory of coexistence was taken as proof of revisionism. His personal prestige was strong enough to enable him to continue editing his works, which were published in West Germany. His students, including Ágnes Heller, who was at the forefront, signed in Korčula (Yugoslavia) a protest against the invasion of Czechoslovakia. Together with other Marxist participants of the summer school, they experienced the same fate as their Czechoslovak colleagues, Kosík and Strinka. They lost their jobs and subsequently left their homeland. Like the objections of other "revisionists," their criticisms were not only directed against Soviet Marxism-Leninism but focused on the character of the Soviet system itself. The sociologists of the Budapest School (A. Hegedüs, Mária Márkus, Marc Rakovski) held that the Soviet Union and those countries that follow its "model" of development had not succeeded in building socialist societies but had carried out the industrial modernization of their countries under noncapitalist relations of production. Rapid industrialization under such conditions required the creation of a specialized management apparatus that usurped political power. The bureaucratic structures of those countries are not secondary or peripheral phenomena but are essential characteristics of such a society, which is neither developing toward true socialism nor regressing toward capitalism.[17] Similar theories were advanced long before World War II by Fritz Sternberg and Richard Lowenthal and have recently been elaborated in the works of B. Horvát, S. Stojanović, and H. Lefèbvre, who have analyzed "statism" as a specific social system.[18]

Having surveyed certain "rightist revisionist" tendencies as perceived by their dogmatic critics and defined by their proponents, we shall summarize the essential characteristics of that "revisionism":

1. The ideological roots of Eurocommunism are to be found in the Marxist philosophy that is labeled and condemned as rightist revisionism in the countries of Eastern Europe. Those ideas have expanded in influence and today

are subscribed to by all important European Marxists, some of whom (until recently) had endorsed Soviet Marxism-Leninism. At present there is no significant group of Marxists in Europe that represents Soviet Marxism-Leninism. We can say without fear of exaggeration that the process of theoretical differentiation—as an expression of a definite historical movement—is complete. There are few individuals with the reputation of Marxist philosophers and few student groups of sectarian character who represent Soviet Marxism-Leninism. Consequently, we can state, using the vocabulary of our political opponents, that the victory of "rightist revisionism" in Western Europe is complete.

2. The dogmatic conception of Soviet Marxism-Leninism has remained unchanged in its Stalinist nature.[19] It was accepted by many communist parties as their official philosophy, which proved to be an ideological and a political mistake. Soviet Marxism-Leninism caused great damage to those parties, much of which has not yet been repaired. First, there was a real degeneration in Marxist thought—the voluntary abandonment of the party by some of the best Marxist thinkers or the exclusion of others from membership in the party—weakening the workers' and progressive movements, undermining the influence of Marxist thought, and causing the ideological and political sterility of such mass organizations as political parties and unions. The degeneration was evident in the dissipation of the leftist cultural vanguard that played a significant role in Europe after World War II, when the Marxist intelligentsia influenced leading cultural organizations, journals, and newspapers—a necessary relationship for any mass political movement. Intellectual youth, especially student groups whose role in revolutionary movements is always significant, similarly deserted the parties. The implicit reason for that desertion was the conceptual sterility of Soviet Marxism-Leninism, a dogma that renders its proponents incapable of following the complex processes and

problems of modern industrialized society. The explicit reason for the desertion was the inability of the bureaucratized communist and socialist parties to make their programs ideologically richer and more elaborate. The efforts of Eurocommunists are aimed at overcoming the long-lasting crisis, at winning back Marxist thinkers and creators of culture, at reviving the cultural vanguard, and at restoring the ideological and political influence that existed in the years after the last war.

3. "Rightist revisionism" represents a return to the "authentic" thought of Marx. It does not necessarily represent a "return" for everybody because for some philosophers (for instance, Lukács, Korsch, Gramsci, and some members of the Frankfurt circle), Marx's thought retained its validity between the two world wars despite all the attempts to exert countervailing pressures and criticisms. We can speak instead of the revitalization of Marx's thought, especially the thought of the young Marx. Differences between authentic Marxist thought—so-called critical, humanist-anthropological Marxism—and the philosophy of praxis, on one side, and Stalinist Marxism-Leninism, on the other side, are so profound that it is difficult to foresee a compromise or a dialogue, not even for political reasons. It can be said that today two Marxisms exist that cannot engage in peaceful coexistence. Perhaps it would be better to speak about one and only one Marxism and its severe Stalinist revision. Marxism is the expression of the independent and creative thinking of individual Marxist philosophers, sociologists, and other social and political scientists, whereas Stalinism is the dogmatic, politically controlled, dependent tool of political bureaucracy and its servants. It is not an exaggeration to say that from the authentic Marxist viewpoint, Soviet Marxism-Leninism represents a dogmatic, apologetic, pseudoscientific revision and abuse of original Marxist thought. It will prosper only as long as it is supported by bayonets. But one cannot sit on bayonets for long.

4. It should be evident that creative Marxism, or rightist revisionism according to the terminology of the U.S.S.R., is not the consequence of a direct negation of Soviet Marxism-Leninism. It arose from studying the original thought of Marx, Engels, Lenin, and other Marxists and from profound contributions to their thought. It was renewed through re-solving many problems arising from social development by applying Marxist explanations. Authentic Marxism can be considered the sensitive enrichment of Marxism. It is always sensitive and open to various conceptual currents in contem-porary society that look like "smuggling bourgeois ideas" or "falling under the influence of foreign ideologies" to dogma-tists, who have isolated themselves behind walls, wires, and tanks. Texts of a polemical character that refute the bureau-cratic dogma of Soviet Marxism-Leninism represent an insig-nificant percentage of the works of creative Marxism. The need to deal with concrete problems has always been more important than duels with the advocates of a sterile ideology.

5. A critical relation to Stalinist and post-Stalinist Marxism-Leninism has always meant a critical relation to the Soviet system, for it is obvious that Soviet Marxism is an integral part of that system. The characteristics of Soviet Marxism-Leninism demonstrate the function of the ideology as well as the nature of the political system: The two are interdependent. Soviet Marxism's dogmatic and apologetic character is suitable for the bureaucratic control of public opinion, which in fact has been eliminated in the name of the "dictatorship of the proletariat" and "the leading role of the party." The pseudoscientific character of Stalinist and neo-Stalinist Marxism accords with an uncritical relation to Soviet reality and with the practice of verifying "social cognition" through "higher reason" or by "wise leadership." Its neglect of the anthropological basis of Marxism and of the theory of alienation in particular formed the basis for the fetish of the "dictatorship of the proletariat," "the proletarian state," and

"the vanguard of the party." "Real socialism" has become a social mythology beyond all scientific criteria. It is obvious that the positivist and organicist elements of Stalinist and neo-Stalinist Marxism imply the denial of the role of the individual in the name of the "masses," the denial of communist humanism and personalism, that is, Marx's thesis that social organization must serve the "free development of the individual."

6. The representatives of creative Marxism subscribe to principles of socialist order and models of socialist organization that are based on the principle of the self-determination of man not only as *homo politicus* but as *homo economicus* and ultimately as *homo humanum.* Yugoslav Marxists from the praxis circle advocate self-governing socialism in this context. Some are discussing many variations and nuances of the concept. But all are discussing self-determination in terms of industrial democracy, de-Stalinization, debureaucratization, and decentralization. The reputation of the praxis group stems primarily from the fact that it created a coherent conception by connecting the fundamental principles of Marxism with a definite and realistic conception of self-governing socialism.

Marx set forth the political meaning of an epistemological conflict:

The chief defect of all hitherto existing materialism—that of Feuerbach included—is that the thing *[Gegenstand]*, reality, sensuousness, is conceived only in the form of the object *[Objekt]* or of *contemplation [Anschauung]*, but not as *human sensuous activity, practice,* not subjectively. Hence it happened that the *active* side, in contradistinction to materialism, was developed by idealism—but only abstractly, since, of course, idealism does not know real, sensuous activity as such.[20]

Persons unfamiliar with the spirit of Marxist philosophy and its connection with revolutionary practice may find it difficult to understand why Marxists engage in such fierce debates over what is apparently a purely philosophical or epistemological problem: Is knowledge or perception based on the Marxist reflection theory, or is it based on the theory of praxis? The dispute may appear scholastic, but it is basic to an understanding of the Marxist dialectic and to the relation of man to society and to the external world. It affects the nature of the revolutionary subject itself. Counterposed in this dispute are not only philosophers and abstract thinkers but interpreters and representatives of Marxist individualism. One side is presented as the "bureaucratic vanguard" and the other as the "revolutionary movement," that is, individuals and groups that claim the right to participate in the transformation of society. The dispute is as old as the revolutionary movement itself, but it has taken this specific form in the formulation of Marxist theory since the October Revolution.

Because the dispute may appear abstract, we will summarize its content: Soviet theorists counterpose Lenin's reflection theory to that of the praxis philosophers, although Lenin, following Hegel, expressed serious reservations in his *Philosophical Notebooks* about the theory that he had defended in *Materialism and Empirocriticism.* The representatives of the philosophy of praxis attack Soviet Marxism-Leninism-Stalinism because their reflection theory has remained on the plane of traditional, contemplative Platonic thought. Because they separate the subject from the object, that is, spirit from matter, and ignore the fact that the object is the objective work of human historical practice, that is, created by human interaction with the external world through which man changes not only the world but himself, the subject and the object react together and continue the process of becoming.[21] Soviet Marxism-Leninism, with the reflection theory as its basis, has remained on the level of prebourgeois philosophy, for it has not reflected the active role of the subject in the creation of the objective world—a role that was stressed by such German idealistic philosophers as Kant, Fichte, and Hegel, who reflected the activism of the industrial epoch that was inaugurated by the modern bourgeoisie. Lenin developed his materialistic theory from the Russian tradition that was based on the French materialism of the seventeenth century. Only later did Lenin recognize the significance of Hegel for Marxism. He recommended that Marxists in the Soviet Union form clubs to study Hegel's philosophy.

It is significant that Stalin intervened in the debate between the mechanists and the idealists in the 1930s and gave Soviet Marxism its markedly pseudoscientific form. After the political liquidation of Trotsky and Bukharin, Stalin made himself the "major philosopher" of socialism and intervened in philosophical disputes that had developed freely until that time. He succeeded in asserting his interpretations and conceptions, which became obligatory. From Deborin he appropriated the scientific position concerning the division of the "materialist dialectic" (*Diamat*): the dialectic of nature, the methodology of all the natural sciences, the dialectic of history, and historical materialism, reducing the historical dialectic by rendering it a subbranch of the general dialectic. From the mechanists he retained the vulgar materialist conception according to which the objective world is considered separate from consciousness, or the subject that reflects that objective world—a reflection verified through practical activities.

The Yugoslav philosopher P. Vranički commented on Stalin's concept of history:

Stalin understands laws in the sense of classical mechanics, the calculus of probability, statistical laws, and above all, the laws of trends, which are much more important for understanding historical development, and, for him, do not exist as a problem at all. That is why Stalin can completely, undialectically, examine history under the aegis of natural laws and see historical laws in such a way that they are not affected at all by the conscious activity of mankind; therefore, his characteristic his later years. The problematic anthropology of Marxism is expressed in the theory of alienation, and therefore there is formulation of historical materialism as merely the extension of dialectical materialism to the study of social life and the application of the assumptions of dialectical materialism to social phenomena, the study of society and the study of the history of society.[22]

Stalin believed that it was necessary to intervene in the field of philosophical thought and Marxist theory. Thus in January 1931 the Central Committee passed a resolution about the journal *Unter dem Banner des Marxismus,* which had been published by the followers of Deborin. Deborin's followers were dismissed, and Stalin's minions were appointed. Stalin demanded that philosophical thought be directly connected with practical political work because, in his opinion, political practice was markedly successful in socialist construction, whereas theoretical work was lagging behind. Therefore, theoretical work had to catch up with practical work. We know, of course, that it is a favorite bureaucratic theme that political practice moves forward rapidly, whereas theoretical work lags behind, for political work is considered the objective creation of socialism, whereas little consideration at all is given to the relationship between socialism and political practice.

In "Stalin's Errors in Philosophy," a paper presented when he was a member of the Politburo of the French Communist party, Roger Garaudy maintained that Stalin distorted Marxism, transforming it into a positivistic concept by separating the dialectic from materialism, or method from theory, and reducing the dialectic to the dialectic of nature. Stalin rejected the principle of negation, the negation of negation; he eliminated the role of philosophy; he introduced a mechanical interpretation of the relation of the base to the superstructure; he rejected the theory of alienation that led to the conclusion that the emiseration of the proletariat under capitalism must be given the same purely economic interpretation as that given to the material impoverishment of the working class. That interpretation does not confront the facts.

Although Garaudy articulated the positivistic distortion of Marxism in Stalinist Marxism-Leninism, his designation of Stalin's fundamental revision of Marxism as Stalin's errors is as ludicrous as if he had called Nero's crime an error in pyrotechnics.[23]

The purpose of Stalin's pseudoscientism, proclaimed as the "objective laws" that guide the construction of Marxist-Leninist political theory, was to camouflage the extreme voluntarism and willfulness of the political leadership, who, under the direction of one man, intended to wield decision-making power in the party. Because such an absolutist, dictatorial practice is alien to genuine Marxism, it was necessary to assert that the wise leadership of Stalin (and all party leaders who were to succeed him, as well as those in countries with statist regimes) respected dialectical development and the objective laws of dialectical development in the construction of socialism. Because of the "objective laws of historical development," the results of antisocialist practice were alleged to be transformed into "real socialism."

The philosophy of praxis has as its aim the exposure of the mystification behind which hides the political voluntarism of a monopolistic group. Gerson S. Sher, in an excellent presentation of Yugoslav praxis philosophers and sociologists, wrote:

But while philosophers of the praxis group may issue from different intellectual traditions, they agree on two essential points. First, they are unified in their belief that the revitalization of Marxism can be effected only by returning to the critical theory of praxis and alienation and to the profound humanism that inspired Marx's work through his life; and second, they are commonly convinced that such a revitalized Marxism is the most effective tool that man has at his disposal for understanding and transforming the world in accordance with his needs. To devote undue emphasis to divergences in theory between individual praxis Marxists is to lose sight of their binding commitment to these goals.[24]

The philosophers of the praxis group reject the artificial distinction between the "young Marx" and the "old Marx," between the "early" humanistic and liberal "anthropological" phase of Marx's thought and the "scientific" Marxism of an intimate relation between praxis and alienation because the historical praxis of mankind is engendering different forms of alienation (political, as statism, economic, as alienated labor, and so on). Both fundamental forms of alienation—statist and economic—exist in the Soviet Union, a hierarchical and centralized organization of productive forces and of political life that generates an extreme form of privation.

The active role of the human being is underlined in a statement by P. Vranički: "We see man as par excellence a being of practice, a being who freely and consciously transforms his own life. . . . Man exists and develops only by transforming his natural and social reality, and . . . in this way he transforms himself also."[25]

The concept of praxis implies a critical position to the world and to man because it not only deals with what is "existing" but with "the not-yet-existing"—the future. Man alienates himself not from a given substance, ontologically predetermined, but from his possible being, his possible realization as a human being, a position similar to Ernst Bloch's "principle of hope." Therefore, his attitude is critical of and negative toward the given reality. The principle of negation possesses a creative function, even a revolutionary role, because it expresses the necessity of transcending the present for the future and the frequently-cited and hated principle of "the ruthless criticism of all that exists."

G. Petrović developed the idea of man as a "creative and self-creative being" and of Marxist philosophy as a "thought revolution":

Is not revolution the most developed form of creation, the most authentic form of liberty? . . . Is not revolution the "essence" of existence, of being in its essence? And if revolution is existence itself, is not philosophy, by virtue of this very fact . . . the thought of revolution? . . . Can philosophical thought be content to reflect upon revolution without participating in it? . . . In short, is true philosophy only the thought of revolution, or is it thought revolution?[26]

The same idea can be found in the editorial introduction to the first issue of *Praxis.*

But if contemporary philosophy aspires to contribute to the solution of the contemporary world crisis, it cannot be reduced to the study and interpretation of its own history; neither can it be a scholarly construction of encyclopaedic systems, much less the analysis of the methods of modern science or the description of the modern usage of words. If it desires to be thought revolutionary, philosophy must orient itself toward the essential human concerns of the modern world and of modern man. . . .

Against the Stalinist conception of philosophy as *ancila politicae,* praxis philosophers have rehabilitated philosophy as an autonomous discipline, believing that the theory has a leading role to play in social and political practice, and have reasserted the responsible and revolutionary role of independent Marxist thinkers. Even more important, theory and practice are not only related at the general societal level—in the form of political organization or of leadership representing class consciousness—but also at individual and collective levels. Collective liberation is not possible without conscious, individual activity; revolutionary transformation presupposes the conscious action of every man. The enlargement of revolutionary subjectivity is considered by Stalinists and dogmatists to be a kind of "bourgeois individualism" and "idealism." (It is curious to note that in a marginal remark in his *Philosophical Notebooks,* Lenin wrote "subjectivity = freedom.") Bureaucratic organization implies everyone's alienation from personal freedom, which has been transferred to the charismatic leader. All praxis philosophers can agree with G. Petrović's statement: "A society is socialist to the extent that it opens possibilities for the free, creative development of every man." Those who contend that human freedom has already been realized in the socialist countries are obliged to repudiate the theory of alienation. (Most Soviet sociologists admit that the phenomenon of alienation does exist in the Soviet Union—for example, religion—but only as a remnant of bourgeois society.)[2][7]

With real social democracy in mind, Korsch and Lukács insisted between the two wars that so-called scientific Marxism had reduced the role of the subject in history and in the formation of socialist consciousness by counterposing so-called objective laws of development in the name of a positivistic interpretation of evolutionism. In this way, it was possible to eliminate the revolutionary substance of Marxist thought and grant "to the final end the role of a superhuman deity"—that is, the final or long-term goals of development had been monopolized by the political bureaucracy that gave itself a godlike role in history. Creative Marxism naturally denies such a role, which is the reason for the bureaucracy's hatred of all representatives of the philosophy of praxis.

Repressing the anthropological basis of Marxist humanism and negating the role of every subject in his creative aspect, Stalinist positivism, basing itself on "objective laws," interjected fatalism into human consciousness, that is, the notion that socialism can be developed only by a fated scheme outside and above the consciousness and the responsibility of individuals; the individual is not free in his historical action and has no specific responsibility for its development. The philosopher of hope, Ernst Bloch, rose against this fatalism. Because man is not determined in his relationship to the future in the sense of an external necessity, this fatalism engenders a demobilizing effect on revolutionary action, on every individual, and on the whole movement—except on those who control the movement's institutions. Fatalism became the means of institutionalizing a movement, separating it into an active core, or vanguard, and a passive mass. The gap between matter and consciousness that Stalinist positivism found in nature was imposed on society as the gap between the passive masses and the active elite. Whereas creative Marxism, or the philosophy of praxis, is the expression of the revolutionary movement itself, of the broad mobilization of all progressive forces, Stalinist positivism is the expression of an institutional movement and the rule of an elite that controls state institutions.

NOTES

1. See, for example, the books by Leopold Labedz, *Der Revisionismus* (Cologne, 1965), and by Helga Grebing, *Der Revisionismus. Von Bernstein bis zum "Prager Frühling"* (Munich, 1977). Grebing has otherwise correctly interpreted the different "revisionist" Marxist movements in Europe. Many references have been taken from her book.
2. Quoted from *Ideologie des Sozialdemokratismus in der Gegenwart,* edited by the Academy of Sciences of the U.S.S.R. (Moscow, 1970; Berlin, 1971), p. 325.
3. For more details on the constitution of "Marxism-Leninism-Stalinism," see Predrag Vranički, *Die Geschichte des Marxismus,* 2nd ed. (Frankfurt a.M., 1974).
4. The text of this declaration is quoted from "Erklärung der Weltkonferenz der kommunistischen Parteien in Moskau, 14-16. 11. 1957," *Einheit,* (1957), vol. 12, no. 12.
5. See the very interesting analysis of the similarities between American functionalism and Soviet Marxism in Alvin Gouldner, *The Coming Crisis of Western Sociology* (New York/London, 1970).
6. Alfred Kosing, "Verfälschung und Preisgabe der materialistischen Dialektik durch den modernen Revisionismus," in *Deutsche Zeitschrift für Philosophie,* (1972), vol. 20, pp. 204-215.
7. A detailed report on the persecution of the praxis group in Yugoslavia was published by Mihajlo Marković and Robert S. Cohen, *Yugoslavia: The Rise and Fall of Socialist Humanism: A History of the Praxis Group* (Nottingham, 1975).
8. Kosing, *op. cit.*
9. "Aktualny problemy marksistkoi filosofii," (Moscow, 1974).
10. For the development of Yugoslav socialism and Marxism after 1948, it is useful to consult Wolfgang Leonhard, *Die Dreispaltung des Marxismus, Ursprung und Entwicklung des Sowjetmarxismus, Maoismus und Reformkommunismus* (Düsseldorf/Vienna, 1970); Vranički, *op. cit.,* vol. 1-2; Ludvig Vrtačić, *Der jugoslawische Marxismus. Die yugoslawische Philosophie und der eigene Weg zum Sozialismus* (Olten, 1975); Gudrun Lamân, *Das jugoslawische Modell. Weg*

zur Demokratisierung der Wirtschaft (Frankfurt a.M./Cologne, 1976); Branko Horvát, "Essays on Yugoslav Society," *IASP,* New York, 1972; Gerson S. Sher, *Praxis* (Bloomington/London, 1977); Grebing, *op. cit.*
    11. See Grebing, *op. cit.;* also Martin Jänicke, *Der dritte Weg, Die antistalinistische Opposition gegen Ulbricht seit 1953* (Cologne, 1964); Ernst Bloch, "Philosophische Aufsätze zur objektiven Phantasie" in *Gesamtausgabe der Werke* (Frankfurt a.M., 1969), vol. 10; Ernst Bloch, *Revision des Marxismus* (Berlin, 1957); and the contributions of O. Gropp, G. Handel, H. Ley, K. Hager, and others; Fertwig Manfred, *Deformationen. Die Rebellion der Intellektuellen in der DDR* (Frankfurt a.M., 1977); Peter C. Ludz, "Freiheitsphilosophie oder aufgeklärter Dogmatismus?" in Ludz, *Ideologiebegriff und marxistische Theorie (Opladen, 1976).*
    12. Ernst Bloch, "Hegel und die Gewalt des Systems," in Bloch, *Über Methode und System bei Hegel* (Frankfurt a./M., 1970), pp. 70-89.
    13. *Nowa Kultura,* no. 17-19, 1957 (Warsaw).
    14. "Diese gesamte 'leninistische' Theorie ist aber kein ausreichender theoretischer Ausdruck für die *praktische Bedürfnisse der gegenwärtigen Entwicklungsstufe des internationalen proletarischen Klassenkampfes,* und ein als das ideologische Fundament jener leninistischer Theorie dienende materialistische Philosophie Lenins ist aus diesem Grunde auch nicht die dieser heutigen Entwicklungsstufe entsprechende revolutionäre Philosophie des Proletariats." *Marxismus und Philosophie,* 1st ed. (1923). Edited and introduced by Erich Gerlach (Frankfurt a./M., 1966), p. 60.
    15. The significance of K. Korsch for industrial democracy, or workers' self-management, is presented in B. Horvát, M. Marković, R. Supek, "Self-governing Socialism," *IASP,* vol. 1-2, New York, 1975.
    16. Georg Lukács, *Schriften zur Ideologie und Politik,* ed. Peter C. Ludz (Neuwied and Berlin, 1967; 2nd ed. 1973) p. 612.
    17. For the Hungarian situation, see Grebing, *op. cit.,* pp. 203-213.
    18. See particularly H. Lefèbvre, *De l'Etat. 1. L'Etat dans le monde moderne, 2. Theorie marxiste de l'Etat de Hegel à Mao, 3. Le mode production etatique.* The book by Branko Horvát dealing with "statism" as a particular social system will soon appear in English. See also R. Supek, "Statist and the Self-governing Model of Socialism," in A. Barton, C. Kadushin, B. Denitch, *Yugoslav Opinion-making Elites* (New York, 1974).
    19. About the constitution of official Soviet Marxism-Leninism by Stalin, Mitin, and Yudin during the thirties in the Soviet Union, see Vranicki, *op cit.,* vol. 2.

20. Marx & Engels, *Basic Writings on Politics & Philosophy,* edited by Lewis S. Feuer, (Garden City, New York, 1959), p. 243.

21. See Alfred Schmidt, *Beiträge zur marxistischen Erkenntnistheorie,* (Frankfurt a./M., 1969; 2nd ed., 1971).

22. See Predrag Vranički, *Historija marksizam,* 3rd. ed., (Zagreb, 1978), vol. 2, pp. 211-220.

23. Roger Garaudy in *Cahiers du communisme,* no. 7-8, Paris, 1962. See also R. Supek, "Once More about the Alternative: Stalinist Positivism or Creative Marxism?" *Praxis,* no. 6, 1965.

24. Sher, *op. cit.,* p. 67.

25. Predrag Vranički, "On the Concept of Praxis," *Praxis,* Int. ed. no. 1 (1965), p. 42. This issue of *Praxis* is dedicated to the clarification of the concept of praxis. (Articles by B. Bošnjak, G. Petrović, D. Grlić, R. Supek).

26. Quoted by Sher, *op. cit.,* p. 103.

27. For more information on the Soviet conception of alienation, see Adam Schaff, *Entfremdung als soziales Phenomen* (Vienna, 1977).

R. V. Burks

TITOISM
AND EUROCOMMUNISM

Among Westerners concerned with the East-West confrontation, the emergence of the phenomenon known as Eurocommunism has aroused considerable puzzlement, provoking a spate of learned literature. Moreover, Eurocommunism has presented American policymakers—especially those responsible for the North Atlantic Treaty Organization and the defense of Western Europe—with thorny, intractable, and controversial decisions. The stability of Italy, for illustration, would seem to require the admission of the *Partito Comunista Italiana* (CPI) to membership in a coalition government. Otherwise shaken, terror-ridden Italians would have to acquiesce in the continuation of minority Christian Democratic governments. At the same time, the acceptance of the *compromesso storico* proffered by the communists and the formation of a two-party government in Italy appear to most observers to threaten the internal security of the

NATO defense system, not to mention the common fear that communists in the government would sooner or later take over, expelling the Christian Democrats by force, by fraud, or by a judicious admixture of the two.

The Eurocommunists would, of course, much prefer that the United States not use its influence to make more difficult their accession to a share of power through the formation of coalition governments, and there are elements among them that would even welcome American support of their political enterprise. As a first step in the analysis of the Eurocommunist problem, it will be worthwhile to present as succinctly as possible the arguments advanced by the Eurocommunists to justify their position in contemporary history and then to examine briefly the revolutionary doctrine that has been formulated by the most prominent and influential of the Eurocommunist factions.

According to the Eurocommunists, their movement began on the night of February 24-25, 1956, at the twentieth party congress of the Communist party of the Soviet Union (CPSU) when N. S. Khrushchev made his "secret" denunciation of I. V. Stalin. That act had the unintended consequence of raising for West European communists what could be called the Russian question—a matter that their leaders had endeavored, until then successfully, to keep out of intraparty discussion.

Khrushchev's secret speech, Eurocommunists assert, represented for the Western cadres a traumatic experience. Until then knowledge of the purges, the gross violations of individual rights, and the forced labor camps had been filtered through the intense ideological convictions of the Western parties as simple slander or as countermeasures provoked by dangerous enemies. After some consideration of the unfiltered information provided by the Soviet first party secretary, the Westerners were forced to conclude that the first socialist state was capable of grievous error either because it was liable to such an infirmity as the personality cult or because of the hard task of primitive accumulation that Russian backwardness had dictated.

The same year that marked the delivery of the secret speech also witnessed (and not accidentally, as the Soviets would say) the Hungarian uprising and the Polish October. One consequence of those upheavals was the ideological re-action that caused a world conference of communist parties, assembled in Moscow in 1957, to declare that revisionism had become the main danger to the movement. Thus in reacting to Khrushchev's famous denunciation of Stalin, the Hungarian theoretician György Lukács warned that substituting Lenin and his doctrine for Stalin and Stalinism could also lead to dogmatism; in East Germany Ernst Bloch and his students demanded peaceful coexistence with social democracy, the inclusion of the contributions of Bukharin, Luxemburg, Trotsky, and even Kautsky in the sacred literature of the movement, and the introduction in socialist countries of workers' councils. András Hegedüs, prime minister of Hungary under the redoubtable Rákosi and the Budapest school, went further by asserting that the Soviet government had not built a socialist society but had instead carried out the industrialization and modernization of Russia under conditions of noncapitalist industrial relations—a process that had resulted in the creation of a managing bureaucracy that had usurped political power. It was in the midst of this ferment that a group of Yugoslav theoreticians gathered around the new journal *Praxis* (published since 1964 in Zagreb) and began to reformulate what they called critical Marxism.

According to the Eurocommunists, however, the emergence of right revisionism was by no means the only cause for the revival of critical Marxism. There were other factors, such as the development of a multiplicity of socialist models—the Yugoslav, the Chinese, and the Cuban, in addition to the Soviet—and, more generally, the increasing complexity of Soviet society, for which socialist interpretations had to be formulated and socialist solutions had to be found. Perhaps this complexity, not right revisionism or the multiplicity of models, was the seedbed of Eurocommunist thinking. In any case, all three developments raised questions concerning the long-range aims of socialism as well as the role to be played by the industrial proletariat in socialist societies. Since 1956, when Ernst Bloch took up residence in the West, setting thereby an example followed widely by Marxist philosophers, all significant Marxist thinkers, according to the Eurocommunists, have dwelled outside the Soviet camp, and all serious Marxist theoreticians have been either forerunners or formulators of Eurocommunist positions.

Significantly enough, the Eurocommunists insist, the Dubček experiment, coming thirteen years after Khrushchev's secret speech, proved enormously popular with the West European parties. The experiment was popular because it seemed to promise a socialist state of democratic and pluralist character in which the party could retain its leading role. The rapid chain of events in Prague appeared to indicate that the Soviet variety of the socialist system as well as its potential for gross error contained a built-in mechanism of regeneration that would enable it to evolve in a direction acceptable to Western Marxists.

The Soviet occupation of Czechoslovakia proved to be the turning point for Eurocommunists. What kind of socialism was it that had to be forced on a mature industrial proletariat who had abolished capitalism? What kind of socialism was it that had to eliminate communist leaders who enjoyed the enthusiastic support of the masses? The Soviet occupation of the Czech lands could not be explained by attributing it to a backwardness that had been substantially overcome or interpreted as a reflection of a cult of personality that had already been condemned. Something fundamental was involved.

If the Soviet Union did not provide a model for the highly industrialized countries of Western Europe, how were the communists of the West to justify an organizational existence separate from that of the West European socialist and labor parties? Shortly after the events in Prague, Soviet First Secretary L. Brezhnev defined right revisionism as a flirtation with social democracy—a courtship that, he added tartly, could lead to a negation of the leading role of the party in socialist countries and to the loss of socialist achievements. In brief, the Russian question had at last been raised, and Eurocommunism, in gestation since February 1956, had been born.

According to the Eurocommunist account, the West European parties had achieved organizational and political independence from Moscow in the early postwar period. But until 1968 the ideological bond had not been loosened, for it had been easier to implement organizational independence by allowing the sleeping ideological dog to lie. Nor had party leaders entertained any wish to surrender the domination of their memberships sanctioned by democratic centralism—a mastery that would erode in debate and argument once the Russian question was formulated. But with five Soviet divisions stationed in Bohemia, the home of the most pro-Soviet and pro-Russian of all the Central European peoples, the process of ideological emancipation could no longer be contained.

In its determined opposition to American imperialism and in its unflinching support of liberation movements in the third world, the Soviet Union remained progressive, it was argued. But the Soviet collossus could no longer serve as a model for the countries of the advanced industrial West. The Western parties began to speak of social pluralism and parliamentary democracy, although with varying degrees of intensity, clarity, and commitment. The national authenticity of each party was stressed. As the Western comrades regarded the defense of national independence as their special tasks, they opposed any further extension of Soviet territory and power. The *Parti Communiste Francais* (PCF) came to support the French nuclear deterrent, and the CPI found it easier to conceive of a mature socialism within the confines of NATO than outside it.

Not surprisingly, the Eurocommunists assert, many Western communist leaders found it increasingly difficult to maintain the practice of democratic centralism. Internal party debate was unavoidable on a question as vital as the relationship with the Muscovite lodestar. Moreover, if socialist society was to be pluralist in character, why must the communist party itself retain a monolithic posture? The leaders fell back on the time-honored position, until then honored only in the breach, that party discipline was a matter of scrupulous adherence to party strategy once that strategy had been determined in open party discussion.

The debate is still in progress. The debaters must analyze the nature of the Soviet state. Is it in some sense socialist, or is it not? And based on the answer to this question, what should be the relationship of the revolutionary movement to the one-time capital of the world revolution? And what role should the West European communist parties play in the evolution of that relationship?

The conception of the Soviet Union held by a Western party is reflected in that party's self-image. If it is determined that the Soviet party has not been struggling to found an ideal workers' state but has instead worked (unconsciously to be sure) to create a cruel and exploitive despotism, then the Western affiliate must reject the Soviet paradigm and shop around for new ideas and a new purpose. If the Western party is to maintain a coherent organization and a sense of forward movement, it must find a new model of the good society that it wishes to build. Eurocommunists recognize that after fifty years of Stalinism, that will not be easy.

So far various positions have emerged in the debate: that

of the Italians; the position presented by Santiago Carrillo, leader of the Spanish party, in his much translated *Euro-comunismo y Estado*;[1] and that put forward by the Yugo-slav revisionists. The Yugoslav teaching exists both in an official version, primarily the work of the now disgraced Milovan Djilas, and in opposition dress, as represented by the group around the Zagreb journal *Praxis*. This coterie had come to dominate the faculty of philosophy at the University of Belgrade as well as the departments of sociology and philosophy at Zagreb. Unhappily, both groups have been deprived of their right to teach, and the journal *Praxis* has been suppressed (1974).[2] The influence of the group is well established beyond the Yugoslav frontier, however. It held summer-school classes on the island of Korčula in the Adriatic to which Marxist theoreticians from the West repaired regularly, and the editorial board of the international edition of the journal reads like a *Who's Who* of non-Stalinist Marxism.

The praxis advocates seem likely to play greater roles in the ideological turmoil that besets the Western parties than those played by the proponents of any other school. The praxis people have the distinct advantage of representing a much more important and successful party than do either the Italians or the Spanish. They combine a strongly held anti-Soviet position with residence in a socialist country. In *Euro-comunismo y Estado* the Soviet Union is presented as socialist and therefore capable of being brought back into the fold by a revolution leading to a change of government, whereas in the praxis teaching (as in the official Yugoslav doctrine), the Soviet system is treated as a form of state capitalism that can only be returned to the path of Marxist righteousness as the consequence of a general revolutionary upheaval—one that would change the class structure as well as the government. But whatever the course of the argument, the internal crisis of each Western party is likely to be both prolonged and severe.

* * *

It should be worthwhile to encapsulate praxist doctrine in a few paragraphs before attempting a critical evaluation of the Eurocommunist movement as a whole.

In the praxist view, the teaching of Marx and Engels, originally a critical and an open system of thought, has been thoroughly revised by its Russian champions, this revision taking the form of Marxism-Leninism (not to mention the now discredited and even forgotten Marxism-Leninism-Stalinism). The key to Russian revisionism is the positing of inexorable laws of development that leave scant room for either the initiative of the individual or for the respect of the human personality. Marxism-Leninism in fact teaches that the worker is so limited in his outlook toward capitalist exploitation that he can do no more than mitigate his economic plight by organizing unions and conducting strikes. Therefore to initiate and manage the revolutionary upheaval foreseen by Marx, a class of professional revolutionaries would have to be recruited from the intellectual elite. The ultimate effect of this reading of Marxism is to make of Soviet Russia another version of the class society, the planned capitalism of the USSR becoming even more exploitive and reactionary than the unplanned capitalism of the West.[3]

By denying the individual human being any role in history, Marxism-Leninism vests all power in a communist party that is only a surrogate for omnipotent bureaucracy that has at its disposal—even if it does not own—the means of production. The ruthlessness and thoroughness with which this bureaucratic machine exploits the working class of the Soviet Union exceed anything produced by capitalism. The bureaucratic machine has refused to tolerate the existence of public opinion. It has forbidden its new socialist intelligentsia to engage in creative activity. It has even isolated itself from any "foreign influence" by conducting a continuous search for new enemies. And it is every inch as etatist, that is, concerned with the magnification of its own power, as its capitalist rivals, if not more so.

In the Marxist language of the praxist philosophers, Euro-communism is the necessary antithesis of Marxism-Leninism and the Soviet model. Eurocommunism rejects Marxism-Leninism as a doctrine adapted to the modernization requirements of a backward country. It therefore repudiates the Soviet model of socialist society and attempts to formulate a socialism appropriate to advanced industrial countries with democratic traditions. It denies any leading role to the Soviet party, insisting instead on the sovereignty and independence of national communist parties. Eurocommunism, in short, represents a belated return to the critical Marxism of the founding fathers.

Historically, the dominance of the Soviet party within the world Marxist movement tended to swallow up critical Marxism and obscure its followers from public view. The Western parties have paid dearly for this domination. The costs include ideological sterility, for Marxism-Leninism is incapable of coping with the complex processes of modern industrial society; the dissipation of the intellectual resources of the revolutionary movement; and the large-scale defection of youth.

Rudi Supek, perhaps the leading praxist, has summarized the distinctive core of the doctrine.[4] The conception of man has been broadened from *homo politicus* to *homo economicus* and ultimately to *homo humanum,* the latter serving as the central figure in self-governing socialism. Man, furthermore, is self-determined: There are no objective laws of development. Praxis theoreticians understand man not as a product of society but as a unique, unhistorical, and socially undetermined being. History does not make man, rather the reverse is true, and everyone, not only the elite, has a say in the historical process. Soviet rejection of these postulates and capitalist acceptance of them explain why the alienation of the workers is greater under the red banners of Marxism-Leninism than under the bloody flags of laissez-faire.

Because the individual is the maker of history rather than its victim, everyone must have the right to engage in unsparing criticism in any field whatsoever, a right that Marxist-Leninists believe should be exercised only by those who dwell in the shadows of bourgeois society, for otherwise ordinary citizens would be free to criticize communist leaders—a great inconvenience. In short, praxists believe in freedom of speech and freedom of the press. Praxis adherents believe in human rights as against the interests of a bureaucratic single party, although this stand opens them to the charge that they have become de facto advocates of social democracy—an accusation that they find troublesome. It follows that Marxist praxists are also advocates of democracy not only in the political realm, where, they believe, it has been achieved in Western industrial countries, but above all in industry, which, they believe—in conformity with the official Yugoslav position—should be managed by the workers. Worker management is what Eurocommunists mean when they speak of the hegemony of the working class—their pale and emaciated substitute for the dictatorship of the proletariat.

In the view of the praxis group, the process of theoretical reconstruction initiated in 1956 has now been completed, and the ultimate victory of Eurocommunism in Western Europe is assured. There exists in that part of the world no significant body of Marxist intellectuals who are willing to defend the tenets of Marxism-Leninism. Henceforth the competition within each party will pit an authentic, critical Marxism created by independent minds against a Marxism-Leninism that is nothing more than the tool of the bureaucratic despots in the East. Between these two forces there can be no compromise, and within the Soviet empire the needs of internal security will require not only a sharp differentiation between the two philosophies but the physical suppression of critical Marxists as well.

* * *

As an intellectual pedigree, a history of ideas, Euro-communism is striking and insightful. It rests on the assumption that conviction is a decisive element in communist behavior, that when communists are persuaded by events that their beliefs are wrong, they will change their views and work out a more effective approach to the better social order that is their dream, as has been done by such leading cadres as Josip Broz-Tito, Imre Nagy, Alexander Dubček, and Enrico Berlinguer as well as by such theoreticians as Lukács, Bloch, and Supek. This emphasis on the integrity of communist conviction is perhaps the most important contribution of the Eurocommunist exegesis.

But the Eurocommunist explanation, I would argue, is only true as far as it goes; it is not sufficient because it ignores the practical side of communist politics—the question of power. The perfervid belief of the militant is rooted as much in his need for power in order to realize his dream as it is in his experience of defeat. An analysis that compares the power relationships that brought about Yugoslav revisionism—either in its official or in its oppositional form—to the power factors that helped produce the Eurocommunist movement as a whole will, I believe, have at least as much explanatory power as the doctrinal or ideological approach. The argument is not that Yugoslav influence played no role in shaping Eurocommunist ideology—it did so in the past and very probably will do so in the future—but that Euro-communism may come to the same doctrinal position as Titoism and for the same basic reason: the question of power.

In my view Eurocommunism began not with the occupation of Czechoslovakia on the night of August 23-24, 1968, nor on the night of February 24-25, 1956, when Khrushchev delivered his famous philippic, but rather on June 28, 1948, with the expulsion of Yugoslavia from the Cominform.[5] Eurocommunism began then because the Yugoslav

Communist party (CPY), which had fought its way to power in a three-way civil war, had by no means achieved the support and the confidence of the majority of the population. It could not then, as it cannot now, gain a majority in a free election, as its bold experimentation with semifree electoral processes showed. Expulsion from the Cominform created for the CPY a veritable crisis situation, for the party was thereby deprived of Soviet subsidies that had made possible the pursuit of extremist policies in the face of bitter opposition from below. To compensate for this loss (surely a heavy one, for Stalin himself—no mean judge of power relationships within the bloc—believed that the Yugoslav cadres would have to overthrow the "clique of Tito, Ranković, and Kardelj" and come crawling for forgiveness in order to survive), the party had to expand substantially its base of popular support within the country.

Moscow had, for example, given the regime in Belgrade a political subsidy in the form of an unspoken guarantee of Soviet military intervention in the event of its collapse, what I referred to elsewhere as a political landslide. The loss of this political subsidy could only be offset by (1) abandoning the forcible collectivization of agriculture; (2) limiting the role of the political police in order to provide such rights as freedom of conversation (a right different from freedom of speech); and (3) decentralizing the regime in order to permit local authorities some say in the decision-making process.

There had also been an economic subsidy, created by including Yugoslavia in the socialist system of barter trade that guaranteed the sale of inferior Yugoslav manufactures as well as a secure supply of critical raw materials at fixed prices. The loss of the economic subsidy was offset by partial reliance on market forces—the invention of a socialist market, as it were—in the hope of raising the efficiency of the economy to such a level that Yugoslav manufactured wares would one day compete in the world market. Examples of this greater reliance on market forces include permitting unemployed or underemployed Yugoslav workers to migrate to the countries of the Common Market in search of employment, developing the tourist trade as a major source of hard currency, and vesting decision-making authority in managers of individual enterprises.

The Soviet Union had also given the CPY an ideological subsidy: membership in a revolutionary movement of world-wide dimension as well as a sense of total immersion in the wave of the future. Because of the CPY's isolation and un-popularity on its own terrain, the Soviet ideological subsidy was of awesome importance in maintaining cadre morale and discipline. The problem facing the CPY leadership—and now we return to the issue of ideology—was how to develop a position that (1) would restore cadre morale and loyalty by putting Moscow in the wrong and Belgrade in the right; (2) would make possible the decentralization of a taut regime without letting matters get out of hand; and (3) would make possible a Western financial subsidy without the regime's appearing to have sold out to the capitalists.

The solution of this ideological conundrum was brilliantly conceived. The Muscovite center, it was alleged, had itself fallen into deviation, reverting to the practices of bureau-cratic despotism. Belgrade alone in the socialist world carried forward the Olympic flame of the true faith, concretized domestically by the transfer of power in the factories to elective workers' councils and internationally by a foreign policy of nonalignment in a world rent by conflict between capitalist and "socialist" exploiters.

Through the introduction of political, economic, and ideological substitutes for Soviet subsidies, Belgrade reached a *modus vivendi* with the population that it ruled, achieved a higher rate of growth in gross national product than that of any other socialist country, acquired a financial subsidy from the West sufficient to cover Yugoslavia's hard currency deficit stemming from crop failures, created a bloc of non-aligned third-world states, and became a center of world communism that competed with Moscow and Peking.

Italian revisionism—the revisionism of a party out of power—is rooted in the same basic problems as that which faced the Yugoslav communists: broadening the base of popular support for the party, although for the purpose of winning elections rather than of stabilizing a regime threatened with collapse. The Italian approach to this problem was preconditioned in much the same way as was the Yugoslav, by the experience of armed resistance to the Nazi occupier. For the sake of brevity our purview in Western Europe will be limited to the CPI, which, I would argue, has advanced farther along the Eurocommunist road than any other party.[6]

Resistance in fact recreated the CPI phoenixlike after it had virtually been destroyed in the prisons of Italian fascism. Under the conditions of resistance, the CPI learned to collaborate with non-Marxist forces, such as the guerrillas fielded by the *Partito d'Azione,* and even to work with and accept the support of the Western powers, including the archcapitalist United States. During the resistance, furthermore, members of the intelligentsia achieved positions of great importance, if not dominance, in the Italian party leadership. Cooperation among social forces, unusual among West European parties, contributed in the postwar period to the great flexibility of the Italians in matters ideological.

Reborn and reconstituted during the conflict, the CPI possessed another unusual advantage. It could draw on its experience under fascism as interpreted by a major Marxist theoretician, Antonio Gramsci, who died a martyr's death in prison. Like the bulk of his comrades, Gramsci had been impressed by the broad support that fascism had won from the ranks of Italian labor as well as from the peasants in the villages. Like them, he believed that once fascism was overthrown, the minions of conservatism would rally around the Roman papacy—that internationale of world reaction—in order to block progress. Gramsci reasoned that in the Marxist scheme of historical epochs, the road to socialism in Italy would be longer and more arduous than elsewhere in Western Europe and that before communist power could even be imagined, there would have to take place, as a precondition, a great liberalizing transformation of Italian society.

Thus at the very time that the CPY was broadening its popular base in order to replace the subsidies that it lost from abroad, the CPI was attempting to build an electorate sufficiently large to make impossible the formation of any government without its participation and thereby prevent a return to reaction.

Achievement of the CPI objective required, as a matter of principle, acceptance of the democratic process that could lead to a pluralist society; otherwise no one but the party faithful would vote the party ticket because of the fear that the first free election won by the communists would be the last. The CPI leadership went so far as to assure the electorate that not even a 51 percent majority would be taken as authorization for socializing Italian society; *that* would be undertaken only if and when the overwhelming majority of the voters favored it. The communist delegation to the Italian parliament worked assiduously to promote the interests of their constituents and to introduce legislation designed to get on the statute books rather than to stir up controversy. Communist-controlled local governments became for Italy models of probity and efficiency, taking care not to dig too deeply into the pockets of the nervous middle class.

To their acceptance of pluralism and parliamentarianism the Italian communists added the practice of *presence,* the notion that devoted Marxists should be posted in all the dugouts and trenches of capitalist society to prevent or at least to warn of any turn to the fascist right or any mobilization of reaction under Vatican guidance. Thus practicing Catholics were not excluded from membership in the party, and the party, exfoliating front organizations, reached out for alliances even with non-Marxist elements.

The CPI also proclaimed an Italian road to socialism, emphasizing its independence from Moscow by criticizing Soviet handling of dissident intellectuals, by condemning the occupation of Czechoslovakia, by accepting the European Community and endorsing its enlargement, and even by expressing its willingness to cooperate with the North Atlantic Treaty Organization.

There are analogies with the Yugoslav case. The conversion of the CPI to parliamentary democracy and social pluralism is analogous to the introduction of worker self-management in Yugoslavia in the sense of being the fundamental doctrinal change that made possible the expansion of the party's popular base. The practice of seeking a universal *presence* is the analogue of the CPY's greater reliance on market forces in the sense that the erection of a special barrier to middle-class fascism is an effort to stabilize the system as a whole, as is the attempt to raise the productivity of Yugoslav industry to world standards. Finally, the Italian road to socialism is the counterpart of the Yugoslav policy of nonalignment.

It is my contention that the power situation of a communist party is at least as potent an explanation of the Eurocommunist phenomenon as is its ideological pedigree. One reinforces the other. As long as the threat of nuclear war hangs over Europe, as long as the Soviet economy remains dependent on importing from the West the principal products of the continuing scientific and technological revolution, as long as the rate of growth of Soviet GNP continues to decline, and as long as the Common Market progresses toward the unification of Western Europe, there is no use in waiting for Godot. And once a communist party reaches that conclusion, then it must concern itself with achieving power through the parliamentary process and within the framework of a pluralist society or else fall apart. That the invention of Eurocommunism can be ascribed to the Yugoslav party results from the fact that that party was expelled from the communist comity by the same Godot and even though ensconced in the seat of power, found it necessary to broaden its narrow popular base in order to remain enthroned.

The two explanations, the ideological and the political, are closely related, but they are also different, as an examination of their policy consequences will make clear. The praxis people contend that Eurocommunism represents a complete breach with the Soviet Union and Marxism-Leninism and is a new and more vigorous form of social democracy. The threat that Eurocommunism poses in the long run is not to the beleaguered Italian government or to NATO but to the extremist left in Italy and to Soviet influence in Western Europe. American policy, instead of opposing CPI participation in the Italian government, should foster such collaboration. In so doing there would be little to lose and the stabilization of Italy and NATO to gain.

The political explanation of Eurocommunism leads to suspended judgment. Are there not limits to the Europeanization of communism or to the further evolution of revisionism—limits set by the question of power itself? The importance of this question became apparent in Yugoslavia in 1971 when a major crisis revealed the extent to which the Croatian people rejected the party and its regimen of ethnic equality in favor of a separate national existence. A political landslide began in Croatia in 1971, and the Croatian communist regime would probably have given way to a nationalist one had it not been for Tito's threat to send the Yugoslav People's Army to occupy the deviant republic. The difference between Croatia in 1971 and Czechoslovakia in 1968 is that the Croats were convinced that Tito would carry out his threat, whereas the Czechs refused to believe that Brezhnev would follow through on his.

The conclusion that CPY leaders drew from the Croatian crisis was that they had to rebuild the central party apparatus that had been partially dismantled as a consequence of decentralization begun in 1952 and had to reinforce the practice of democratic centralism; in short, they decided to return to Leninism, a word that had almost disappeared from the Yugoslav socialist vocabulary. In other words, those who believed in the Yugoslav federation found it necessary to return to Leninism and democratic centralism in order to prevent the dissolution of the state. Leninism, the party, and democratic centralism stand in the way of Yugoslavia's repeating the unhappy fate of the Hapsburg monarchy (which in its ethnic problems the federation so much resembles). Were it to succumb to ethnic pressures, Yugoslavia would leave an additional heritage of tiny, economically unviable nation-states with ethnically indeterminable frontiers. Yugoslav society cannot be fully pluralized—heaven forbid that one should speak of democratizing the Yugoslav polity—without threatening the dissolution of the federation.

It follows that if American policy were to be reversed and the CPI—if not the first Eurocommunist party in the field, then certainly the most Eurocommunist of all—were permitted to form a coalition with the Christian Democrats, the expectation would be that the new government would prove capable of containing not the centrifugal force of nationalism, which has destabilized the Yugoslav federation, but the revolution of rising expectations that is at the bottom of Italy's semibankruptcy. It appears that if Italian society is not to collapse of its own weight, Italy will have to impose harsh measures, such as the restoration of labor discipline, austerity in consumption, the rigid regulation of currency and capital flows, and the suppression of terrorist activity by extraordinary police procedures. Living standards will have to stagnate or even decline. Before such changes could take place, however, would not the communists have to become dominant in the coalition, and would not the unions have to submit to government control, retaining only the right to engage in wildcat strikes? Would not a great expansion of governmental regulation of the economy be necessary together with a disproportionate growth of bureaucracy? Would not a substantial expansion of the police power and of police activity be called for, perhaps even the replacement of the rule of law with an Italian equivalent of socialist legality? Can any party but one practicing democratic centralism implement such measures? Is not the democratic centralism of the Italian Communist party the one available counter to the revolution of rising expectations?

Does not the argument that we have advanced lead to the conclusion that what Italy really needs is a small dose of communist dictatorship? That democratic centralism could prove vital to the salvation of parliamentary democracy and social pluralism in Italy is not only the ultimate paradox but is the ultimate Marxist contradiction as well. The paradox raises moral questions for America's policymakers. Is it not one thing to subsidize and protect a Marxist-Leninist Yugoslavia in defiance of the Soviet Union, promoting thereby a revisionist evolution of a totalitarian system, and quite another thing to push an Italian parliamentary government in the direction of dictatorship? These questions that proceed from the political explanation of Eurocommunism must be answered. Questions concerning the effect of CPI government participation on NATO security should also be answered.

There is, however, an alternative scenario that should be taken into account if the political explanation of the Eurocommunist phenomenon is to be considered. Like the CPY, the CPI has changed some of the components of democratic centralism. As the CPY abolished party cells in all government offices and industrial plants, so the CPI has replaced its cellular structure with a sectorial organization. But should the *compromesso storico* not receive America's blessing, requiring the CPI to enlarge its electorate substantially beyond the 34 percent that it received in the general election of 1976 in order to make parliamentary government impossible without communist participation, would not the practice of democratic centralism become so eroded that the CPI, having diluted its Leninist discipline, could do no better coping with the interminable Italian crisis than the enfeebled Christian Democrats have done? Or could not this erosion have already taken place?

During the acting out of either of these two scenarios there might well come a time when the Kremlin might feel forced to cut its losses and expel the Western comrades or at least some of them from the European communist brotherhood. Brezhnev has already threatened to invoke this sanction. The breaking point could come because Moscow could no longer bear the weight of Western party criticism on the subject of human rights—a subject concerning which the European communist regimes have very little tolerance—or because Western party participation in European Community governments raised too many questions concerning the possibility of multiparty coalitions in Eastern Europe—a contingency not lightly to be dismissed. Such excommunication, which would be analogous to the Cominform declaration of 1948, might well result in the transmutation of the expelled party or parties into organisms fully representative of critical Marxism or social democracy if there is a difference.

Should this happen, one unanswered question would remain. Would party cadres as well as those who regularly vote the communist ticket *all* follow the leadership into the social democratic fold, or would important numbers secede and form a new, more militant, and pro-Muscovite party on the far left? Might it not happen again?

We do not know, of course, largely because we are still for the most part ignorant of the answer to another question: Why do the masses of Italians and French vote the communist ticket election after election, even decade after decade? Two assumptions are often made concerning the motivation of the communist electorate: It is a protest vote that would melt away if such intractable evils as unemployment were overcome; in any case, this electorate is ignorant of the true conditions obtaining in the countries of socialism. Some thirty years of studying communist regimes and movements leaves me somewhat doubtful on both counts. The correlation between working-class support and communist adherence made in Western analyses—which sometimes serve as mirror images of communist teaching—is greatly overstated.[7]

It is even less clear that the communist electorate is so woefully ignorant of the conditions of life under socialism or of what would happen in a West European country under conditions of Soviet military occupation and Marxist-Leninist takeover. It is not at all inconceivable that this electorate thinks of pervasive police control, forced labor camps, and bloody purges as condign punishment for those who communism has taught are responsible for the current oppression and deprivation of communist voters. Nor would these voters be averse to finding themselves suddenly elevated into the places of those who had been overthrown and whose talents, assiduousness, and capital reserves they have not been able to match under a competitive system. We really do not know because the hard evidence is lacking. On this score the Western literature on communism remains for the most part silent.

NOTES

1. Barcelona, 1977. The English translation was published in London in the same year.

2. They did not, however, lose either their salaries or their privilege of going abroad when invited by foreign universities. The standard work on the *praxis* group is Gerson S. Sher, *Praxis: Marxist Criticism and Dissent in Socialist Yugoslavia* (Bloomington, Ind., 1977). For a review,

see Bogdan Denitch in *The American Historical Review*, LXXXIII (1978), pp. 1295-1296.

3. See Rudi Supek's chapter in this volume. Supek served as joint editor-in-chief of *Praxis* virtually throughout its stormy history and has become the principal spokesman of that school.

4. *Ibid.*

5. For a more detailed exposition of my explanation of the Yugoslav phenomenon as well as a marshaling of the evidence on which that view is based, see R. V. Burks and S. A. Stankovic, "Jugoslawien auf dem Weg zu halbfreien Wahlen?" *Osteuropa* (Stuttgart), XVII (1967), pp. 131-146; R. V. Burks, "Liberalization of Dictatorship: The East European Experience," a paper presented to the 1968 annual meeting of the American Political Science Association, 18-page mimeograph; R. V. Burks, *The National Problem and the Future of Yugoslavia* (Santa Monica, California: the RAND Corporation, P 4761, 1971), 74 pp.; and R. V. Burks, "The Problems Facing the Yugoslav Communist Movement," in Andrew Gyorgy and James A. Kuhlman (eds.), *Innovation in Communist Systems* (Boulder, Colorado, 1978), pp. 99-104. The most recent general work on the Yugoslav regime is Dennison Rusinow, *The Yugoslav Experiment* (Berkeley, 1977). For an evaluation, see R. V. Burks in the *Slavic Review*, XXXVII (1978), p. 335.

6. For the analysis of the Italian party I have depended primarily on Donald L. M. Blackmer and Sidney Tarrow (eds.), *Communism in Italy and France* (Princeton, 1975).

7. This is a central conclusion of the *Dynamics of Communism in Eastern Europe*. For a study of the communist electorate in Western Europe, see R. V. Burks, "Catholic Parties in Latin Europe," *Journal of Modern History*, XXIV (1952), pp. 269-286. In order to isolate and account for the Christian Democratic electorate it became necessary to deal with the socialist and communist electorates as well.

Peter C. Ludz

EUROCOMMUNISM AND ITS INFLUENCE ON THE SOCIAL DEMOCRATIC PARTY IN WEST GERMANY

1. Preliminary Remarks

In recent years and more forcefully since 1977, the phenomenon of Eurocommunism has assumed not only European but global significance because of what it portends for both the United States and the Soviet Union. The Americans are concerned with its effects on the political and social stability of Western Europe and the Atlantic Alliance; the Russians are concerned with its political and ideological effects on the Warsaw Pact countries of Eastern Europe and beyond. The West European perspective, specifically, the West German perception of the problem, is of special consequence not only because the Federal Republic of Germany (FRG) is the cornerstone of European stability but also because West Germany is the most important European ally of the United States.[1] The attitude of the ruling social democratic government of the FRG toward Eurocommunism is thus also a matter not only of European but of global significance.

It is true that because the French left, epitomized by the French Communist party (PCF), failed to obtain a majority in the National Assembly elections held in March 1978 and because support for the Italian Communist party (PCI) declined in the local elections in May 1978, the immediate concern with Eurocommunism appears to be receding.[2] But irrespective of whether it continues to occupy the limelight of political and scholarly debate, the potentiality and the reality of Eurocommunism will affect European and international developments for several reasons:

A. Eurocommunism reflects the objective situation of world communism and the fact that Moscow has lost its dominant position. Eurocommunism is no uniform movement; instead, it is characterized by ever-growing variations and nuances. Thus at least in Europe, Eurocommunism is engendering a momentum of insecurity and instability: It is producing ideological claims that may menace the existing ideological vacuum in Western Europe. Eurocommunism should therefore not only be regarded as another schism in world communism. Its capacity, which was reinforced by the policy of detente, to endanger the status quo in Europe should be analyzed. Analysis has to take into account the fact that conservative political circles in Europe, on the one side, and numerous leftist groups, on the other, oppose Eurocommunism as strongly as do some top officials of the CPSU.

B. In political and sociological terms, Eurocommunism mirrors a specific sociopolitical dynamism that has increasingly shaped the domestic policies of Western industrial countries for many years and has thus influenced their foreign-policy decisions to an increasing extent. In this context, I mention the labor unions, their roles in domestic policies, and their relations with communist, socialist, and social democratic parties or with specific factions within individual parties.

C. Eurocommunism affects not only the East-West conflict but also the North-South conflict in international politics.

2. Some Paradoxes of Eurocommunism

Our factual knowledge suggests that there is not a uniform Eurocommunist movement, a theory, or a program adhered to by the two largest Eurocommunist parties (the PCI and the PCF) that dictates strategies to be followed and tactics to be used. This state of affairs seems surprising if one considers that in principle all Eurocommunist politicians and ideologues put more emphasis on the historical period identified as the road to socialism than on the goal to be reached, that is, socialist society. However, not even Gramsci formulated a consistent theoretical program for the PCI despite the fact that after Togliatti, he is considered the most important theoretician.[3]

The need for a deeper understanding of Marxism became especially urgent after the Second World War, when the keepers of the rigid theory that is the official Marxism-Leninism of the Soviet Union and those who propounded the theoretical vacuity of the social democratic parties in Western Europe squared off. The rediscovery of Gramsci (as well as Lukács) is above all traceable to the advances made by such intellectuals as Lucio Colletti, who joined the PCI in the late 1940s and sought, through the study of Gramsci as the national heir to the historicism of Vico and Croce, to uncover the sources of Marxism that had been buried under Stalinism, including Marx's own writings.[4] The Italian intellectuals who joined the PCI at that time found in Gramsci's works a "rejection of 'economism' " and "positivist scientism," that is, a rejection of the "crude materialism" and "false objectivity" of Bukharin's *Theory of Historical Materialism* (1921).[5] Even if Western observers, according to a recent statement by Frane Barbieri,[6] who in 1975 coined the term Eurocommunism, regard Eurocommunism as an "ideologically fluid and vague phenomenon" that nevertheless has "instrumental qualities," it is true that countless intellectuals in the 1950s and 1960s sought clarification of their own theoreticopolitical positions *within* the communist parties of the West, not *outside* them.[7]

Among the paradoxes of Eurocommunism, especially Italian communism, is the fact that communists "will be unable to throw themselves unequivocally into the practice or support of democratic government but will prefer to cultivate the situation of being both in the government and in the opposition simultaneously."[8] No Western analyst has so far been able to provide a plausible explanation of this paradoxical position. Does it stem from the "divided nature" of the Eurocommunist parties or from their Leninist "dual strategy"? Without proposing that sole importance be accorded to the Leninist theory of strategy and tactics for an interpretation of European communism, I want, however, to recall that in the course of history, and particularly with respect to the so-called coalition policy, Leninist movements have always seized all opportunities that would bring them to power. Eurocommunism can be regarded as a Leninist movement because Eurocommunists still refer to Lenin as their forefather, even though one can question whether they are only paying lip service to Lenin. Some observers argue that very often Berlinguer and Marchais have had to assume dogmatic attitudes in their public statements because their party bureaucracies are run by thousands of Stalinist-trained cadres. In my opinion, this explanation is plausible, but there may be other factors to be considered.

Additional contradictions in Eurocommunism include the Eurocommunists' intention to draw a line of demarcation between themselves and the socialists or, even more distinctly, the social democrats and at the same time to stake everything on a "convergence" of "all democratic and socialist forces" that may develop in an uncertain future. This split attitude can be observed in Carrillo. With respect to the goals of the PCE, he wrote: "We shall not . . . abandon the revolutionary ideas of Marxism; the ideas of the class struggle, historical materialism and dialectical materialism; the conception of a worldwide revolutionary process which is putting an end to imperialism. . . . We are not returning to social democracy!"[9] On the other hand, Carrillo is searching for a platform on which the communist parties may unite with the socialist and social democratic parties: "The 'Eurocommunist' strategy aims to bring about a convergence with the Socialist and Social Democratic parties, with the progressive Christian forces, with all the democratic groups that are not the henchmen of monopoly-type property."[10] This paradox is usually resolved by employing an argument that has been voiced by Italian party politicians and ideologues since Gramsci advanced it. Social developments have to be understood "not as static," but as "fluid" and permanently changing processes.

Another paradox of Eurocommunism relates to the fact that Eurocommunist leaders have created an atmosphere of "liberalism" around themselves and profess "reformist" and "conciliatory, collaborationist" policies, while adhering to the organizational *modus vivendi* ("democratic centralism") of their party and reinforcing the principles of strict party discipline.[11]

To some extent orthodox theoreticians such as Louis Althusser and Etienne Balibar recognize these and other paradoxes, contradictions, and inconsistencies in the PCI and the PCF. Althusser, in addressing himself to the new theoretical orientation of the PCF at the twenty-second party congress in Paris in 1976, made specific reference to the situation of world communism: "Paradoxically, the revolutionary movement has never been so powerful in the world now that the third world movements for liberation and economic independence have been joined to the anticapitalist struggle in the imperialist centers. But paradoxically, at the same time the crisis of the international communist movement, both open (the Sino-Soviet split) and masked (the conflict between the Western communist movement and the USSR), has never been so acute."[1][2]

These and other features of Eurocommunism make the leaders of the communist parties in Western Europe appear unreliable—even to some of their followers or former adherents. For instance, one of the reasons why the *Il Manifesto* group split from the PCI (in 1970) was spelled out in ideological terms: The PCI is no longer a revolutionary party in the sense of Marx and Lenin. Also, more recently, the leader of the Italian Socialist party, Bettino Craxi, sharply attacked the "Leninist," "Asiatic" communism of the PCI and even extended his attack to Gramsci, whom he called a totalitarian.[1][3] Berlinguer, replying on the occasion of the national festival of *L'Unita* in Genoa (in the middle of September 1978), tried anew to give a clear account of the Italian road to communism. He drew a line of demarcation between the Italian Communist party and the communist parties of Soviet Russia and Eastern Europe at one end and the social democratic parties at the other. He confirmed democratic centralism as the major principle of organization without abandoning either civil liberties or the goals of socialism.[1][4] On the whole, however, Berlinguer once more postponed the necessary clarification of his position.

3. The Strategy of the Historical Compromise

Most Western observers and politicians realized that Eurocommunism was exerting an impact on European politics after the Italian Communist party won 32 percent of the vote in the 1975 regional elections and after it gained more than one-third (34.4 percent) of the popular vote in 1976. The saliency of Eurocommunism in European politics had to be recognized when Berlinguer's "strategy of the historical compromise" *(compromesso storico)*, inspired by Togliatti, yielded some success.

Many Western observers consider the strategy of the historical compromise an expression of the growing flexibility of international communism. This flexibility can be traced to several roots. The ideological strategists surrounding Berlinguer, for example, Segre, Pajetta, Amendola, Napolitano, and others, point to the fact that as long ago as 1957, Togliatti announced "polycentric communism."[15] Some Eurocommunists subscribe to this view. Carrillo, for example, calls Togliatti the pathmaker of modern, pluralistic communism in Europe.[16] Other observers emphasize the 1968 invasion of Czechoslovakia by the Warsaw Pact countries as the fateful event. It united the three most important communist parties in Western Europe—the PCI, the PCF, and the PCE—on a pseudo-anti-Moscow platform, thus causing the rise of *Euro*communism. Finally, the tendencies in the individual West European communist parties toward autonomy, reformism, and regionalism are considered to have exerted a decisive influence on the growth of what today is called Eurocommunism.[17]

The historical compromise has never been defined as a strategy or as a program. "One is never told what it will do."[18] Berlinguer and the other PCI leaders can probably only sell the new line as long as they remain deliberately vague and ambiguous about its direction. Some Western observers point to the fact that Amendola, a powerful representative of the PCI's right wing, sees the historical compromise as a potential "copy" of the Grand Coalition between the SPD and the CDU in West Germany in 1966. By joining the Christian Democratic party in the Grand Coalition and governing with their representatives for three years, the Social Democratic party proved that it was trustworthy and socially responsible. Thus the road was paved for the party to win the chancellorship in 1969.[19]

4. The SPD Delimits Itself from Eurocommunism

Like the communists, the social democrats rank problems of delimitation very high.[20] Focusing on their public espousals may assist our understanding.

A. Some Official SPD Statements

The SPD strategy of delimitation from Eurocommunism includes official statements denying Eurocommunism as an all-inclusive phenomenon. If there ever existed a Eurocommunist movement, it is argued, it would have to be sought in Yugoslavia. There communism is rooted in the history experienced since 1941—the history of resistance and of the fight against Stalinism since 1948. Yugoslav communism had developed remarkable democratic qualities.[21] Unlike the PCI, the Yugoslav League of Communists took a clear stand against the Soviet Union and in support of Europe—for a Europe that should accept contributions from the United States. It is often recounted in SPD circles that Tito, in one of his speeches, referred to hegemony (of the USSR) ten times but only once to imperialism (of the USA). The leaders of the SPD seem to want to support Yugoslavia politically, economically, and socially and to strengthen its position as a stabilizing factor in Southern Europe.

Other official and semiofficial statements by SPD politicians highlight Eurocommunism as a phenomenon resulting from the communist parties' adaptation to social changes in Western Europe. They reject the notion that Eurocommunism may change the political profile of Western Europe in the foreseeable future. They assert that the communist parties will integrate themselves into the existing political system of Western Europe. From this point of view, the decisive task of the social democratic and socialist parties of Western Europe is to raise the living standard of Southern Europe to a level commensurate with that of Northern and Central Europe—a task beyond the means of the communist parties. The major positive function of Eurocommunism would therefore be to help stimulate evolutionary forces in Eastern Europe and perhaps even in the Soviet Union.

Conservative forces in the SPD, such as the former secretary of defense Georg Leber, raise another variant of the meaning of Eurocommunism. Not unlike certain circles in the CDU/CSU opposition in the West German parliament, Leber sees Eurocommunism as a danger. His argument is based on the following assertion: With the help of Eurocommunist parties, the Soviet Union would not only be able to threaten or even control Europe militarily but also ideologically and would eventually be able to consolidate its control over Western Europe.

The official line that, for example, Herbert Wehner, Willy Brandt, and Bruno Friedrich have presented to the West German parliament and public and to the international community is based on the preceding arguments. (Leber's position appears to be marginal.) Such presentations demonstrate that the SPD is not ambiguous in its attitude toward Eurocommunism. But Eurocommunism is a challenge to the party, which becomes evident when the theoretical-programmatic dimensions of the problem are analyzed.

It is clear that the theoretical vacuum of the 1960s, which has become manifest in the SPD since 1968, reflects a structural problem that has led to the wild and uncontrolled importation of theories. Theoretical borrowing has been employed by all JUSO groups, in particular, the so-called Stamokap faction, that is, the faction that derives its identity from its opposition to "state-monopolistic capitalism" (in German: *Sta*ats*mo*nopolistischer *Kap*italismus) and antirevisionists. The theoretical vacuity of the SPD can be attributed to mixing together the eclectic theoretical strivings of Andre Gorz, Herbert Marcuse, and Ernest Mandel, on the one hand, and Eduard Bernstein, Ferdinand LaSalle, Richard Loewenthal, as well as Paul Tillich, Erich Fromm, and Martin Buber, on the other.[22]

B. SPD Platforms as Responses to Eurocommunism
Social democratic leaders aim at developing a general "theory of democratic socialism," whereas Eurocommunist leaders and ideologues, also using the words *democracy* and *socialism,* try to design a more specific theory tailored to Western Europe. Such a Eurocommunist theory envisages a long period of transformation under the leadership of the working class. However, both the social democrats and the communists seek to promulgate supranational political platforms. For the social democrats, this platform would serve the interests of the social democratic and socialist parties of the Federal Republic of Germany, Austria, and Sweden.[23] For the communists, it would incorporate a variety of documents associated with the PCI as well as with the PCE.[24]

This striving to achieve a supranational orientation was preceded by attempts to coordinate national programs. Thus the programs adopted by the Socialist party of Austria (in 1958), the Social Democratic party of Germany (in 1959, i.e., the so-called *Godesberger Program*), and the Social Democratic Workers party of Sweden (in 1960) display similarities. All three define freedom, justice, and solidarity as "basic values." August Bebel, Ferdinand Lassalle, Jean Jaurès, and Eduard Bernstein are referred to by all three parties as the progenitors of democratic socialism. Moreover, quite a number of similar goals can be found in the policy platforms of the three parties:
   —increasing the influence of the unions and so-called citizens' initiatives in democratic decision making;
   —full employment;
   —more workers' codetermination;
   —more democratization but less bureaucratization;
   —a mass-oriented cultural policy;
   —restrictions against multinational corporations;
   —state-planned investments;

—the development of Europe as a "sovereign political entity."[25]

By comparison, the theoretical, programmatic declarations of the Eurocommunist parties seem to be vague. Only some contours of a program can be discerned:

—emphasis on a national road to socialism or communism;

—reform (although of far-reaching impact), instead of revolution;

—independence from the East and from the West, that is, from the USSR and the USA.[26]

The number of classical theorists invoked by the West European communists is greater than that cited by the social democrats. In the first place, Marx, Engels, and Lenin are always mentioned. Their ideas are reviewed once in a while and even frankly discussed within the Italian and Spanish communist parties. In the second place, Gramsci (and sometimes Vico and Croce) and Togliatti are invoked in Italy, Gramsci, Togliatti, Althusser, and Balibar in Spain. Gramsci's term hegemony, for example, has been the object of continuous discussions, leading to the conclusion that his concept of hegemony was aimed at redefining "the nature of power in modern societies in more comprehensive terms, allowing for the articulations of the various levels or instances of a given social formation, political, cultural or ideological. . . . "[27] He interpreted hegemony to mean predominance rather than revolutionary force. In order to achieve hegemony, the working class would have to become conscious of its existence as a class and prove its legitimacy by pursuing activities in the political, cultural, and ethical fields.[28]

Considering these and other attempts at definition, Gramsci can rightly be judged the most far-seeing thinker of the socialist-communist movement in Western Europe. Carrillo identified the major aspect of the post-Gramsci discussions about hegemony: The focus of the debate is "whether the working people in the developed capitalist countries can impose their hegemony without resorting to the dictatorship of the proletariat."[29] Gramsci's concept of hegemony should not, of course, confer on him the label of a pure Leninist. His attempts to formulate a concept of hegemony appropriate to Italian society and the Italian working class, however, point to the semantic insecurity of an ideology in flux. This ideology in flux appears to reflect the ongoing sociohistorical change of the PCI and Italian society at large.

Social democrats delimit themselves from communists, and vice versa. But both also send out signals that indicate mutual interests and common views. Citing Carrillo, I have demonstrated that the attempts of the communists to delimit themselves from the social democrats and the stressing of mutual interests can exist side by side. But there are also different nuances. These nuances can be explained by ascertaining the climate that prevailed on the dates when the respective statements were issued, by analyzing the objective political situations, by comparing the relative strengths of specific groups and the relative prestige of speakers within the parties, and as far as the PCI is concerned, by analyzing the consciously-employed *correnti,* that is, the channeling of differing conceptions and representative statements.

Recently SPD leaders set the boundaries of approach to the Eurocommunists in their draft platform for the European election in 1979, in which they argued that insofar as the Eurocommunists had not taken a clear stand on the Soviet dictatorship and bureaucracy or on the issues of human rights and freedoms in Eastern Europe, they are "political adversaries."

Thus for the SPD, the major questions with respect to Eurocommunism remain:

—How far will the Eurocommunists go in criticizing social and political conditions in the Soviet Union and Eastern Europe?

—Does Eurocommunism provide evidence for the political and ideological erosion of the Soviet system?

—Have not leading representatives of socialism (such as Kautsky, Luxemburg, and Bernstein) and even communists (like the Austrian Marxists Franz Marek and Ernst Fischer) again and again warned of or attacked the "dictatorship of the proletariat" in its Stalinist form?[3][1]

—Beyond a very widely-conceived political philistinism and the parties' dependence on it, will the left be willing to share the burden of Western European defense spending?

With equal firmness but by applying different arguments, the Eurocommunist leaders Carrillo, Azcárate, Berlinguer, Amendola, Napolitano, and even Marchais define their positions vis-à-vis the socialists and social democrats:

—The social democrats do not aim at transforming capitalist society; instead, they administer it.

—By their "superreformism" the social democrats closed all routes toward revolutionary change.

—The social democrats let themselves become integrated into state-monopolistic capitalism, thus functioning as "one of its governmental variants."

—Finally, the social democrats set too high a value on formal civil liberties.[3][2]

C. Are There Any Ideological and Structural Similarities Between the Social Democrats and the Eurocommunists?

The most interesting political observations seem to be that both the social democrats and the Eurocommunists are persistent in their opposition to all *collectivisme à la Russe,* on the one hand, and in their critical attitude toward the United States, on the other hand. Certainly, nuances exist. But if national and international party platforms are compared in these respects, they may well provide the bases for concluding that attitudes toward the USSR and the USA constitute a political rationale for cooperation between social democrats and Eurocommunists in the long run.

The convergent attitudes toward the USSR and the USA

can be explained in terms of historical and political events. The Eurocommunists, responding to the twentieth CPSU congress (1956) and the invasion of Czechoslovakia by the Warsaw Pact troops (1968), became more and more skeptical of the Soviet brand of "proletarian internationalism." The social democrats lived through a period of disillusionment brought about by the Vietnam War and Watergate. By and large, social democratic politicians have the impression that the United States considers problems of international politics from the viewpoint of military strategy and security. One also hears from leading SPD politicians that American officials regard Vietnam as a strategic mistake. Some see the core of the problem but do not perceive its significance. Also, economic measures taken by the American government since the beginning of the oil crisis have contributed to the SPD's critical attitude toward the United States.

It is important to take each party's rank and file into consideration—especially because the social composition of party membership has changed. For many years a definite trend has been observed: Workers are leaving both the communist and social democratic parties, whereas intellectuals and members of the lower middle classes are joining in greater numbers. As early as 1972, Willy Brandt noted that workers made up only 24 percent of the SPD membership. This percentage has since declined. Between 1971 and 1978, most of the SPD's 650,000 new members were students, teachers, other intellectuals, and members of the new middle class. Similar developments have taken place in the youth organization of the SPD, the JUSOS, and in the ranks of the young socialists. At the 1972 JUSO congress in Oberhausen, 42.05 percent of all the delegates were students; 25 percent were pupils; 21.09 percent were white-collar employees; and only 4.08 percent were workers and craftsmen.[33]

Thus the social composition of the SPD has changed. A similar trend has been a matter of debate within the PCI.

Gramsci foresaw this development in *Historical Materialism and the Philosophy of Benedetto Croce* and other works.[34]

5. SPD Approaches to Eurocommunism

Despite the apparently successful attempts of the official SPD to delimit itself from the Eurocommunist parties, there exist influential groups within the SPD that sympathize with certain Eurocommunist ideas. These groups are located left of center of the spectrum that can be drawn from the SPD. (See the chart below.) In 1978 they included members of a group of intellectuals surrounding Horst Ehmke, some of whom were based at the Research Institute of the Friedrich-Ebert-Stiftung in Bonn; individuals such as Karsten Voigt and Heidi Wieczorek-Zeul, as well as the "Leverkusener Kreis," and another group represented by Peter von Oertzen (and strongly influenced by Ernest Mandel); furthermore, other members and affiliates of the JUSOS and members of the most powerful labor unions (for example, IG Metall), Ehmke, Voight, Wieczorek-Zeul, and von Oertzen were all members of the SPD board *(Vorstand)*, which consisted of thirty-six persons.

The SPD groups and individuals sympathetic to Eurocommunism in one way or another are attracted by the Eurocommunists' adherence to some kind of revolutionary fervor, their belief in the ideology of the class struggle, their will to autonomy (vis-à-vis the USSR and the USA), their acknowledgment of certain dogmatic principles associated with Marx, Engels, Lenin, and Luxemburg, that is, their genuine devotion to the tradition of the international workers' movement. These SPD members have great confidence in the ability of Eurocommunists to bring about sociopolitical changes; some may even believe that Eurocommunists can be more effective than social democrats. Disregarding ideological and semantic problems, they have narrowed their perspectives. They focus their attention on the Eurocommunists' intention (and

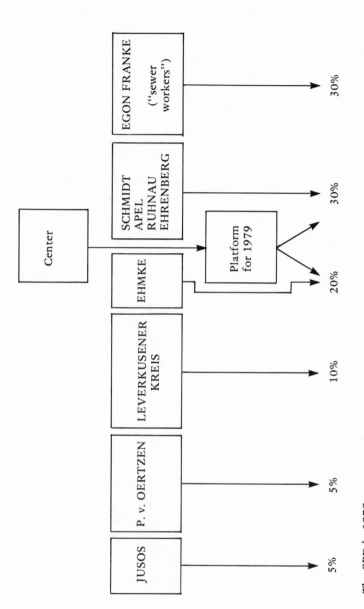

The SPD in 1978
(percentages estimated on the basis of voting pattern at the 1977 party congress in Hamburg)

presumed capability) to solve the problems of Western industrial societies with the help of insights derived from Marxism and socialism. They stress the political fight against the re-emerging powers of conservatism[35] as a possible rallying point to unite social democrats and Eurocommunists. These social democrats welcome the Eurocommunists for taking the risks of the "venture called political democracy."[36]

Furthermore, some groups within the SPD, as well as some Eurocommunists, believe that bipolar politics should be broken up by moves emanating from the Western or Eastern bloc. The driving forces behind such moves in the West are supposed to be generated by social policy demands (i.e., workers' codetermination, state planning of investments, humanization of work, and the emancipation of women). This conception of social policy, transcending policies of defense and security, is designed to play a leading role in future Western politics.

These groupings within the SPD, the PCI, and the PCE base their views on similar perceptions of political and socio-economic change in Europe. They regard the following developments as major factors promoting change:

—the CSCE, especially the Helsinki accords of 1976;
—the general crisis of Western industrial societies that has produced different forms of social and political pluralism;
—the increasing significance of the North-South conflict;
—changes in world communism.

The social democrats and communists who hold these views look for support from the outside, neglecting those social aggregates and strata from which were recruited the traditional voters of their parties. SPD subgroups do so in order to stay in power; PCI subgroups embark on this path because they want to come to power. The main approach that they all use to get public support is displaying an offensive attitude toward the Soviet Union and Eastern Europe, on the one hand, and toward the United States, on the other.

They assert that even though the Soviet Union and the United States take initiatives in European politics, as far as the programmatic dimension of ideology and social policy is concerned, the superpowers continue to play only a defensive role. Thus such groupings on the margin of the SPD and within the PCI are optimistic about their ability to influence anti-Soviet feelings in Eastern Europe and anti-American sentiments in Western Europe.

6. Recent SPD Strategies and Tactics Toward Eurosocialism and Eurosocial Democratism

Aside from programmatic delimitations, the SPD has begun systematically to review its role in European political history. Thus SPD ideologues point to the fact that in 1925 some members of the party (e.g., Breithaupt) demanded stronger relations with France. August Bebel and Jean Jaurès have been cited (for example, by Chancellor Helmut Schmidt) as representatives of this point of view. The social democrats also assert that they have always supported the idea of an active policy toward the West and have opposed the isolation and the encirclement of Soviet Russia by the West (including Germany).

Such arguments suggest that there exists some basis for cooperation between the SPD and the PS in France. Indeed, for more than two and a half years, three joint SPD-PS commissions (on defense policy, economic policy, and European questions) have met on a regular basis. Delegates of the PS, among them Cot, Rocard, and Huntzinger, visited Bonn several times. SPD delegations, headed by Brandt and later by von Dohnanyi, met with PS representatives in Paris. There is no doubt that the PS attitude toward European politics differs from that of the SPD. For example, the PS not only envisages bipolarism as a threat but stresses the danger of accelerating military-technological developments in the United States. PS leaders—Mitterrand himself and one of his spokesmen, Cot—emphasize the threat of a "new Gaullism." Despite all these differences, cooperation between the PS and the SPD continues.

German-French relations at the party level are paralleled by governmental contacts, for example, official and personal contacts between President Valery Giscard d'Estaing and Chancellor Helmut Schmidt. Their official dialogues concentrate on European monetary matters, that is, the foundation of a European currency system, and on the European Parliament. Especially remarkable in this context is Chancellor Schmidt's "turning to Europe." Schmidt had been considered an "Atlanticist." His recent and unmistakable moves in the direction of European solidarity may well mark a turning point in the history of postwar Europe.

One can discern in the relations between the SPD and the PS the growing power of social democratic and socialist parties in Western Europe: The social democratic and socialist parties of West Germany, Holland, Luxemburg, Belgium, England, Denmark, Ireland, and, in part, Italy (Craxi) constitute a powerful bloc.[37]

7. *Summary*

1. The phenomenon called Eurocommunism is evaluated in different terms by different groupings in the SPD. However, they all seem to agree in principle with the official line that Eurocommunism evolved from social change in Europe in a manner that suggests that communism has adapted to the sociopolitical conditions of the West European system. This view implies that the communist parties of Western Europe would rather integrate into the European sociopolitical system than bring about spectacular change.

2. Eurocommunist ideas appeal to many intellectuals and some party politicians in the SPD. As intellectuals have always done, these SPD members dream of a "united working class" that will determine political affairs throughout Western Europe.

3. The majority of the political leaders of the SPD ascribe to Eurocommunism the specific function of promoting the political erosion of Eastern Europe. With regard to the Federal Republic of Germany and Western Europe, they recognize Eurocommunism as a potential danger. Eurocommunism, in their view, may be successful in filling the ideological vacuum in the Western democracies. Thus their overall strategy and specific platform have been designed to fill that vacuum and to draw boundaries between the SPD and the communist parties of Western Europe.

---

*It was Ludz's intention to revise this paper on the basis of a lecture entitled *SPD, SED, and Eurocommunism,* which he delivered at Harvard University in late October 1978, reflecting his reconsideration of events that had taken place since he prepared the paper. I have emended and expanded his text and notes with reference to the outline of his Harvard lecture.

As the coeditor of this volume, Ludz intended to write the afterword. Toward that end, he prepared a handwritten outline entitled *Actual Problems of Eurocommunism and Eurosocialism.* He considered Eurocommunism one of the most fascinating phenomena today to be analyzed from the standpoint of the social sciences, and he believed that those who seek to analyze it must take into consideration theories and methodologies from various disciplines and subdisciplines. Using this multidisciplinary approach, he intended to discuss Eurocommunism in terms of political theory and the history of political ideas, political sociology—with reference to the role of the elite within party organizations and apparatuses—comparative politics—domestic and foreign—party politics and organizational behavior, political economy and its relation to ideology, the sociology of international relations, focusing on how policy is formulated in terms of national and international interests, statistics of voting and electoral behavior, and policy analysis. All these disciplines and subdisciplines, in Ludz's view, could and should be applied in analyzing the phenomena of Eurocommunism, Eurosocialism, and Eurosocial democratism.

In distinguishing Eurocommunism, Eurosocialism, and Eurosocial democratism, Ludz identified the constituents of Eurocommunism as the *Partito Communista Italiano* (PCI), the *Parti Communiste Francais* (PCF), and the *Partido Socialista de Espana* (PPS); Eurosocial democratism as the *Sozialdemokratische Partei Deutschlands* (SPD), and the

Socialdemokratiska arbetar partiet (SAP). He included the Yugoslav Communist party as a special case.

Ludz's view of the problems of Eurocommunism and his ideas about how to approach them led him to formulate three political questions, which he considered of particular importance: (1) How is the socialist model of neoreformism to be realized? (2) What effects will Eurocommunism have on the socialist states of Eastern Europe? (3) From the perspective of sociological analysis, what roles will be played by the new middle class, that is, members of the service sector and the intelligentsia? Ludz understood that the phenomena of Eurocommunism and Eurosocialism reflect social and political changes in Western and Southern Europe, particularly in the parties of the left. But he intended to investigate whether they were also expressions of a new nationalism, political economism, political regionalism, or fragmentation in Western Europe.

Ludz advocated a holistic approach to Eurocommunism. In this connection, he noted (and deplored) the deficiencies of the official American view. In the United States, Eurocommunism and Eurosocialism are interpreted as expressions of a changing political fashion. The rise of the left is considered the consequence of political and economic breakdown. As a European observer, Ludz found this judgment rather surprising. Indeed, representatives of the American administration, and even some American political scientists, have referred to the relationship between the Social Democratic party of Germany and the proponents of Eurocommunism as the expression of some kind of low-level crisis, whereas their real or actual concerns should be and are the breakdown of the international economic system, problems of protectionism and inflation, socioeconomic dislocation, and the developing competition between the United States and Japan, on the one hand, and between the United States and the Federal Republic of Germany, on the other. In Ludz's view, the Americans neglect or fail to understand the correlations between newly-emerging class structures and political developments in Western Europe.

In other words, the official American view reflects the kind of thinking that focuses on established institutions such as NATO and the European Security Conference (ESC), rather than on processes of social (domestic) change, although the latter appears to be exerting a growing impact on international politics. To a certain extent, however, this impact has been acknowledged, albeit as "pluralization" or "fragmentation." But these terms are only applied to the structures and processes of the international *economic* system. This American view, which appears to center on institutions, may also explain the simplistic dichotomization of the left and the right that hinders an analysis of the new middle classes—among whom are members of the service sector—social democracy, and the "new socialism," the new sociopolitical phenomena in Western Europe.

Many American observers seem quite content to describe recent phenomena in Western Europe by affixing to them such labels as new nationalism, new revisionism, and new reformism. They shrink from analyzing actual political and socioeconomic structures, from speculating about their potential consequences within each country, and from drawing comparisons based on crossnational research. Western European observers in general, and the social democrats in West Germany and the communists in Italy in particular, wonder why American officials avoid such questions as: How do the parties of the left look at social and political changes in their own and other West European countries? What part do those parties play or want to play in changing West European society? In the light both of European developments and East-West relations, Ludz sought to bring the European and American perceptions of Eurocommunism, Eurosocialism, and Eurosocial democratism into line.

G. L. Ulmen

NOTES

1. The seriousness with which the phenomenon of Eurocommunism is viewed in the FRG is attested to by the number of recent books that have appeared, for example, Adolf Kimmel, ed., *Eurokommunismus* (Cologne, 1977); *Eurokommunismus im Widerspruch,* edited, translated, and introduced by Manfred Steinkühler (Cologne, 1977); Alfons Dalma et al., eds., *Eurokommunismus—Italien, Frankreich, Jugoslawien, Portugal* (Zurich, 1977); Heinz Timmermann, ed., *Eurokommunismus—Fakten, Analysen, Interviews* (Frankfurt a/M., 1978); Wolfgang Leonhard, *Eurokommunismus: Herausfoderung für Ost und West* (Munich, 1978); C. M. Hutter, *Eurokommunisten—Lenin's treue Jünger* (Krefeld, 1978).

2. The May 1979 congress of the PCF put an end to the party's seven-year partnership with the PS. In June 1979 the PCI, for the first time since 1948, lost ground in the national elections.

3. It is thus not surprising that there is no consensus concerning what Eurocommunism means or what criteria should be used to evaluate the parties. Recently some analysts, for example, the Yugoslav Rudi Supek, have even maintained that the word is incorrect inasmuch as "Eurocommunism" also exists in Japan. According to this inter-

pretation, Eurocommunism means nothing more or less than the adaptation of communist doctrines and party organizations to the conditions of modern industrial society. But such a loose definition obscures more than it reveals.

4. See Lucio Colletti, "A Political and Philosophical Interview," in *Western Marxism: A Critical Reader*, ed. *New Left Review*, Verso Edition (London, 1978), pp. 315 ff. Disenchanted, Colletti left the PCI.

5. See John Merrington, "Theory and Practice in Gramsci's Marxism," in *Western Marxism*, ed. *New Left Review*, pp. 140 ff.

6. Manfred Steinkühler, "Gespräch mit Frane Barbieri, der den Ausdruck 'Eurokommunismus' praegte," in Steinkühler, ed., *Eurokommunismus im Widerspruch*, pp. 389 ff.

7. Neil McInnes, *Euro-Communism* (Beverly Hills, London, 1976), p. 61.

8. See, for example, Enrico Berlinguer, "Gedanken über Italien nach den Ereignissen in Chile," in Steinkühler, ed., *Eurokommunismus im Widerspruch*, p. 96. See also Annette Jost, "Italien-Kommunisten an der Macht," in Timmermann, ed., *Eurokommunismus—Fakten, Analysen, Interviews*, pp. 67 and 73.

9. Santiago Carrillo, *Eurocommunism and the State* (Westport, Conn., 1978), p. 133. Title of the Spanish original: *Eurocomunismo y Estado*.

10. *Ibid.*, p. 104.

11. See Neil McInnes, *The Communist Parties in Western Europe* (New York, London, 1975), p. 137. See also *Euro-Communism, op. cit.*, p. 44.

12. Louis Althusser, "The Historic Significance of the 22nd Congress," afterword in Etienne Balibar, *On the Dictatorship of the Proletariat*, trans, Gragane Lock (London, 1977), p. 194.

13. Quotes from Craxi's article were published in the Swiss newspaper *Die Weltwoche* (September 6, 1978).

14. See *Frankfurter Allgemeine Zeitung* (September 18, 1978), p. 1.

15. See Sophie G. Alf, introduction to the German edition of Eric J. Hobsbawn and Giorgio Napolitano, *Intervista sul PCI* (Roma, 1975), p. 31. Title of the German edition: *Auf dem Weg zum "historischen Kompromiss": Ein Gespräch über Entwicklung und Programmatik der KPI*, (Frankfurt a./M., 1977). The interview was also published in English: *The Italian Road to Socialism: An Interview by Eric Hobsbawn with Giorgio Napolitano of the Italian Communist Party*, trans. John Cammett and Victoria DeGrazia (Westport, Conn., 1977).

16. Carrillo, *Eurocommunism and the State*, pp. 110 ff.

17. See William E. Griffith, "Das Problem des "Eurokommunismus,"'

Amerika und West Europa: Gegenwarts-und Zukunftsprobleme, ed., Karl Kaiser and Hans-Peter Schwarz (Stuttgart, Zurich, 1977), pp. 218-243.

18. McInnes, *Euro-Communism,* p. 38.

19. *Ibid.*

20. SPD efforts to delimit itself from Eurocommunism received additional momentum from the party's competition with the ruling Communist party in East Germany—the Socialist Unity party of Germany (SED). Therefore, a few words concerning the SED's stand on Eurocommunism may be in order. The close link between the SED and the CPSU remains in effect, but the SED no longer extends only a helping hand to the CPSU in international politics and with respect to Eurocommunism. The SED's major motivation vis-à-vis Eurocommunism derives from its belief that it cannot afford to become isolated from movements in world communism and world politics. At the European summit meeting of the Communist parties in East Berlin in the summer of 1976, the SED had to play two roles at the same time: (1) strengthening the Soviet Union and condemning anti-Sovietism (conceived of as anticommunism) and (2) acknowledging to a greater extent than did the CPSU the autonomy of the communist parties in Western Europe. A manifestation of this second endeavor was the fact that unlike all other East European parties, the SED published the complete text of the summit speeches in its official paper, *Neues Deutschland.* The SED would like to act as a broker between the communist parties of Western Europe and the CPSU and other East European communist parties. In pursuing this objective, the SED has been competing with the SPD. The SED has frequently sent delegations to Paris and Rome and occasionally to Madrid. From the standpoint of the PCI (Calamandrei), the SED's policy is very "sensitive." It is not looking for assistance with respect to the German question but is striving for acknowledgment and contacts and a cautious acceptance of the Italian position. From the standpoint of the PCE (Aczarate), the SED's policy consists of listening attentively but not commenting: It is "sensitive," expressing friendly attitudes. On the other hand, the SED is determined to fight such deviations as those of Rudolf Bahro, who was influenced by Gramsci, the praxis group in Yugoslavia, and other ideological strains of Eurocommunism.

21. The Yugoslav experiment began in the Second World War when the Communist party in the Partisan Movement asserted its independence from the Red Army. It was the first party to embark on a course of de-Stalinization, as early as 1948. It was the first party to experiment with "models" for a European Marxism and European socialism-communism. It was also the first party to experiment with political

regionalism. Thus it is not surprising that the word *Eurocommunism* was coined by a Yugoslav, the journalist Frane Barbieri, in 1975.

Important ideas about the new socialism were developed only in Yugoslavia and especially in the praxis group in Zagreb and Belgrade between 1966 and 1970. The praxis group sought to give material form to symbolic expressions borrowed from the French Revolution, such as "liberté, egalité, et fraternité." They view the French Commune as *the* example of "real democracy." They maintain that "democracy is not a matter of procedure" but a matter of cold determination, a matter of autogestation, of democracy. Following the praxis group, many Eurocommunists also want a new state. However, those who want it are not administrators and managers, who ostensibly know something about economics and finance, but intellectuals, humanists, artists, and philosophers. Moreover, the Eurocommunists, in their critique of the praxis model, argue that it is nineteenth-century totalism *(totalisme)* and that the Yugoslav communists fail to recognize the need for partial theories. To be sure, the theory of alienation is important in order to specify the flaws in all industrial societies, but the Eurocommunists, in arguing for self-management, stress the decentralization of social power and the extension of human rights.

22. Horst Heinemann, *Theoriediskussion in der SPD: Ergebnisse und Perspektiven* (Frankfurt a./M., 1975), pp. 224 f.

23. See Willy Brandt, Bruno Kreisky, and Olaf Palme, *Briefe und Gespräche, 1972-1975* (Frankfurt a./M., 1975), *passim.*

24. See, for example, the joint declaration of the PCI and the PCF in *L'Unita* (November 18, 1975) and the joint declaration of the PCI and the CP of Great Britain in *L'Unita* (April 30, 1976).

25. Quoted from the draft of the platform formulated by the German Social Democratic party for the European parliamentary elections in 1979. See *Soziale Demokratie für Europa: Programm der Sozialdemokratischen Partei Deutschland für die erste europäische Direktwahl 1979*, photocopied draft of August 1978.

26. Giorgio Napolitano, in the interview conducted by Hobsbawn, *The Italian Road to Socialism,* pp. 88 ff.

27. John Merrington, "Theory and Practice" in *Western Marxism,* ed. *New Left Review*, p. 150.

28. See John M. Cammett, *Antonio Gramsci and the Origins of Italian Communism* (Stanford, Ca., 1967), p. 204; Christian Riechers, *Antonio Gramsci: Marxismus in Italien* (Frankfurt a./M., 1970), pp. 194 f.

29. Santiago Carrillo, *Eurocommunism and the State,* p. 149.

30. SPD Draft Platform, see note 24, p. 68.

31. See Hartmut Jaeckel, "Eurokommunismus zwischen 'Diktatur des Proletariats' und sozialer Demokratie," *Sozialismus in Theorie und Praxis*, ed. Hannelore Horn et al. (Berlin, New York, 1978), pp. 441-451.

32. Santiago Carrillo, *Eurocommunism and the State*, pp. 104 f. and 133.

33. Horst Heinemann, *Theoriediskussion in der SPD*, p. 232.

34. In a sense, Gramsci, when speaking of the "organic intellectuals" and the role of the "cultural intelligentsia" in the party, predicted those changes in the communist parties' social structure. In the early 1920s he dealt with the psychological problems arising from such socio-structural changes, emphasizing the loss of identity of modern man and the possibility of regaining an identity through party-controlled cultural institutions. See Antonio Gramsci, *Philosophie der Praxis: Eine Auswahl*, ed. and trans. Christian Riechers (Frankfurt a./M., 1967), pp. 27 ff., 131 ff., 405 ff., 431 ff.

35. Willy Brandt and Herbert Wehner are also concerned with the strengthening of the "right" as a danger to national and international politics.

36. See Horst Ehmke's preface to Timmermann ed., *Eurokommunismus—Fakten, Analysen, Interviews*, p. 9.

37. In the elections to the European Parliament in June 1979, the Socialists and Social Democrats won 112 seats, the Christian Democrats 105, the Conservatives 63, the Liberals 41, and the Communists 44.

Part II The Ideological and Political-Theoretical Foundations

Bernard E. Brown

FRENCH COMMUNISM

Every leader and spokesman of the French Communist party has asserted, whenever the question has been raised, that there *is* an ideological foundation of French communism. It is the body of knowledge known as Marxism-Leninism, to whose German-Russian base such distinguished French "theorists" as Maurice Thorez, Jacques Duclos, Waldeck Rochet, and now Georges Marchais have added their contributions. The official rules of the party make it crystal clear: The activity of the PCF is "based upon Marxism-Leninism," described generously as a "scientific view of the world, method of analysis, and guide to action." The fundamental principles of the PCF are always set forth in Marxist phrases, such as "dialectical and historical materialism," that convey an overpowering sense of certitude, rectitude, and infallibility.

It is beyond the scope of this paper to review the Marxist theory of ideology or to offer yet another exercise in Marxist scholasticism. But the theme of this volume is ideology and communism; and, in fact, it is useful to approach the phenomenon of communism—especially when it is a mass movement, as in France—by focusing attention on its ideology. Doubtless it would be useful also to center our collective endeavor on organization, or the social composition of the leadership, or on other features of communist parties; but that is not our task. In any event, ideology has always been and remains such a striking concern of communist parties that systematic study surely will be rewarding—provided that we avoid falling into the trap of engaging in polemical exchanges or purely literary criticism. The ideological component of French communism will therefore be viewed first from the vantage point of the leaders themselves. As we have seen, invariably they have claimed Marxism-Leninism as a heritage, a guideline, an inspiration—in short, as a foundation.

But we encounter immediately a puzzling problem. In Marxist terms how can ideology be a "foundation" for French communism or anything else? Ideology is only part of the "superstructure" of a society. The "material basis" of a society consists of productive forces and relationships. In modern capitalism the productive forces are the laws or innate tendencies of the economy (above all, the drive for profit requiring increasingly intensive exploitation of the proletariat), which come into conflict with productive relationships (an increasingly revolutionary proletariat that eventually refuses to be exploited). Throughout history every social class creates an ideology that justifies its rule or its revolt. Hence the "foundation" of French communism can be only material, that is, a working class made ever more revolutionary by the very process of capitalism. Marx complicated the issue even more—as he invariably did because of the ambiguity of key concepts—when in another context he referred to ideology as essentially a deformation of reality, a "false consciousness" that directs attention away from material interests.

Thus ideology reflects the material base of society; at other times it interacts with and changes these material interests and sometimes distorts material interests.

If the material base of society consists only of productive forces and relationships, then there is need neither for communist parties nor for bourgeois intellectuals like Karl Marx, Friedrich Engels, and Nikolai Lenin. Workers will be made revolutionary by the process of capitalism, not by reading the literary production of Karl Marx. Let the workers then become revolutionary by themselves; guidance from above or without is superfluous, even dangerous. Marxism in this sense is the ideological foundation for the liquidation of the French and all other communist parties. But to wait for the masses to choose the right path is viewed by PCF spokesmen as "vague petty bourgeois anarchism." In responding to demands for the democratization of the party after the defeat of March 1978, Marchais vowed never to yield to the "cult of spontaneity and anarchism"—because to do so would make it impossible for the party to play its role of vanguard.[1] In truth, the leaders of the French Communist party have never been greatly concerned with philosophical problems. Whatever his other talents, Georges Marchais will never go down in history as a creative Marxist theorist. Insofar as the problem of ideology is considered at all, French communists accept wholeheartedly the Leninist formulation: The workers by themselves will only develop a trade-union consciousness and therefore require knowledge "brought from the outside" by professional revolutionaries in order to play their historical role.

Is the ideology of Marxism-Leninism therefore miraculously transformed from superstructure into base? Or is the knowledge "brought from the outside" merely a set of tactics that serves the shifting interests of the party? Critics and defenders of communism alike are caught up in the controversy and argue on both sides of the question. For some the

Soviet Union remains a revolutionary force in the world seeking to bring about the triumph of world socialism by any
appropriate means; for others the only reality is the interests
of the clique in power in the Soviet Union, who use an ideology drained of all content simply to justify whatever tactic
(from the Nazi-Soviet Pact, to the purchase of American
wheat, to either an alliance with or hostility to Yugoslavia,
and so on) will strengthen their hold. The same controversy
takes place over the ideology and tactics of mass communist
parties in parliamentary democracies. Are these communist
parties committed to Marxist ideology (identified with a socialist transformation of society conducted by themselves);
or are they above all seeking to preserve their luxurious party
headquarters, limousines, summer homes, control of municipalities and trade unions—with power as the be-all and the
end-all?[2]

The debate is not only endless but inconclusive. It is impossible to "prove" that ideology is either foundation or
superstructure. What kind of evidence would be required to
show that the PCF, for example, subordinates ideology to
tactics, or the other way around? It is not even clear what is
ideology and what is tactic, much less whether one is being
subordinated to the other. The irreducible ambiguity of the
controversy is a reflection of the inherent contradiction between Marxist and Leninist elements of present-day communist ideology. Ideology is at times superstructure and at times
the knowledge brought from the "outside" that reshapes consciousness and transforms a society. When communists come
to power in backward societies, they may use their ideology
as a way of bringing about changes that would never have
been produced by the normal play of social forces and productive relationships. Depending upon the interests involved
and the political situation that obtains, ideology is foundation or tactic, both, or neither.

Nonetheless, it may be suggested that there is a relationship, however loose, between ideology and the tactics of communist (and all other kinds of) parties. This relationship is not viewed fruitfully as cause and effect nor as base and superstructure; but the relationship is real and, for our purposes, highly significant. Let us postulate for a moment that a communist party has at least some of the characteristics of a church (not an outlandish proposition), with a theology, hierarchy, ritual, dominant personalities, procedures for recruitment and initiation, communion, excommunication, discipline, symbols, seminaries, schools, and so on. It is beyond the power of any analyst to prove that Catholicism—or Protestantism, Judaism, Hinduism, Buddhism, Islam, and so on— is the one true religion and that all others are false. Nor can we demonstrate that theology is more important than ritual, or the other way around. But, as Max Weber pointed out, theology (or ideology) may be related to historical and political factors—for example, the unequal development of capitalism throughout medieval Europe and Asia.

The study of ideology can be rewarding. But it depends on what we are looking for. Validity and causation are beyond proof. Mass communist parties today are facts of life in France and Italy, expressions of an underlying reality. The French Communist party has regularly received about 20 percent of the popular vote (from a low of 18.9 to a high of 28 percent) in all legislative elections since the Liberation. It is an organized manifestation of a profound social and political movement within the French polity. The ideology of the PCF is an *indicator* of that movement. If an important change takes place in that ideology, it is reasonable to assume that a corresponding change is taking place in the movement itself.

Ideology and Modernity

Let me first place the question of communist ideology and tactics in the broader perspective of working-class politics and political change in France. Since the breakup of feudalism and the explosion of scientific knowledge in the late eighteenth century, it is possible to distinguish three major currents of opinion (or ideology, if you prefer) within the French left: social democracy, authoritarian socialism, and libertarian socialism. Each of these currents of opinion corresponds to important structures of political activity, such as parties and trade unions; that is, the three currents do not merely provide a range of possible reactions to modernity; they are also organized sectors of political life. At the present time the major organizational expression of the social democratic or reformist current is the Socialist party, successor to the SFIO; the major organized expression of the authoritarian current is the Communist party, whose ancestry can be traced, prior to the Congress of Tours in 1920, to the revolutionary wing of the working-class movement. Libertarian socialism has, by its very nature, discouraged organization and hierarchy; it manifested itself in the past and manifests itself today as well mainly in cultural and intellectual circles and in the propensity toward syndicalism. In May 1968 the libertarian movement was carried forward in spectacular fashion by a network of anarchist, surrealist, and situationist groups.

The left in France—and in all other industrial societies, for that matter—has always been deeply divided. Two major issues have set apart socialists, communists, and libertarians: acceptance or rejection of parliamentary (known within house as bourgeois) democracy as a statement of the rules of the political game; and acceptance or rejection of modern society (and all of its associated features, such as science, technology, giant industry, urbanization, hierarchy, bureaucracy, rationality, impersonality). In principle all three groups reject the capitalist version of modern society; that has never been an issue within the French left, at least not as an abstract proposition. At the risk of some oversimplification, I suggest that the Socialist party represents that portion of the

French working class—along with intellectuals and some middle-class and peasant elements—that fully accepts both parliamentary democracy and modernity (although a few traces of both authoritarian and libertarian currents can be found within its left wing today, for example, in the CERES, some elements of the old PSU, and among some advocates of a largely undefined "autogestion"). Socialist party leaders have come to accept the institutions and practices of parliamentary democracy, the notion that competing political parties appeal to the sovereign electorate, which decides in a free and fair election which party or coalition of parties shall govern. They seek to attain their goals within the framework of the parliamentary system, with opposition parties always enjoying the right to organize and press their views. For the most part, they also view the transition from feudalism to parliamentary democracy and from agrarian to industrial economies as not merely change but as progressive change. They try to defend the interests of the working class and other social groups within an increasingly industrial and scientific society. Through socialism they hope to make the industrial economy more productive and the industrial society more equitable.

Since its creation in 1920, the Communist party has been clearly and distinctly set off from the Socialist party on the first issue, that of parliamentary democracy. It has associated itself with a version of Marxism and Leninism that is skeptical, even contemptuous of bourgeois democracy—always perceived as an instrument of the dominant or capitalist class in its incessant and intensive exploitation of the working class. The Communist party competes in the electoral process and participates in the parliamentary game; but its attitude ranges from open declarations that it will use the opportunities afforded it by the bourgeoisie to bring about the overthrow of the whole rotten system of capitalist exploitation to affirmations that bourgeois democracy is a transitional stage to "advanced democracy," itself a transitional stage to "real democracy" or socialism. As for the modernizing process, the Communist party for the most part is wholeheartedly in favor of rationality, science, and technology—provided that modernization proceeds ultimately under the auspices of a "liberated" working class. In practice the Communist party finds itself defending the interests of many "small people" who are being modernized out of existence; but such "Poujadism of the left" has little effect on its principles.

The major and up to now unbridgeable gulf between the socialist and communist currents within the French left has been the profound attitude of each party to parliamentary (or bourgeois) democracy—with all that it implies for the protection of individual liberties, pluralism of political parties, and freedom of expression. Acceptance of parliamentary institutions has also disposed the socialists to be more optimistic about the efficacy of reform (adopted through the parliamentary system, of course) and to be hostile to the kind of collectivism that exists in the Soviet Union. Perhaps the single most important "test" of socialist and communist attitudes toward parliamentary democracy is their respective appraisal of the Soviet Union. For socialists, what exists in the Soviet Union is a horrible example of authoritarian rule and state capitalism to be avoided at all costs; for communists, the Soviet Union is the world's first socialist state and the major progressive force in the world. Whatever socialism "in the colors of France" may be, whatever "aberrations" may occur in the Soviet Union, French communists still believe that the Soviet Union is a socialist and a progressive society.

The third current—libertarian socialism—is a pervasive influence in French intellectual life. It has affected even the organized Socialist and Communist parties in recent years. Libertarian socialists reject parliamentary democracy (as do communists), but they also reject the Communist party, all other oppressive hierarchies, and, above all, the greatest bureaucratic enterprise of all, the Soviet state; that is, they are hostile to *all* bureaucratic and hierarchic structures, whether parliamentary or communist. They also either repudiate outright or are profoundly skeptical of the modernizing process itself, which they believe is at the root of the alienation of mankind from its labor and its essential humanity. In mounting their attack on modernity, the libertarians draw inspiration from Proudhon, Bakunin, and the "young" Marx.

It is in this perspective that I propose to examine the relationship between ideology and tactics in the French Communist party. What is important is not the question of causation, or validity, but the relationship between both ideology and tactics, on the one hand, and the underlying divisions within the French working class and the left as a whole. The currents here described run fast and deep. But periodically the leaders of the French left are driven to explore the possibility of bridging the gaps, of creating mutually satisfactory agreements or even alliances so that the interests of the working class or the people generally can be forwarded. But how can a synthesis be achieved, in view of the internal contradictions mentioned above? One possibility is the triumph of one of the currents over the other two—which has so far proved to be unattainable. Another possibility is a change in ideology and tactics that will facilitate agreement and ultimately perhaps the unification of the left. Most observers agree that the French Communist party has changed in the past decade. Has the change been sufficiently great to permit an alliance with the other major party of the left and ultimately perhaps the unification of the left and the revolutionary transformation of French society? Rather than review the whole history of the Communist party since the Congress of Tours, I propose to focus attention on one decision concerning ideology, analyze it in depth, and then appraise the significance and import not only of the doctrinal change, but of the doctrine itself. The most intriguing doctrinal change in the past decade was the abandonment of the "dictatorship of the proletariat" at the twenty-second party congress. Does this decision portend a transcending of the internal rivalries and contradictions of the French left? What does it tell us about the changes taking place in that portion of French society that recognizes and expresses itself through the Communist party?

1. Dropping the Pilot Light

On February 4, 1976, the secretary-general of the French Communist party, Georges Marchais, presented the report of the central committee to that party's twenty-second congress. For some observers Marchais' report, like that of Khrushchev twenty years earlier, marked a break with the Stalinist past. Before fifteen hundred delegates Marchais announced that the phrase "dictatorship of the proletariat" no longer figured in the proposed new version of the party rules. "Consequently," he continued, "and conforming to the request of all the federal conferences, we propose to the congress that it decide to abandon the notion. We propose also to the congress that it charge the central committee about to be elected to submit to the next party congress the necessary modifications of the preamble to the party rules." That preamble states that the PCF bases its action on Marxism-Leninism, has as its goal the transformation of capitalist society into a collectivist or communist society, believes that the liberation of the French people from the chains of exploitation requires the conquest of political power, and that "this power, whose forms may vary, is the temporary dictatorship of the proletariat."

For party leaders the proposed change is an indication of a policy that is "really new"—as Marchais has repeatedly asserted—a "democratic path to socialism." Democracy and liberty were presented as the arms of struggle for the transformation of French society and, at the same time, as the fundamental characteristic of the new society.[3] After the twenty-second party congress, *democracy* and *liberty* became the constant points of reference in PCF ideology. How to achieve socialism? Through democracy and liberty. What would distinguish the new socialist society? Again, democracy and liberty "pushed to their extreme." The enormous slogan adorning the stage of the amphitheater in which the party congress held its meeting summed it up: "a democratic path to socialism—a socialism for France."

In the French context is thus posed one of the most critical questions of contemporary politics—and political science. Is there a movement of communist parties in industrial societies toward greater independence from the Soviet Union and toward acceptance of parliamentary democracy and civil liberties? Students of European politics today are examining the evolution of mass communist parties—especially those of France, Italy, Portugal, and Spain—for signs of basic change. The future of these nations depends in large measure on the authenticity of "Eurocommunism" as a departure from the classic model of Marxism-Leninism. If the PCF remains a hard-core Marxist-Leninist party, then the left in France will continue to be divided into authoritarian, reformist, and libertarian movements, all working at cross-purposes. But if the PCF evolves in the direction of social democracy (and if, in its view, the Socialist party also determines to "break with capitalism"), then the divisions of the French left may be transcended and the political balance will necessarily swing in its direction. A close analysis of ideological debate within the party should offer valuable insights concerning the reality—or surreality—of Eurocommunism.

In view of the enormous significance ascribed by party leaders to the doctrinal change adopted by the twenty-second party congress, it is curious to note that in the preliminary document circulated beforehand no mention whatsoever was made of an intent to change the preamble to the party rules. The preliminary document was drawn up three months before the scheduled meeting of the twenty-second party congress. All party members had a chance to read and discuss it in their cells; such discussion has always been an important aspect of "democratic centralism." On January 7, 1976, less than a month before the congress was to meet, a party militant from Epinay-sous-Sénart contributed a statement to the "tribune of discussion" in *l'Humanité* suggesting a new version of the party rules that would better adapt the notion of dictatorship of the proletariat to the realities of the class struggle without actually using the phrase. The following day Georges Marchais was interviewed on radio; he was asked, among many other questions, what he thought of the statement that had just appeared in *l'Humanité* concerning deletion of the dictatorship of the proletariat. Marchais voiced his agreement, adding modestly that "the congress will decide." He gave his personal opinion: In 1976 the phrase "dictatorship of the proletariat" no longer corresponded to what the communists want. "It has an intolerable meaning, contrary to our aspirations, to our doctrine." Even the word *proletariat* no longer was appropriate because the communists want to rally the majority of all salaried workers.

In the three weeks that immediately preceded the party congress, debate in cells and sections revolved almost entirely around the proposed doctrinal change. Only a few intellectuals—notably, Etienne Balibar and others close to Louis Althusser—were openly critical. Balibar's defense of orthodox Leninism was published in *l'Humanité's* "tribune of discussion" on January 22. He warned that giving up the phrase would mean yielding to the ideological pressure of the opposition, thereby running the risk of underestimating the contradictions, the intensity, and the importance of the class struggle. In the next day's *l'Humanité* a member of the political bureau, Guy Besse, painstakingly refuted Balibar's argument. Placing emphasis on the continuing revolutionary nature of the party, Besse said that it was precisely in order better to liquidate capitalism that a new and democratic path to socialism had to be traced. In all, some 22,705 delegates to 98 "federal conferences" within the PCF voted on the proposal to drop the phrase "dictatorship of the proletariat" from the party rules. Only 113 delegates voted against this doctrinal change and 216 abstained. The party leadership claimed that the procedure was an illuminating example of democratic centralism in action. Jean Kanapa reported proudly to the congress that the intervention of the secretary-general had stimulated and enriched the discussion and that all members of the party expressed themselves freely, including opponents of the proposal. The doctrinal change finally was debated and approved by the full congress.[4]

The Case for Democracy

In his report to the twenty-second party congress, Marchais built up slowly to the doctrinal change. The first half of his speech contained no surprises. He denounced the shortcomings of French capitalism, the continued degradation of living conditions, the crisis into which French capitalism was plunged, the total inability of the "masters of France" to fight their way out of the impasse, the menace of world imperialism, and so on. More than ever France needed a transformation of society from capitalism to socialism. But how to bring it about? Here was the innovation that, according to subsequent statements of party leaders, marked the twenty-second party congress as historic: by the democratic path. Hence the phrase "dictatorship of the proletariat" was no longer appropriate.

The argument can be recapitulated. (1) Marchais sought to clarify the meaning of democracy and liberty and their relationship to socialism. (2) He then dealt with the relevance of the Soviet model. (3) To stress the unique conditions in the West, Marchais analyzed the distinctive characteristics of French society and the role of the working class. Democracy and liberty, the Soviet model, the changing nature of the working class in advanced capitalist society—these were the three major aspects of the doctrinal change.

For Marchais it is ludicrous that apologists for capitalism and imperialism should talk of a "free world" in opposition to communist dictatorship or should suggest that under communist rule opposition parties would be eliminated and dissenters thrown into concentration camps. These troubadours of capitalism and imperialism have things the wrong way around! It is the capitalists who are the opponents of liberty and democracy; and it is none other than the communists who are the champions of liberty. Marchais spoke so glowingly of democracy and liberty that the unsuspecting listener might mistakenly have believed that he was secretary-general of a social democratic party and that his patron saint was John Stuart Mill, not Marx or Lenin. "In truth, there is only one party in France that raises high in all circumstances the flag of liberty, one, sole party that denounces violations of the rights of man wherever they occur without exception—and that is the French Communist party. It is for us a basic orientation, a question of principle. We fight for a society in which each man and each woman will be masters of their destiny and wherein their personalities can blossom. For us, socialism and liberty are inseparable." Nothing could be further removed from the minds of communists than total conformity, or the "communism of barracks," in which everyone (and everything) is poured into the same mold. Here, then, is the major reason why "dictatorship of the proletariat" no longer figures in the party rules: It does not correspond to the "reality of our policy." Why talk about "dictatorship" when the communist goal is "liberty"?

The PCF thus emerges as the supreme guardian of liberty and democracy in French society. Marchais embraced as his own the moving commentary of Pablo Neruda in his *Memoirs*—a commentary repeated on numerous occasions as an eloquent declaration of communist intentions and policy: "I want to live in a world where there will be no more excommunications. I shall not excommunicate anyone. . . . I shall not say to someone else: 'I shall not publish your poems, your creative work, because you are anticommunist.' I want to live in a world where people will be human beings only, without any other titles, without being obsessed by a rule, by a word, by a label. . . . I want the immense majority, the only majority, everyone, to be able to speak, write, read, blossom." In a communist France there will be no censorship, Marchais vowed, no single party system, no official ideology, no suppression of dissidents.

When Marchais and his colleagues speak of their ideal democracy, outsiders are bound to ask whether they have in mind the Soviet Union. If so, how do the French communists explain censorship, forced labor camps, the suppression of dissent, and the other unpleasant features of (or rumors about) the Soviet Union? Marchais approached this question head on. He frankly admitted that the PCF does not intend to take the same path as did other people "who have already realized the socialist transformation of their societies." He did not deny that under the conditions that prevailed in Russia in 1917 and during the civil war that followed, the dictatorship of the proletariat was necessary in order to ensure the success of socialism. But under other conditions, a democratic path may be possible. The very triumph of socialism in half the world offers an opportunity for people still subjugated by capitalism to try new ways of achieving the revolutionary transformation of society. Despite the immense gains registered by the socialist countries, Marchais reserved the right to criticize what appears to be "erroneous"—for example, repressive measures that violate freedom of opinion, expression, or creation. "We cannot agree that the communist ideal, whose object is the happiness of mankind and for which we call upon the workers to fight, can be stained by unjust and unjustified acts."

Marchais' comments before the congress were elliptical, hesitant, and coupled with effusive tributes to the accomplishments of the Soviet Union. The PCF disapproved of the invasion of Czechoslovakia in 1968, expressed its support for the dissident writers Siniavski and Daniel, and in December 1975, after a film on Soviet forced labor camps was shown on French television, demanded a formal explanation from Soviet authorities, affirming in advance that in the absence of a satisfactory reply, it would express "surprise and the most categoric disapproval." Time and again Marchais stated that serious differences continued to exist between the French and Soviet parties over Marxist theory and the relationship between socialism and liberty. The PCF spoke up in defense of Solzhenitsyn, the mathematician Plioutschtch, Sakharov, and other dissidents. When French television organized a debate on the Stalinist trials and purges, the PCF delegated Jean Kanapa (known as a hard-liner) to convey its condemnation of Stalinism. The image presented to the French people was that of a Communist party sincerely devoted to the protection of individual liberties everywhere in the world, without exception even for the Soviet Union.

Finally, Marchais explained that although the proletariat is the core, or heart, of the working class, it does not represent the totality either of the working class or, obviously, of all those who contribute their work to society. The socialist power envisaged by the PCF will be an emanation of all who work, and therefore the concept of a "proletariat" is now too restrictive. He thus prepared the way for an appeal to almost all elements in French society.

After four days of discussion, the 1,500 delegates of the

twenty-second party congress of the PCF *unanimously* approved Georges Marchais' report. As an indication of the importance of the doctrinal change, three of the four paragraphs of the final resolution dealt with the deletion of the phrase "dictatorship of the proletariat" from the party rules, stipulating that it should no longer be cited as one of the party's goals and charging the central committee to submit appropriate amendments of the party rules to the next party congress.

2. Canon to the Left, Canon to the Right

Most party militants greeted the doctrinal change with an almost audible sigh of relief; "dictatorship" is not generally considered a nice word or an admirable reality. But a handful of intellectuals, mainly those associated with Louis Althusser in Paris, believed the proposed change incompatible with the Marxist theory that should be the guiding light of the revolutionary movement. Chief among the critics of Marchais within the orthodox Marxist-Leninist wing of the party was the philosopher, Etienne Balibar. He voiced his objections immediately, during the debate that preceded the twenty-second party congress; shortly thereafter he published a best-selling book, entitled *Sur la dictature du prolétariat,* in the series edited by Althusser for Maspero.

Balibar pointed out, quite correctly, that Marchais' new line had serious implications for Marxist theory. Dictatorship of the proletariat for Marx was the counterpart of dictatorship of the bourgeoisie. Before the revolution, the dominant class is the bourgeoisie, which controls all the instruments of coercion, using them to carry out its exploitative policies. First consequence of the doctrinal change: The counterpart notion—dictatorship of the bourgeoisie—must also be abandoned. The Marxist criticism of capitalism is thus vitiated. Second consequence: The Marxist theory of the state comes under attack. Either the state is nothing but an instrument of the dominant class, or it is something else. Hold out the hope that there is a democratic path to socialism, and the state becomes more than a tool of exploitation: It performs or may be able to perform useful functions for the workers and the whole society—exactly as argued by "bourgeois political scientists" and social democratic reformers. How then defend the need for revolution?

Another consequence: Renounce the dictatorship of the proletariat and inevitably one scraps the very idea of the proletariat—converted instead into diversified workers who have claims and make demands on the state. All along the line, the ideology of the bourgeoisie and of social democrats is vindicated: There is no proletariat; the state is a useful instrument of the larger society; it reconciles the legitimate interests of differing classes. Gone are the class struggle, the fight against capitalism and the state, and the fight for socialism. The last indignity inflicted upon the revolutionary movement by the doctrinal change is to leave the working class utterly defenseless against the bourgeoisie in the unlikely event of a revolutionary transformation of society. Without a dictatorship of the proletariat, the workers would be unable to ward off the inevitable counterrevolution.

For Balibar and the critics within the PCF's left wing, Marchais has caved in under pressure from bourgeois ideologues. Theorists of pluralism and social democracy seek to depict Leninism as a gigantic historical error of the working-class movement. They wish to liquidate the Leninist theory of the dictatorship of the proletariat "by substituting for it the ideology of reformist and technocratic socialism and, incidentally, its permanent by-product, anarchism."[5] Balibar's criticism of Marchais is not to be confused with that of the hard-line Stalinists within the party. For Stalin, he noted, dictatorship of the proletariat was simply a hierarchy of institutions under the orders of the party, with the masses attached to the party by a series of transmission belts. Balibar reflected the influence of May 1968, with its emphasis on revolutionary salvation to be achieved through the creativity and the spontaneity of the popular masses.

The May revolt is even more evident in the views of Louis Althusser, the philosopher who had inspired a Maoist defection among young communists in the early 1960s—even though he himself finally chose to remain within the party. Althusser's critique of the twenty-second party congress was set forth in a public lecture at the Sorbonne in December 1976 (published by Maspero several months later as a pamphlet) and also in three articles in Le Monde in April 1978, after the defeat of the left in the legislative elections.[6] For Althusser, as for Balibar, to drop the dictatorship of the proletariat is to dissipate revolutionary consciousness of the nature of capitalism (dictatorship of the bourgeoisie) and of the state as exclusively a tool of class exploitation. The twenty-second party congress deprived itself of the opportunity to think through the implications of the destruction and the withering away of the state; it assumed that a simple change in juridical formula would suffice to determine the meaning of socialism. Swept aside is the real problem: how to revolutionize the structures, practice, and ideology of the state apparatus in transforming and transcending the division of social labor and creating new relationships between the masses and a state that will be compelled to wither away and be replaced by new forms of popular organization? The "democratic path to socialism" turns out to be "democratic adventurism," concluded Althusser, signaling the abandonment of Marxist principles and the party's revolutionary mission.

Althusser then turned to the demand that was to agitate the critics of Marchais more than anything else after the defeat in the legislative elections in March 1978: to give militants more of a say within the party. There was no real discussion or debate in the twenty-second party congress, exclaimed Althusser—thus denying the claims of party leaders. Only a few unimportant amendments were adopted, and the speakers merely repeated what was in the preliminary document. It is time, contended Althusser, to permit lively differences of opinion to be expressed within the party, to put an end to the practice whereby the party bureaucrats think for the militants. The "democratic" aspect of the party is an illusion; only the "centralist" aspect is real. So-called collective discussion is a play on words. "The discussion (that of the *whole* party) can be termed 'collective' only *in its result,* it is not 'collective' *in its effective reality.* Members of a cell never discuss except among themselves, then their delegates among themselves in the sections, and so on—all this in separate and watertight compartments that go from the base to the summit."[7] The real decisions are made in secret by a small unofficial group, including the secretariat, part of the political bureau, and a few experts or collaborators from the central committee. In short, Althusser and other left-wing communists finally discovered, almost sixty years after the creation of a Leninist Communist party in France, that the structures of that party are designed to permit the leaders to bring "knowledge from the outside" to the masses, who are organized in such a way that they can never challenge the official policy; they can only carry it out. For having arrived at that conclusion previously, the critics of the party had long been treated as lackeys of capitalism.

What alternative is offered? Here Althusser revives the spirit of the May revolt. Go to the people, who in their spontaneity will generate revolutionary sparks and create innovative structures. The party made a mistake in May 1968, according to him, in cutting itself off from the revolutionary masses simply because it was not in full control of the situation. The party now prefers to withdraw into its fortress rather than venture out and run the risk of "disappearing"—

in reality, finding itself—in the masses. Althusser's position is a challenge to the basic structures of all communist parties and systems: The party should be completely separate from the state both before and after the revolution if a descent into Stalinism is to be avoided. The party, in his vision, must be an instrument of the destruction of the bourgeois state *and* of the withering away of the proletarian state.[8]

The debate over dictatorship of the proletariat is the latest explosion of a perennial controversy within the French left, going back at least as far as the rivalry among Proudhon, Bakunin, and Marx in the early nineteenth century. Through the criticism of Balibar and Althusser is revived a vision of revolution as achieved by the spontaneity of the masses rather than through an organized hierarchy that can erect itself into a power above the people. The new socialist society will not be another, more rational version of modern society—with its dehumanizing division of labor and subordination of humanity to impersonal science and technology; instead, the division of labor will be transcended. New social and political forms will be devised to ensure the supremacy of human beings over the things that they create and the structures through which they cooperate. Conveniently, the details will be left to the "popular masses" to deal with later. Even within the PCF today, then, there is a small group still sensitive to the appeals of anarchism, still hostile to all forms of hierarchical domination, still distrustful of the modern society that gave birth to the socialist movement in the first place.

For other militants within the party, the decision to abandon the dictatorship of the proletariat is a step in the right direction but does not go far enough. Perhaps the leading, certainly the most vocal, critic from the "right" (or perhaps the "West") within the party is Jean Elleinstein—assistant director of the Centre d'études et de recherches marxistes, sometime communist candidate in legislative elections in the Latin Quarter, and prolific author. For Elleinstein, the PCF has done what critics all along said it could never do: It has "exorcised the specter of the dictatorship of the proletariat" and has done so "clearly, forthrightly, without subterfuge, on the basis of principle, and not by bluffing as some would like to make us believe."[9] He thus defends the new party line against the criticism of both Althusser and of Stalinist hard-liners like Jeannette Thorez-Vermeersch.

Elleinstein has been one of the principal popularizers of the doctrinal change, explaining how it is possible to reconcile it with both Marx and Lenin. Marx, he pointed out, used the phrase only eleven times and in a highly theoretical sense in order to describe the class content of the new socialist state as opposed to that of the capitalist state. Certainly it was not Marx's intention to call for dictatorial methods and the suppression of public liberties! It was Lenin who further developed the notion of dictatorship of the proletariat—"to be exercised in a peaceful manner, without army, without police, and without bureaucracy." But the peculiar conditions of the Bolshevik revolution and the civil war made proletarian rule a real dictatorship. "That is why it was necessary to abandon the expression of dictatorship of the proletariat, because it entailed an ambiguity in the position of the PCF." French communists now prefer the risks of democracy and of a peaceful revolution that might take a long time to the tragedy of violent revolution and civil war. And by basing a democratic socialism on pluralism and public liberties, Elleinstein concluded, the new society will be radically different from that in the Soviet Union, China, or any other communist country.[10]

Elleinstein described himself not as a social democrat (social democracy throughout Europe, in his view, has been a failure in that it has continued to seek merely to administer capitalism), but as a *democratic socialist*—another way of saying Eurocommunist, that is, someone who believes in "political democracy plus socialism."[1][1] Although Elleinstein was echoing the very words of Marchais on the importance of liberty, independence from the Soviet Union, and democracy within the party, his illustrations of each notion suggested that there were differences of interpretation on each point. After the defeat of the left in March 1978, these differences suddenly came to the fore. It was then evident that Elleinstein had been popularizing a view of Eurocommunism radically different from that entertained by party leaders, despite the similarity in terminology. In a series of articles that appeared in *Le Monde* (after being turned down by the party press), Elleinstein charged that the party had been defeated because its leaders were reluctant to continue the march toward democratic socialism. They have not kept up with changes in French society in the past several decades. His indictment is far-ranging: The party has not followed through on its decision to eliminate all traces of Stalinism; it has not undertaken a thoroughgoing critique of Soviet policy in Eastern Europe; it has not deepened its critical analysis of the Soviet model of socialism or probed the reasons why the Soviet Union is now an "antimodel." The party accepts in theory the idea that the revolution will be a long and gradual process; but by insisting on a hoary language of class struggle ("make the rich pay"), it is less appealing to many forward-looking people than the Socialist party. Finally, the party has not changed its structures sufficiently. It should rehabilitate the victims of past purges—Marty, Tillon, Garaudy, for starters; admit some of its historical errors—such as its endorsement of the Nazi-Soviet Pact; and increase the "democratic" and cut down on the "centralist" elements within the party structure. The party leaders could hardly have appreciated being characterized as "ambiguous" or stuck in midstream—reluctant to push the logic of their own doctrinal change to its logical conclusion—and in some ways in retreat from their own positions.[1 2]

As party leaders sought to contain internal factionalism, Elleinstein's position within the party became increasingly difficult. In a long interview on television on August 9, Marchais berated Elleinstein for declaring that the party pays no attention to dissenters. Why does not Elleinstein acknowledge, asked Marchais, that the secretary-general of the party received him for three hours, that his arguments were discussed one by one, and that on a number of points the wayward critic admitted his errors? Elleinstein replied immediately (not in *l'Humanité*, but in the all-too bourgeois pages of *Paris-Match*) that he had made no such admission of error. The discussion ended, he reported, by a finding that disagreement continued on all the problems brought up! Once again Elleinstein called upon the PCF to break completely with Stalinism (of which Marchais' statement was an obvious example), adding a call to the socialists to break just as completely with their policies of class collaboration and managing capitalism—thereby arousing the indignation and the anger of Mitterrand as well as the hostility of Marchais. He echoed the historic demand of the libertarian left for a "third solution" that would be neither the social democratic management of capitalism nor the experience of the so-called socialist countries, but rather "something new, capable of preventing the decay of the West and of renovating our society on bases that will promote more justice and humanity in the relations among men." He neglected, however, to describe any structures or to offer concrete policies.[1 3]

The tendencies here described as "left" and "right" are—at least so far—still within the PCF. The critique of Balibar and Althusser is more profound and is a greater threat to the current party leadership than that of Elleinstein. But the arguments on both left and right go beyond personalities; they express ambiguities and dilemmas within the French revolutionary movement. All involved in the dispute reject capitalism and seek to create a socialist society under the leadership of the Communist party. But there has always been a group within the revolutionary movement that rejects any dilution of the class struggle and banks on the revolutionary impulse of the workers to keep the new society on a correct course of authentic liberation. And there has always been a rival group that emphasizes the need for a corps of professional revolutionaries, holding divergent ideas, however, on the proper relationship between leaders and masses. In the ferment let loose by the May revolt, these old issues suddenly flared up again. Balibar and Althusser draw inspiration from Trotskyists and Maoists, who retain their commitments to class struggle. Elleinstein has some sympathy with the antimodernizing outlook of anarchists and surrealists, especially on the dangers of technology, despite their "adventurism." The debate that began with the creation of a socialist movement in the early nineteenth century and that led to the great fission between democratic and authoritarian factions at the Congress of Tours in 1920 has now surfaced (in attenuated form) within the Communist party itself.

3. The Center Holds

If we believe Balibar and Althusser, the PCF has abandoned the class struggle; if we believe Elleinstein, the PCF has not gone far enough in adapting its policies and structures to the modern world. Which side is correct? From the point of view of the party leaders, of course, neither. The party continues to believe in class struggle, remains authentically revolutionary, and has adapted its tactics to new conditions. In defending themselves against charges from both left and right, party leaders have reassured their followers and enlightened observers: Marx and Lenin continue to be the patron saints of the French Communist party. The time is not yet ripe—and never will be—for the entry of John Stuart

Mill into the galaxy of communist superstars.

Union of the French People

Rejection of dictatorship of the proletariat does *not* imply, all leaders of the PCF have stressed, acceptance of social democracy. The "democratic path to socialism" is via the *Union of the French People,* which is a far cry from the spirit of parliamentary or bourgeois democracy. Marchais explained the tactic carefully in his speech to the twenty-second party congress: "We want to rally all the creative forces ('forces vives') of the nation against the barons of big business, we want the Union of the French People." In this vast assemblage there is room for all the victims of capitalism, including managers, engineers, technicians, intellectuals, peasants, and Catholics. We do not ask you to become workers, Marchais assured all members of the social categories just enumerated; remain what you are, and contribute your special talents to the construction of the new socialist society.

But in this Union of the French People, two crucial points must be kept clearly in mind: (1) The working class will maintain its integrity and play the role of vanguard in the struggle for democracy and socialism; and (2) there is only one party of the working class, one party of revolution—the Communist party. Without its vanguard and its revolutionary party, there is no Union of the French People. Why does the working class play the role of vanguard? Here Marchais falls back on the orthodox concepts that seemed to be abandoned with dictatorship of the proletariat but miraculously have come back to life. First, the workers create "the essence of wealth" (in Marxist terms they create value), and by their number and role in the productive process, they are a massive force. Second, the workers bear the brunt of the exploitation inflicted upon all the victims of capitalism; hence they are the group most interested in pushing the battle against capitalism to its ultimate and inevitable conclusion, that is, to socialism. Third, concentrated in factories and enterprises, the working class has developed its struggle against capitalist exploitation, for which purpose it has created powerful trade unions and disposes of a revolutionary party—the PCF, which is the *only* party that has refused to manage capitalism, the *only* party that has always called upon the workers to fight against reformism and class collaboration, the *only* party that has always fought against authoritarianism, colonial wars, and encroachment upon national sovereignty and for democracy and socialism (as properly defined and understood).

Crucial for a correct view of the "new" communist ideology and tactic is the PCF perception of the Socialist party, its designated partner in a future left government. In a secret speech to the central committee immediately after the signing of the Common Program in 1972, Georges Marchais assured his colleagues that no concession whatever had been made to the ideology of social democracy and that the Socialist party would be compelled to accept a subordinate position within the left alliance in the long run.[14] When the secret speech was made public three years later, socialist spokesmen professed to be shocked; but in fact Marchais and other communist leaders had never concealed their intentions or calculations. In the logic of the Union of the French People, it is necessary that the Socialist party be relegated to a subordinate position; otherwise the march to socialism will never take place. As Marchais summed up in his speech to the twenty-second party congress: "It is true that the Socialist party remains a reformist party," and the fact that it signed the Common Program has not brought about any change. Its reformism stems from the whole history of the Socialist party (a sordid tale of class collaboration); from its lack of a coherent theory (that is, the PCF version of Marxism-Leninism); from the social composition of its leadership (overwhelmingly middle class and intellectual); and from its long policy of electoral cooperation with the right, especially in governing municipalities. As a final blow, the Socialist party was accused even of continuing to claim the heritage of Leon Blum!

The PCF leadership thus considers the attacks of the left wing (from critics like Balibar and Althusser) to be completely unjustified—and rightly so. What has changed is the phraseology but not the reality of dictatorship of the proletariat. The reality continues to be a vanguard role for the working class and for the only revolutionary party of the working class, namely, the Communist party. So long as these two points are upheld, the much-acclaimed doctrinal change is of minimal significance. The party has packaged somewhat differently the policy previously termed dictatorship of the proletariat.

But what about the other elements of the "democratic path to socialism"—the emphasis on democracy, liberty, pluralism of parties, alternation in power, repudiation of the Soviet model, and independence from the Soviet Union? Scrutiny of declarations made by communist leaders brings to light immense loopholes and qualifications at every point in the argument. Therefore, it cannot be demonstrated by either the critics or the admirers of the PCF that a significant doctrinal evolution has taken place. The phrases are different; the central meaning remains the same. New labels have been placed on old bottles; the "appellation" has been strictly "contrôlée" by the PCF. Let us look more closely at the loopholes and qualifications.

Liberty

The PCF now puts itself forward as the indefatigable, indeed, the only champion of liberty in France—including liberty of opinion and expression, assembly, demonstration, opposition, publication, religion, and so on. These liberties are to be extended and guaranteed. The PCF has even proposed a new bill of rights to be incorporated into the constitution. But the communists insist that they have not become advocates of "liberty" as that term is understood by the bourgeoisie and by liberals; and in explaining what they have in mind, all the old concepts reappear. To begin with, the communists remain firmly opposed to one so-called liberty, and that is the "liberty" to exploit workers, if one can indeed speak of liberty when dealing with the right to oppress a whole class. Liberty under capitalism is the privilege that capitalists have of extending and intensifying their exploitation. That kind of liberty will be eliminated; or rather, it will not be considered liberty at all. As René Andrieu put it: You do not leave a fox at liberty in the chicken coop![15]

Liberty is thus not merely negative; it is positive. "We have an infinitely higher and richer conception of liberty," explained Marchais. It is the possibility given each person to realize himself or herself completely, to develop creative faculties and human personality, to participate effectively in social and political life, and so on. "That full and complete liberty can only exist on condition that it cease to be the privilege of a few in order to become the good of all. That is the path of human progress."[16] In other words, real liberty cannot exist under capitalism; it can only materialize under socialism. But not only will a handful of capitalist exploiters be affected. As we have seen, the Socialist party is undeniably a reformist organization that eventually will be used by the capitalist class as a barrier on the road to socialism. The refrain is all too familiar: No freedom for the enemies of freedom—defined to mean all those who advocate capitalism, class collaboration, and exploitation of the workers or who block the only party of the workers in its task of constructing socialism.

The communists also defend themselves convincingly against the charge that they are sacrificing the revolution and the consolidation of socialism to the exigencies of bourgeois liberties. If they were to sit back quietly and allow the capitalists to destroy the gains of the working class, they would be nothing but despicable social democrats. As Marchais explained in his speech to the twenty-second party congress—and this has been repeated even by dissenters like Elleinstein—there is also the liberty to "guarantee" completion of the revolution that is only begun by the enactment of the Common Program. The struggle of the masses will progressively modify the balance between the social classes to the benefit of the working class and in favor of socialism. Reactionaries will continue to pursue their nefarious schemes. But the workers will be given extended "liberty" to advance their cause within their enterprises by making sure that their representatives (and they have only one party, be it remembered) have fair access to television and *"that the police will be democratized."* Precisely because they share control of the state, the workers will use "efficacious means" to fight against economic sabotage, to make known and support their views, "to defeat their opponents politically and ideologically." The workers will then be even stronger in their "liberties"—now identified with their use of state power. It is by wielding their expanded power (that is, liberty) that they will develop their struggle and drive the "grande bourgeoisie" toward withdrawal and defeat. Let it not be supposed, commented one of the leading communist intellectuals, Pierre Juquin, that the flowering of "liberty" will be permitted to "disarm" the working class. "You can well believe that the communists will not allow the left to be massacred without acting. Appropriate means are foreseen: prohibition of parties resorting to armed violence or calling for its use; democratization of the army and of the police, and, above all, weakening of the power of money."[17] The logic is inexorable: Advocacy of capitalism or class collaboration is hardly to be considered within the province of liberty; instead, the workers are to be "free" to make sure that reactionary forces (including those treacherous social democratic reformers) will be deprived of the possibility of turning back the clock.

Pluralism of Parties

One of the stumbling blocks in the long negotiations between the PCF and the PSF leading to the signing of the Common Program was the question of pluralism of parties and the right of the opposition to vote the left out of power. The PCF negotiators thought it outlandish at first to make reference to party pluralism and at one point suggested that it would be sufficient to offer guarantees to all parties accepting "socialism"! Suddenly, however, the communists not only accepted the principle of pluralism but became fervent advocates. Marchais has proclaimed that no one party— not even the Communist party—should have the task by itself of realizing the profound transformation of socialism. What is needed is collaboration, alliance, union of all progressive social forces. "We do not believe it is healthy for our country that one party, whichever one it might be, directs alone the affairs of the nation. The risks are too great for democracy."[18]

Again, however, terms are used by the communists in a sense completely different from accepted usage among liberals and social democrats. Parties represent different interests and the aspirations of different social groups, points out Marchais. But we have already seen that for the communists only the PCF is the authentic revolutionary party of the working class. Other parties must therefore represent the interests either of antagonistic classes (such as the bourgeoisie) or of social groups that accept the vanguard role of both the working class and of its only party, the PCF. Of critical importance is the role of the Socialist party, which has the historic task of bringing to the cause of socialism the allegiance of groups that hesitate to ally themselves directly with the PCF. If the Socialist party were to reach beyond that role and seek, for example, to dominate the left alliance, perhaps even to dominate and reduce the influence of the PCF (which is, of course, precisely its goal), then it would be objectively serving the interests of big business and reaction.

Perhaps the best indication of what communists mean by "pluralism" of parties was offered by Marchais after the signing of the Common Program. Many people mistakenly believe, he complained, that communist states are always one-party monopolies. Not so! For example, in Bulgaria, Poland, and East Germany there are multiparty systems (referring to peasant, liberal, and Catholic parties tolerated by the dominant communist parties). Here are fine examples of communists and noncommunists "collaborating" in the inspiring task of building socialism. In this context PCF theory on pluralism of parties is illuminated. Communist-dominated front organizations would have the role of mobilizing popular support for a regime led by the only truly revolutionary party of the working class. Inasmuch as Marchais' musings are read not only by his followers but also by his socialist allies, the impact of the alleged doctrinal change is considerably diminished.[19]

When public opinion polls indicated in the year that preceded the legislative elections of March 1978 an increase in socialist strength (with a projected 30 percent of the vote compared to about 20 percent or less for the PCF), a specter began to haunt the communists—the specter of being wiped out by the socialists. If socialist candidates indeed were to average 30 percent of the vote and communist candidates only 20 percent in each legislative district, then the candidate of the left on the second ballot almost everywhere would be a socialist. It appeared that Mitterrand had won the gamble—and that Marchais had lost—in agreeing to an alliance of the left through a Common Program and mutual desistance on the second ballot. The socialists have never concealed their plan to become the "first party of the left," thereby bringing about a dramatic shift in the balance of political forces in France. Time and again communists returned to the statement made by François Mitterrand shortly after the signing of the Common Program, when he explained to the members of the Socialist International at a congress in Vienna that at least three of the five million people who voted for the Communist party are really social democrats and could be brought into the fold through an appropriate left alliance. Throughout the negotiations on "updating" the Common Program, socialists made it clear that they would not permit the Communist party to exercise the "dominant influence" that its leaders demanded. At that point communist spokesmen charged that the Socialist party had become the chosen instrument of the capitalist class. The alliance of the left disintegrated as communists and socialists alike pointed out that the goals of the two parties were totally incompatible.[20]

Soviet Model

According to Marchais, there is today a serious conflict between the PCF and the Communist party of the Soviet Union regarding democracy and liberty. The way to deal with dissidents is through argument and debate, says Marchais, not censorship and repression. But PCF leaders reject the apocalyptic views of some (unnamed) critics concerning the systematic violation of liberty in the Soviet Union. "Their exaggeration," comments Marchais, "is inspired by a bad cause—the hatred of socialism." Violations of liberty in the Soviet Union are merely aberrations. For the PCF the Soviet Union is the first socialist state and remains a socialist state in which economic, social, and even political results are "positive."

Marchais recently observed that the workers in communist

countries "have more rights than in capitalist countries." Elleinstein and other critics seized upon this statement as evidence of the failure of PCF leaders to pursue their analyses of Stalinism, inasmuch as Russian workers do not enjoy even the elementary right to express themselves and defend their interests, not to mention criticizing and opposing the government. It is notorious that trade unions in the Soviet Union are merely transmission belts of the regime. What then can the French communists possibly mean by "rights" for workers in the society that they strive to create? Marchais insisted, in his exchange of unpleasantries with Elleinstein, that "there can be no question of a third way" between social democracy and socialism of the Soviet type. Social democracy is only a brand of capitalism; the PCF wishes to construct a socialist society that, he said, would not be based on "existing models." Marchais has yet to explain how it is possible to reject a "third way" and still depart from "existing models."[21]

The fundamental ambiguity remains. On the one hand, for the PCF the Soviet Union is a socialist society. On the other hand, socialism cannot exist in the absence of liberty, from which it is concluded that there is repression of liberty in the Soviet Union, which remains a socialist society! Any attempt to probe these contradictions is denounced as a pretext for an anti-Soviet or an anticommunist campaign. The theoretical confusion is total.

Foreign Policy

In the struggle to defend the interests of the working class of France, Marchais has stated, the Communist party naturally feels sympathetic toward the workers of the entire world. In cooperating with democratic and progressive forces, the PCF, of course, has special ties with the other communist parties that are in the vanguard of the struggle for peace and socialism. No single communist party, it is true, has the right to lay down the law for the entire movement. It is now necessary to establish a "new type of relationship" among communist parties. There is a fundamental difference, Marchais argues, between communist parties in power (in "socialist societies") and communist parties in capitalist countries. The first group has the responsibility of power and has to cooperate with the very capitalist regimes that the second group is trying to overthrow! This situation admittedly leads to "complications." The socialist countries want to have "peaceful coexistence," but the communists out of power want to bring the benefits of "socialism" to their own countries. Hence they cannot admit any limitations upon their freedom of action in the struggle that they conduct against capitalism.

But in the long run, concludes Marchais, there is no contradiction between the two sets of interests. By struggling against capitalism the French Communist party can restrain the bourgeoisie from seeking its revenge against socialism by launching a cataclysmic war. And if the PCF comes to power and enters a government, it will be in a position to further the cause of peace and disarmament (thus bringing about the defeat of imperialism). In this way is transcended the short-range differences between the Soviet Union and the PCF. Despite all the talk about polycentrism within the international communist movement and how "international solidarity" has replaced "defense of the Soviet Union" as a top priority, the PCF has yet to take a foreign policy position that differs from that of the Soviet Union. The French communists identify the pillar of world reaction as the United States (aided and abetted by West Germany and other capitalist countries), whereas the great progressive force is the Soviet Union, under whose benevolent protection it is possible for socialism to be achieved wherever communist parties come to power. Every foreign policy initiative by the PCF has the intended consequence of weakening the imperialist camp and strengthening the socialist camp. In a way, verbal independence from Moscow enables the PCF to make an even greater contribution to the common cause of "international solidarity" than would meek submission to orders from Moscow.[22]

4. Ideology and Reality

It is a fact that the phrase "dictatorship of the proletariat" was dropped from the preamble to the party rules at the twenty-second congress of the PCF in February 1976, that the party has embraced democracy, liberty, pluralism of parties, and the principle of alternation in power, has criticized violations of civil liberties in the Soviet Union, asserted the polycentric nature of the international communist movement, and has not resorted to excommunication of dissidents in recent years. Social democrats and "bourgeois political scientists" long argued that the Communist party could never change on any of these points or that if it were to do so, it would cease to be the Communist party. Yet the changes have taken place, and the PCF is still not a party "like the others."

It should occasion no surprise that the terminology or language used by the PCF has been overhauled. If a party is to survive, much less flourish, in a parliamentary democracy, it must attune its appeal to the society in which it functions. All parties must be sensitive to the slightest shift in attitude on the part of their clienteles. Even if a party seeks to reshape rather than reflect a society, it must still mobilize electoral and other forms of support. People have to be won over before they can be redirected or manipulated (for their own good, of course). It is inconceivable that the transformation of French society in the period following World War II could leave such sensitive instruments as political parties untouched. The French Communist party has changed for the same reasons that French society, on whose existence it depends, has changed.

It has not escaped the attention of the leaders of the PCF that the working class, even in its broadest definition, is a minority of the gainfully employed population and will remain so in the foreseeable future. In a frankly revolutionary situation it would suffice if there were merely concentrations of workers in key cities, as was the case in Russia in 1917. But in a society in which the tradition of elections is deeply rooted, a successful party must be able to organize or at least to dominate a popular majority. To put it brutally, if the PCF were to confine its appeal exclusively to the working class, it would be forever shut out from the prospect of coming to power. The Communist party is therefore under great pressure to jettison some of its proletarian symbols and slogans if it is ever to hope to lead a popular majority. A tactic such as the "Union of the French People" admirably serves the particular needs of the PCF. An overwhelming majority of the people, all more or less victims of capitalist exploitation, will be assembled around the working class (which in itself is admittedly less than a majority). But the major trade union happens to be controlled by the communists, and the PCF proudly puts itself forth as the only revolutionary party of that vanguard class! So perfectly tailored for the special position of the PCF is its tactic of the Union of the French People that it is no wonder that the Socialist party rejects it from beginning to end.

Furthermore, relations between workers and the rest of the society have been greatly affected by cultural and social developments. Television has reached into virtually every working-class household in the past two decades. Gone are the times when a worker and his family could live in a separate culture, effectively sealed off from the larger society. Now the messages of all political parties are brought directly into working-class homes and consciousness. Workers have also increasingly shared the values and the life styles that characterize French society. They join their middle-class compatriots in taking holidays on the Riviera, wearing blue jeans, buying records of popular American songs, listening to jazz, exceeding the speed limits (and getting killed) in their own automobiles, and so on. The holiday may be in a camping ground instead of a luxury hotel, the automobile may be secondhand, the blue jeans less fashionable—but the life styles have elements in common. A greater openness and toleration in Communist party ideology correspond to a greater openness—and homogenization—of French society.

The PCF must also take into account a new perception of the Soviet Union by outside observers as well as its own militants and intellectuals. For the French working class, the Bolshevik Revolution was the realization of a dream that had been blasted in France. Every time French workers tried to take power directly in the nineteenth century, they were defeated and then crushed by the bourgeoisie or at least so it appeared to them. The thirty thousand dead of the Commune have weighed heavily in the balance of French working-class politics. In 1917 working-class hopes were transferred in a sense to distant, inaccessible, mysterious Russia. Blocked from power at home, revolutionary workers and intellectuals in France could at least live vicariously in utopia by throwing their support unconditionally to the struggling socialist state, vivid proof that workers could indeed come to power and shape their own destiny. But the revelations of Khrushchev in his secret speech of 1956, the Russian intervention to crush working-class and popular revolts in Hungary, East Germany, and, above all, in Czechoslovakia, the admission that so many of the "bourgeois" critics of the Soviet Union had been correct, and the grim reality of everyday life in Russia, observable even by carefully shepherded tourist delegations, have all contributed to a vast demystification of the Soviet

Union. It is simply no longer possible to maintain the old myths. For some French communists, like Elleinstein, the Soviet Union has become an "antimodel." Even for the party leadership, care is taken to emphasize the "profound differences" between the PCF and the communist parties of Eastern Europe and the Soviet Union on the nature of "socialist democracy" (as distinguished from the social democracy of reformers, of course). That the Soviet model has been called into question in any sense is certainly an important development in the evolution of communist ideology in the West.

But a critical question remains. Have the three major currents within the left—authoritarian, democratic, and libertarian socialism—become any less distinct? Have the changes that we identified permitted a synthesis of these three ideological trends, an alliance or a merger of the political organizations that incarnate them? The answer is no—not yet, probably not for a very long time, perhaps not ever. The currents correspond to historic orientations of different groups in French society; they are continuing if not permanent features of French political life. The parties and other political organizations that carry forward each current have adapted to the new conditions of modern industrial society. In so doing they have evolved somewhat, but the changes so far have taken place well within the underlying rationale of each ideological family. The goals of democratic, authoritarian, and libertarian socialists have *not* changed; only the tactics are different. So long as it proves impossible to synthesize the respective goals of communists, socialists, and libertarians, the integrity of each movement is preserved. Each of these currents can be traced back at least two centuries. A transformation is conceivable only in the event of an enormous shock coming from the outside—Russian military domination and occupation of Western Europe; a war between China and the Soviet Union; an explosion in Eastern

Europe; a collapse of the Soviet regime; or other events beyond the control of the French party. But in an international environment roughly comparable to what exists at present, it is difficult to see how any fusion of the major ideological currents within the left could take place.

How can change lead to an overall situation of "no change"? On every key point of its ideology, the PCF has managed to maintain its distance from social democracy and from libertarian socialism even while modifying its phraseology. As we have seen, the PCF now accepts "democracy" and "liberty" but interprets each notion in such a way as to justify the kind of political system that it has always wanted to create. The Soviet model is in doubt; but no question is raised about the underlying structures of communism or the political consequences of Marxism-Leninism. The Soviet Union is still hailed as a socialist society, even though socialism is supposed to be impossible without liberty. Debates within the central committee are still not made public so that militants in their cells have no way of knowing what kind of support is enjoyed by dissenters; and party leaders have vowed never to permit "factionalism." The basic structure of "democratic centralism" is untouched. And the PCF's support for the objectives of Soviet foreign policy is steadfast.

It is important to place recent doctrinal changes in a larger historical perspective. The abandonment of dictatorship of the proletariat and the advocacy of a "democratic" path to socialism are not entirely new tactics and certainly are not unprecedented in the history of the international communist movement. PCF spokesmen (like Pierre Juquin) have little difficulty in explaining that both Marx and Lenin held out the hope of a peaceful (or a democratic) transition to socialism under appropriate conditions. The "democratic path" may be a departure from the Leninist model created in the Soviet Union after 1917 and especially from the Stalinist model; but in a sense the present PCF tactic is a return to the

Leninist model that preceded the seizure of power.

Lenin was expert in using any slogan or tactic provided that it served the special needs of the Bolsheviks. He at first opposed the soviets, then came out for "all power to the soviets," and then destroyed the soviets. At all times he was consistent in that the tactic furthered the interests of the Bolsheviks. Etienne Balibar cited one of Lenin's declarations (in 1920) in which he argued that it would be utterly ridiculous for communists not to exploit the interests that divide their enemies (even if the divisions were fleeting) or to refrain from seeking agreements and compromises with eventual allies (even if they are temporary, uncertain, fragile, and conditional). The parallel offered by Lenin is to try to climb an unexplored and seemingly inaccessible mountain without sometimes zigzagging or retracing one's steps or using different approaches. It is not possible to triumph over a more powerful adversary, Lenin warned, unless you cleverly and expertly exploit the least little fissure or division among your enemies (between the capitalist classes of different countries or among the various categories that make up the bourgeoisie in a given country) "as well as the least possibility of acquiring an ally that is numerically strong, even if that ally is temporary, hesitant, conditional, and uncertain. Who has not understood this truth has not understood anything at all of Marxism or in general of contemporary scientific socialism."[23] And in fact Lenin was careful to negotiate alliances with other parties both immediately before and after the seizure of power until the point was reached when the Bolsheviks were strong enough to "discuss the theses of the opposition with rifles." Hence the "line" of the twenty-second congress of the PCF is a revival of classical Leninism, free from the rigidities imposed subsequently by the Russians. Flexibility and a certain commitment to pluralism have always been characteristics of Leninism.

The new tactic (or revival of the old) is a sensible approach to the problem of the seizure of power. In the absence of a civil war or defeat by a foreign power, the chances of over-throwing by violence a parliamentary democracy like France are bleak. Were the PCF to storm the bastions of power, it would be crushed. But the chances of being voted into power by a popular majority are also bleak. In France it is unlikely that the Communist party will be able to gain much over 20 percent of the vote in the foreseeable future. The only prospect that the party has to come to power—barring a sensational international development—is not *against* the state but *through* the state, which is the historic lesson of successful revolutions in industrial societies. The party must participate in the state, gain control of key portions of the state apparatus, and use that state power to establish its strategic dominance within the society. To do that the Communist party must have allies (in France, above all, the Socialist party) that will help supply a popular majority but that are too weak to prevent the more dynamic communists from dominating the alliance. As was demonstrated in the period before the elections of March 1978, if the ally is too strong or is likely itself to become the dominant partner, it is preferable for the PCF to break the alliance, retreat into its fortresses (the municipalities that it governs and the unions that it controls), and live to fight another day.

There is another and more recent precedent for the replacement of dictatorship of the proletariat by a "democratic path to socialism." After World War II, all the communist parties of Eastern Europe, with the encouragement of Stalin, declared that there was no need for a dictatorship of the proletariat as a transitional stage to socialism. Because of the victory of the Soviet Union in World War II, a new situation had come into being. It was possible to institute a "popular democracy" in which all forward-looking people and parties could participate. Instead of a monopoly of power by communist parties, which were minorities throughout Eastern Europe, there would be a pluralistic party system—including peasant, liberal, and Catholic parties. Of course, the working class would be the motor force of the new socialist society, and the Communist party would be recognized as the vanguard of the working class. In Bulgaria, Poland, and East Germany there are still remnants of the noncommunist parties; in fact they are and always were front parties created by the communists for the express purpose of providing links to recalcitrant social groups. There is an important difference between the situation of Eastern Europe after World War II and that of France today in that the Red Army had placed the East European communist parties in power in the first place. Nonetheless, strictly from the point of view of Marxist theory, the parallel between the East European conception of "popular democracy" from 1945-1950 and the line of the twenty-second congress of the PCF in 1976 is striking.

The goal of the PCF, its leaders continually assert, is not to participate in government in order to "administer capitalism" but rather to do something with power—to compel its allies to break irrevocably with capitalism and march along with the communists toward socialism. This goal is compatible with a variety of tactics, including the "democratic path" sketched out at the twenty-second party congress. René Andrieu's interpretation of the policy of the Italian Communist party is both typical and highly instructive in this regard. Whether he has correctly understood the intentions of the Italian communists is not important; it is his attitude, as a leading member of the PCF central committee, that counts. Rejecting the charge by Mitterrand that the Italian communists seek to collaborate with the right, Andrieu observed: "In the mind of the Italian Communist party, it is a matter on the contrary of isolating the right by setting in motion a policy of all the popular forces, especially the communists, socialists, and Catholics. The historic compromise in these conditions is conceived as a strategy of the alliance of the forces of democracy and progress. *It is not a third way but a plan of passage to socialism,* taking into account the peculiarities of the Italian situation. . . . The objective is precisely to detach the popular masses from traditional influences and make them swing to the left. . . ."[24] Here we find an extreme flexibility of tactics—which might be either an alliance with the socialists or an alliance with the right—on condition that the outcome is a passage to "socialism" as defined and understood by the Communist party. This line is perfectly compatible with the Leninist prescription for communist parties seeking to seize or come to power.

The distinction made here is between a changing phraseology and a constant meaning. Each phenomenon reflects a social reality. The underlying ideology of the PCF expresses the profound alienation of a portion of the working class and of some intellectuals from the rest of the society or at least from its existing political and social system. Exposing the workers to the national culture through television, for example, may only serve to deepen the alienation of an important part of that class. Familiarity with middle-class life can also breed contempt for middle-class values, even as they begin to percolate through the working class itself. A persistent refrain in the communist press is disgust at what is called the insolence of the rich who flaunt their money and opulent life styles in the face of the workers. In mass meetings a communist orator can always count on arousing his audience when he contrasts indolent luxury and poorly paid honest labor. Resentment of the "beaux quartiers" and of extreme wealth goes deep in the consciousness of French workers; it is not mitigated by habits of social deference (as in Britain) or a widespread belief that high income is the reward for hard work or entrepreneurial ability (as in the United States). For historical and understandable reasons, most French workers look upon the wealthy as parasites or exploiters, in any case, enemies. Many French are also deeply hostile to the profit motive, which is seen as dehumanizing and degrading rather than as a social beneficial incentive for individuals to be efficient and competitive. The notion that people should be rewarded on the basis of their functions within society, that production should be for social use and not personal profit, is widespread among intellectuals and professionals as well as workers. Insofar as that conviction takes precedence over all other considerations (like parliamentary democracy, freedom for capitalist exploiters and their dupes, and so on), a communist party has fertile ground in which to take root.

The PCF for the most part has resisted the temptation to identify capitalism with modern society; in principle it favors the development of science and technology, increased production, and a higher standard of living for all workers. The appeal of the PCF is greatest precisely among those elements in French society that accept the modernizing process (unlike anarchists and surrealists) but who are resolutely opposed to the capitalist version of modernity. Since 1920 the PCF has largely succeeded in appropriating a long tradition of revolutionary socialism, coupling it with active defense of the interests of workers and lower income groups, and creating for that purpose a highly specialized and bureaucratic structure. Ideology serves also as a kind of social cement, holding together disparate elements and giving them a sense of community. To many militants the substantive content of party ideology matters less than the ritual that enables them to participate in social life even while denouncing their social partners.

So long as portions of the French working class and of other social groups (especially intellectuals) continue to be alienated from the central values and the political system of the larger society, the PCF will express and convey that sense of alienation. If the presently alienated workers and intellectuals were to accept gradually the mixed economy and parliamentary institutions that now exist and come to condemn the kind of socialism that prevails in the Soviet Union and Eastern Europe, the PCF, in order to survive, would have to adapt itself to this new reality. But on the basis of the available evidence, such an adaptation has not taken place—itself an indication that the anticapitalist and antiliberal current runs very deep. Workers have been increasingly exposed to the values and the life styles of the middle class; familiarity has not bred respect or brought about social integration. The PCF has given itself the mission of leading to "socialism" a working class that in turn is the motor force of French society. Only when it abandons that mission will the unification of the left be possible. Until then, viewed from the perspective of the other parties of the left, the PCF remains a deadly ally.

NOTES

1. See Marchais' report to the central committee, April 26-28, 1978, reprinted in full, *Cahiers du Communisme,* special issue on the legislative elections of March 1978, p. 42.

2. In using terms like luxurious party headquarters, limousines, summer homes, and so on, I am taking the liberty of quoting statements made to me by several leading socialists, all of whom had been involved in negotiations with the communists, during an informal discussion at PSF headquarters immediately after the defeat of the left in the legislative elections of March 1978.

3. Georges Marchais, *Parlons franchement* (Paris, 1977), p. 198. Marchais' report to the twenty-second party congress is reprinted in full in *Cahiers du Communisme* (February-March 1976), pp. 12-72.

4. See the convenient collection of statements by Marchais, Balibar, and other participants in the debate in the annex of Etienne Balibar, *Sur la dictature du prolétariat* (Paris, 1976), pp. 167-205. See also the report by Jean Kanapa in *Cahiers du Communisme* (February-March 1976), pp. 355-360, and Philippe Alexandre, *Le roman de la gauche* (Paris, 1977), pp. 380-385.

5. Balibar, *op. cit.,* p. 165.

6. Louis Althusser, *22ème congrès* (Paris, 1977) and *Ce qui ne peut plus durer dans le parti communiste* (Paris, 1978), which contain the three articles from *Le Monde* and a long preface.

7. *Ce qui ne peut plus durer . . ., op. cit.,* p. 17.

8. See also Louis Althusser, "Entretien," in *Dialectiques* (1978, no. 3).

9. Jean Elleinstein, *Le P.C.* (Paris, 1976), p. 171.

10. Cf. Jean Elleinstein, *Lettre ouverte aux francais sur la république du programme commun* (Paris, 1977), pp. 51, 57.

11. *Ibid.,* p. 111.

12. See his articles in *Le Monde,* April 13, 14, 15, 1978.

13. *Paris-Match,* August 25, 1978, pp. 36-37, 88. See also Elleinstein's articles in *Le Monde,* August 24, 1978.

14. Marchais' secret report of June 29, 1972, was made public in Etienne Fajon, *L'union est un combat* (Paris, 1975), pp. 75-127.

15. Cf. René Andrieu, *Lettre ouverte à ceux qui se réclament du socialisme* (Paris, 1978), p. 40. In general, see Georges Marchais, *Parlons franchement, op. cit.,* pp. 77-81.

16. Marchais, *Parlons franchement, op. cit.,* p. 81.

17. Pierre Juquin, *Liberté* (Paris, 1975), p. 145. In general, see also G. Marchais, *Parlons . . .,* pp. 205-206.

18. Marchais, *Parlons . . .,* p. 74.

19. Georges Marchais, *Le défi démocratique* (Paris, 1973), pp. 117-130.

20. For characterizations of the Socialist party as a tool of the capitalists: René Andrieu, *Lettre ouverte . . ., op. cit.,* pp. 127-138; Pierre Juquin, *Programme commun: l'actualisation à dossiers ouverts* (Paris, 1977), pp. 167-169; Charles Fiterman, "Construire pierre à pierre," *Cahiers du Communisme* (May 1978), pp. 4-16.

21. Cf. Marchais, *Parlons franchement, op. cit.,* p. 182; and statements on French television, reprinted in *L'Humanité,* August 10, 1978; statement on French radio, reprinted in *Le Monde,* August 19, 1978.

22. Cf. Marchais, *Parlons franchement, op. cit.,* pp. 171-180.

23. Reprinted in Balibar, *Sur la dictature . . ., op. cit.,* pp. 114-115. Curiously, Balibar does not further identify the quotation from Lenin. It is taken, of course, from *Left-Wing Communism, An Infantile Disorder.*

24. René Andrieu, *Lettre ouverte . . ., op. cit.,* pp. 95-96. (My italics.)

Annie Kriegel

EUROCOMMUNISM, FRENCH VERSION

*I. General Considerations: The Union of the Left
and the French Version of Eurocommusism*

In the significant year that ran from spring 1977 to spring 1978, the French Communist party (PCF) triumphed in at least one area: It succeeded in protecting its secrecy from professional party watchers. But the latter's attitude changed from awesome reverence to scornful indignation.

We have to admit that the party was fortunate. It was helped by circumstances: The failure of the French left having been guaranteed practically on the first ballot of the March elections (a surprise even to those rare experts who continued to believe that the majority would finally win), it managed not to reveal itself, which it would have been forced to do, for instance, by not accepting reciprocal general withdrawal, if the results had been reversed or even only more uncertain.

*Translated by Dr. Beatrice Braude

Naturally, the PCF deserves neither the exaggerated respect that it received before March 1978 nor the scorn heaped on it since that date. It has conducted its business more or less as one might have predicted when one became aware of the complex, logical maneuvering that was involved. To the surprise and indignation of its former socialist allies, the satisfaction that it has publicly displayed over having correctly extricated itself does not seem feigned.

Indeed it is a far from ordinary achievement to induce slowly and progressively, through an alternating and complementary game of generalized seduction and pressure on the left wing, the Socialist party (whose membership and, above all, constituency, we are convinced, remains social democratic) to endorse a program, the logic of which must finally cause that party to become involved, even at the cost of an eventual break with its right wing, with an operation so ambiguous that its communist nature would be revealed only when it was too late.

Naturally, it was also possible that the entire communist organization would be affected by such a flaw in conception to the extent that the Union of the Left—at least in a country like France—must, after a period of growth, always and under all circumstances break up. That would be the case, for instance, if one thought that its initial success would inexorably lead only to an excessive growth of the socialist element and that that growth would, from a certain point on, only endanger the communists' ability to control the entire operation.

Thus the only strategy for union that succeeded until the very end, until the establishment of the dictatorship of the proletariat, namely, the strategy for national union in the "popular democracies" after 1945, succeeded perhaps only for reasons not strictly dependent on it. Perhaps it was "condemned" to succeed because the source of its success was external, that is, the prior occupation of the territory by the Red Army.

If this hypothesis is correct, it would be absurd for the communists (and, concomitantly, the socialists) to persist from generation to generation in reworking a strategy that can yield only what it yielded on three occasions: a break before (1978) or after (1937, 1947) taking power. In this connection, the incredible strength of French political mythology can be measured: Neither one socialist nor one communist dissenter has suggested that such a hypothesis should be carefully examined. All sides prefer asserting that if the communists or the socialists had played the game earnestly, the game would have worked.

This hypothesis has the advantage of focusing on the critical point: The communists have in recent years been able to accommodate changes, immediate or long term, in the traditional forms of their control (for instance, by relinquishing the concept of the dictatorship of the proletariat), but they have not questioned the principle of control, the mechanism of which they intend to retain, however discreet, remote, or flexible its exercise has to be.

If no progress is made in this area (and now that the communists are especially interested in "perfecting" democratic centralism, it is highly probable that the twenty-third congress of the French Communist party, to be held in 1979, will take advantage of that preoccupation to overlook this crucial area), we must think either that the Union of the Left is an absurd idea or else that the communists are not interested in its ultimate outcome, for, in their considered opinion, that is not in doubt unless there arises an exceptional situation in which the socialists, repeating the aberrant acts committed in Prague and Budapest from 1945 to 1948, work for their own defeat. This situation would not be improbable if events unfolded, as indeed they did in Prague and Budapest, without recourse to general elections, for although a majority of socialist leaders and militants are capable of going astray out of a mad desire to attain power at any cost, even to the point of taking excessive risks, the socialist electorate is far less foolhardy.

Is it possible that the communists conceive of the Union of the Left only in terms of what it can do for them? Do they return to it periodically only because of the useful by-products that they derive from it? It is true that in 1936 the Popular Front made it possible for them to advance in two directions: They established their legitimacy, and they laid the groundwork for their permanent existence no longer solely on the basis of their theoretical claim but on their practical ability to represent the workers; at the same time, they solidified control over the reunified CGT (Confédération Générale du Travail). In the same way, it can be said, they succeeded between 1943 and 1947, through their expedient of the National Front, in moving up from a legitimacy that had been only social (based on the working class) to a national legitimacy. As a consequence, the Communist party, which had been composed of only a limited network of regional units implanted in the heart of the "working-class fortresses," developed into a nationwide system.

With what useful by-product can the Union of the Left between 1965 and 1978 be credited? This question is not easy to answer. Nevertheless, I venture to propose that this by-product could well be the very recent ability of the PCF to pull itself out of the Stalinist orbit and to shake off its fascination with the Soviet Union in order to put itself in a position in which it would have the leisure to exploit its own heritage, not by breaking with the socialist world but by giving itself more autonomy within it.

Although the meaning and the essence of the French version of Eurocommunism are extrinsic to the Union of the Left, it is the latter, according to my hypothesis, that provided the surge of vitality, prestige, and possibilities without which the PCF's boldness and renewal could not have come about. It is here and here only that these two processes, which people have tended either to confuse or to dissociate, can be linked. The Union of the Left temporarily provided a fairly favorable set of circumstances. It made possible a situation comparable to that of a businessman who experiences a temporary expansion of his credit, enabling him to go ahead with long-needed investments and changes. The investments and changes derived from the Union of the Left found a common refuge under the label of Eurocommunism.

The PCF's "expansion of credit" is visible in its most precious resource: its recruitment of militants. What would have been very risky to attempt with a weakened party, especially one whose majority consisted of old-time militants who had forgotten nothing, became possible as soon as the strategy of the Union of the Left, with its first successes and the hopes that it raised (although unjustified and destined to be dashed), brought the Communist party a large and eager new generation of members. It is from this point of view that the increase in average annual new membership should be looked at: from 40,000 in the sixties to 70,000 in the first years of the seventies and 100,000 and over since 1975. The same assessment can be applied to the jump in total membership from 400,000 to 700,000. (It makes little difference whether these numbers are exact; what counts is the scale of increase that they represent.)

If the Union of the Left from 1963 to 1978 provided the necessary impetus to propel the French version of Eurocommunism on its course, it is easy to understand why the communist leaders poke fun at their dissidents, who, precisely because of Eurocommunism, believe that they must echo socialist complaints and proclaim that the left's final defeat, so close to realizing its declared goal, would mean that this fifteen-year period was a sterile one.

What Thorez had been neither willing nor able to do in 1956, Marchais succeeded in accomplishing without fracas in 1978. Marchais is managing to persuade the communists to continue to work without the assurance that somewhere in the East there exists a perfect society. He is succeeding in lowering their expectations and hopes so that they will no longer be vulnerable to the disappointments that "come from the cold" and yet encouraging their preferences for imperfect socialist society rather than Western society. What is more, he is managing to exalt the purely French dimensions of their communist identity, equating the evil of Western society with the fact that it is not communist and the evil of socialist society with the fact that it is not French.

This is the reason why the French Communist party has not experienced the disarray to which the Socialist party has been prey since 1978. Deprived of the prospect of ruling, and it has been deprived of any prospect whatsoever, the French Communist party seems to have so much work to perform that it can choke its own dissidents with it.

On the one hand, because the Union of the Left is only one of many strategies used by the communists, they can continue to advance it as an abstract slogan even while they are actively destroying its foundation, namely, the participation of the Socialist party. (After all, every union requires that there be two to merge.) Therefore, the same effort that the PCF exerted in contributing to the socialist rebirth is now being exerted to ensure its collapse, and with the same relative success. It is a sad truth that the Socialist party, today as yesterday, defers to the communist way of looking at things. It either screams for union and struggles in a ridiculous vacuum or else looks elsewhere, and consequently on the right, for the help and solace that the left refuses to provide. It then "shifts" to "the right," confirming, after the fact, what the communists had asserted in a baseless accusation.

On the other hand, the French version of Eurocommunism has acquired a consistent image that has been contrived to dispel most of its initial ambiguities and augurs well for the ability of the PCF to continue on its merry way. This image building can be summed up as a refashioning, with delicate touches, of the communist identity. Its working-class structure is jealously retained, its French roots are stressed, and its imitation of the Soviet model is reduced. To say that nothing is going on in the French version of Eurocommunism is therefore an exaggeration. But to say that there is a Chinese kind of schism or even an often severe Yugoslav kind of heresy is saying too much.

Possibly, if the PCF can persuade the Soviets not to panic over complex maneuvers whose results may be as necessary as they are modest (and to inspire confidence on the part of the Soviets, the public condemnation of several dissenters who had particularly irritated Moscow might have done the trick), the party may even be able to afford the luxury of again becoming the "elder daughter of the communist church" in the West in the sense that it would represent for the West what the Rumanian Communist party is for the East: unshakable on the fundamental principles of the system but capable of giving the party an out-and-out nationalist veneer.

In trying to regain the status that it held for a long time within the international communist movement, the PCF is in a good position to win out over its two rivals, the Spanish and Italian Communist parties.

Whereas the Spanish Communist party is debilitated by the quarrel that the Soviets picked with Carrillo, the French Communist party confined the break between Brezhnev and Marchais to the personal level, not in order to take sides against either Brezhnev or Marchais but to ensure that the way to accommodation between itself and the Communist party of the Soviet Union would remain open.

In the same way, the Italian Communist party is marked by a kind of complacence with respect to a suspect liberalism. It also identified itself too closely with one strategy—the strategy of the historic compromise—that it wanted, a little arbitrarily and out of vanity, to become *the* strategy of the time. Apart from the fact that the results of that strategy are minimal and its short-term prospects suggest little progress at all, it is unnecessary to identify the party with any one strategy because there will always come a time when it will be more advantageous to change it. Even if one strategy may seem better adapted than others at a given time, it is wasteful and imprudent to appear to decide *a priori* that adopting one strategy will eliminate prior or concurrent strategies. The French Communist party yielded to neither temptation. It declared itself for liberties, but liberalism is an entirely different matter toward which it does not seem disposed. In the long run, of all liberties, the one that it prefers is its own liberty to choose strategy.

II. The USSR and the French Communist Party

Since it became Eurocommunist, has the French Communist party indulged in "truth" operations, hoping at their termination to pull itself out of the web of old and outdated lies in which it is unnecessarily caught? Yes, partially. It now seems to believe that it must learn to use lies more moderately than in the past. But also, no, partially. It continues to believe that, above all, it must use lies with discretion. It is not enough for the truth to be true; it must be strategically useful. According to the PCF, today's truth must show (1) that Moscow was not always right in disdaining the advice of its local "agents," the communist parties; (2) that the local communist parties possess "secrets" whose revelation could be embarrassing to the Soviet leaders.

Two recent incidents can help us understand the preoccupations of the French Communist party.

Here is a brief account of the first such incident. Having temporarily finished with strictly French business when the left's electoral defeat was sealed in March, Georges Marchais returned to his other interest: the international communist movement. In May 1978 he traveled to Mexico for a visit, which, incidentally, was the first visit of a general-secretary of the French Communist party to Latin America. The visit created considerable stir: Marchais was received by the Mexican president, who was about to fly off for an official two-week visit to the Soviet Union and Bulgaria. But, above all, Georges Marchais was the guest of the Mexican Communist party. His aim in going to Mexico was the same as the motivation that led to his trip to Japan two years previously: to make people understand what he, Marchais, meant by Eurocommunism; to convey that it was not a small regional Latin-European agreement but a conception of communism that would combine and unite two objectives: (1) an unswerving determination to struggle against imperialism (Mexico is at the gates of the imperialist center par excellence, the United States), (2) the determination to obtain Moscow's acquiescence in letting each local party carry on the antiimperialist struggle in its own way—a decision that would prove better for all concerned because Moscow had often erred in its dealings with the local parties.

Georges Marchais brought back from Mexico proof that the Soviet leaders would finally understand the dangers of excessive centralism. That proof was the memoirs published in Mexico City under the title of *My Testimony* by Valentin Campa, seventy-four years old, who was excluded from the Mexican Communist party in 1940 and subsequently "rehabilitated." Marchais immediately had two excerpts translated. They were published in a prominent spot in l'*Humanité* on July 26 and 27, 1978.

What was it all about? In essence, Campa related that as a member of the secretariat of the Mexican Central Committee, he and Hernan Laborde, the general-secretary, and a third comrade, Rafael Carrillo, were "contacted" in September 1938 by an accredited representative of the communist International. The latter's mission was to ask the Mexican

Communist party to take charge of organizing the assassination of Trotsky. The three men "studied the matter with much calm and care" and finally refused. As a result, Campa and Laborde were dragged through the mud and excluded from the party (as "Trotskyites," of course, because they refused to kill Trotsky but also as "opportunists," for the International, in accordance with its usual practices, drew up an indictment in which all kinds of disparate "accusations" were gathered and mixed together). After which, with the help of more obliging comrades, Trotsky was assassinated.

It is too much to say that this was a revelation. Whole libraries are filled with works that demonstrate that Trotsky's assassination was ordered by Stalin and was accomplished by his emissaries. But a secret can be an open secret in the noncommunist world and remain a "party secret" in the communist world. By revealing this "secret," the Mexican and French Communist parties proved—with reference to an old but important case considering what Trotsky represents in the demonology of orthodox communism—that local parties can take liberties in matters declared out of bounds by Moscow. It was not blackmail, but it was a threat, all the more so because in this situation, several revelations, although minor, were made: the role of Vittorio Codovilla, general-secretary of the Argentinian Communist party from 1918 to 1970, who came to the rescue of the Komintern's agent, and the role of Lombardo Toledano, a "fellow traveler" who was until his death vice president of the World Trade Union Federation. Finally, we learned the real reason for which Earl Browder, general-secretary of the Communist party of the U.S.A., was excluded: He was opposed to Trotsky's murder.

But a major secret was also revealed. Even for criminal operations, Stalin, the communist International, and the NKVD made use of the good offices of local communist parties at the highest level, that of the general-secretary. It had been believed that for that kind of operation there were entirely independent channels and departments.

Finally, two secondary observations can be made: (1) Even when excluded from his own party, Campa remained silent, at first because "the Second World War had just broken out" and subsequently for more than forty years; (2) even when "rehabilitated," he did not "rehabilitate" Trotsky or his comrades who, disgusted and shocked, had defiantly withdrawn from the communist movement. On the contrary, in Campa's eyes, Trotsky is still a black sheep, so perverted that he verged on being a collaborator of the class enemy. In short, Trotsky was a "fascist" who "played Hitler's and Mussolini's game." His "elimination" (even today, when telling his story, Campa uses this euphemism) was not necessary because he was "beaten politically." In Campa's statement we can see the Eurocommunist theme according to which "administrative" methods (another euphemism for "strong arm") must yield to the "battle of ideas," for communism has become strong enough to win the battle over the economy.

Nothing prevents us from noting a curious omission that in its way reveals that the Eurocommunist truth of today is the communist truth of instrumental choice. Campa stated that he refused to kill; but he seems not to have entertained the slightest notion that his conscience could not possibly be at peace, for having permitted the killing, he committed a morally reprehensible act—that of not assisting a person in danger.

The second incident is more recent: It began on September 4, 1978, with the publication on the first page of l'*Humanité* of a communique from the political bureau recommending the "fascinating" book edited by "five communist intellectuals" and entitled *The USSR and We. (L'U.R.S.S. et nous)*

We represents the authors, of course, but authors who merge with their party. At least three of them, Francis Cohen, Claude Frioux, and Léon Robel, belong to the oldest generation of communists and have always been known to be completely pro-Soviet in the most orthodox way. The *we* then assumes a very precise meaning, taking into consideration the nuances of communist language in which the *we/they* dichotomy serves an essential affective function: *we*—the communists; *they*—the others, all the others who are not communists. The *we* designates only the community of French communists by banishing the Soviet Union and at the same time introducing into the system of the French communist world a division fundamentally different from the previous division.

Ousted in this way from the affective universe of *we*, what happens to the Soviet Union? Well, everything falls apart, precisely in the Russian meaning of the term, when winter's end transforms the whole country into a quagmire. Nothing very new is evident to a noncommunist reader: The "Stalinist realities" are recalled in broad strokes; it is suggested that the peasants and workers do not yet appear to be directly in power; some of the "brakes" reducing the performance of the Soviet economy are singled out; the "cultural adventures" and the "different forms of ideology" of the last fifty years in the Soviet Union are evoked; so many chapters contain material that has been known for a long time. Only the communists had denied its substance. It is amazing to observe that men who were in the Soviet Union frequently and who were received there like "brothers" have nothing to add to what had been documented without any direct contact with the phenomenon and the society in question.

But that is not the essential point. There are in fact two essential points. The first is that in order to make credible "socialism in French colors" it is not enough for the communists to say that if one day they have the power to do so, they will do things differently from the way in which they were done in the Soviet Union. They feel compelled to add that they will do things differently not because they are

French or are in a different situation from the Soviets, nor because Soviet reality presents dark spots not compensated for by brights spots, but because the Soviet *system* as a prototype embodies fatal errors of conception. The French Communist party is therefore in much the same position as that of the Yugoslav party when Tito rebelled against Stalin. He not only waved the flag of Yugoslav national independence, he also expressed the hope that the Yugoslav brand of socialism would be different from the Soviet system. We know now that the Yugoslav management of their own affairs, the symbol of that originality to which Tito aspired, did not impair very seriously the orthodoxy of Yugoslav society as a socialist society.

But right now the second point is the more important. Throughout their book and in their conclusion, the five authors maintain the dual vision that is at the heart of the communist theory of contemporary society: on the one side, imperialism, and on the other, what they no longer call the *socialist camp* but the *international working class.* If they have revised their image of the "Soviet paradise," that is not at all the case for the "imperialist hell," which they still see only as a "past of exploitation, genocide, and scorn for human values." It is with respect to the international working class that the shoe pinches because, after all, the international working class is only a concept, a theoretical construct, that in order to become concrete and operational, must be based on reality and take on substance, and this incarnation can only be accomplished in and through the Soviet Union.

From that point on, the French Communist party falls back into the situation from which it wanted to detach itself, the situation in which Tito has been locked for thirty years, a nonalignment so ambiguous that at each decisive moment, its mask drops off. Of course, if it behaved like China against the USSR, we would no longer be in the world of heresy but in the world of schism, for the Chinese system is not substantially different from the Soviet system.

III. Eurocommunism, Europe, and the Building of Europe

Summer seems to be a time of clarification—and break—for the communist movement in Europe. During the summer of 1977, the first steps toward the split in the French Union of the Left were taken. During the summer of 1978, there emerged a multiplication of signs that made it possible to eliminate at least one of the interpretations made almost three years ago when the phenomenon called Eurocommunism appeared. Eurocommunism is not and will not be a version of communism characteristic of the West European communist parties, nor is it a revolutionary strategy at the regional level. In short, there does not exist a Latin or a Mediterranean communism any more than there was—in spite of the hopes raised in the recent past—a Latin or a Mediterranean socialism.

We must acknowledge that the French Communist party has done nothing to maintain this illusion. (Quite the contrary.) For one thing, Georges Marchais, in choosing his international activities, devoted himself to showing that his party wanted to develop its relationship with every communist party that is interested in a moderate, "balanced" revision of the working principles of the international communist movement: a revision whose aim involves diminishing the dominating role of the Communist party of the Soviet Union and ensuring an independent capacity for initiative and decision on the part of other member parties. This is the spirit, for instance, that caused the general-secretary of the French Communist party to travel during the past two years to Japan, Mexico, Great Britain, and Rumania. For another thing, Georges Marchais has refused to transform into a platform of mutual action and organization the points of view that he may hold in common with the Italian and Spanish Communist parties on essential theoretical and political questions, such as giving up the principle of the dictatorship of the proletariat and espousing the defense of liberties. In short, although agreeing to give *ideological* meaning to Eurocommunism, he refused to ascribe to it any *geographical* significance or any power to transform itself into a territorially-circumscribed movement. That is why he has not renewed the ambiguous experiment of the first and only meeting that took place in Madrid in February 1977 among the general-secretaries of the three "Eurocommunist" parties.

But Georges Marchais' logic is taking him far beyond those first careful steps. Laying down the principle that each communist party must decide what it is only in terms of the national interest for which it has responsibility and rejecting any form of arbitration other than pure and simple bilateral or multilateral negotiations among directly interested parties, the French Communist party is in the process of giving dual demonstrations, one as humiliating and dismaying as the other, because, it must not be forgotten, both come from a revolutionary movement that derived its original vitality from a dream of universal peace and fraternity after the carnage of the First World War.

First Demonstration: The building of Europe, whose relative success at the beginning of the sixties troubled the unity of the East European communist movement, is now troubling the unity of the West European communist movement. Actually, the establishment of the European Economic Community, in which, to make things worse, the northern social democrats wielded a major influence, risked weakening the solidarity of the communist parties of *all* of Europe, the Europe of the West (and the Common Market) and the Europe (socialist) of the East. Intimations of this concern can be gleaned from the convening of specific conferences of the communist parties of the Common Market countries (Brussels, 1959; Brussels, 1963; Ostend, 1964) and the communist parties of the other European capitalist countries (Rome, 1959; Brussels, 1965; Vienna, 1966; London, 1971; Brussels, 1974).

In a second phase, the problems posed by the expansion—at first from six to nine and then from nine to twelve members—of the Community revealed remarkable differences in the reactions of the communist parties of Western Europe. Whereas the English and Scandinavian communist parties have manifested undying hostility to the membership of their countries in the Common Market, European integration has been for the Italian Communist party since 1971 and for the Spanish Communist party since 1974 the geometric center of their respective *aggiornamento.* But the West European communist parties are no longer at the stage in which differences in evaluation and behavior can be attributed to the assumption by each party of the role of being the sole judge of its national interests but at the stage of divergence and opposition in matters of *mutual* concern: The French Communist party has come out *against* Spain's entry into the Common Market, whereas the Spanish Communist party is *for* it.

In order to evaluate the long-term meaning of such a disagreement, we must remember that in the European Parliament, for instance, the different political groups do not function on a *national* but rather on an international basis. What a disastrous weakening of "international solidarity" within the "European working class" would be observed if the socialist or liberal parliamentarians elected in the various countries of the Community proved capable—as they have demonstrated thus far—of working together in Strasbourg within one parliamentary group and agreeing on a common policy, whereas the communists could not.

Second Demonstration: Even more amazing, the "bourgeois, capitalist, imperialists" are better at finding areas of compromise and agreement and at negotiating among themselves and with the socialist countries than are the communist parties, even though the latter are not in power. A striking manifestation of rigidity, the inability to compromise that is characteristic of interparty communist diplomacy, had already been noted: The Soviet Union, which conceived the idea and presided over both projects, succeeded more easily and rapidly in bringing together the thirty-five concerned states at the Conference on Security and Cooperation in Europe (Helsinki, August 1, 1975) than in bringing the twenty-nine interested communist parties to the All-Europe Conference of Communist Parties (East Berlin, June 1976). Similarly, it would seem that bringing together the president of the French Republic and the king of Spain to meet, discuss, and agree, as was the case in July 1978, is child's play and "in the nature of things" compared with the "impossible mission" of getting Marchais and Carrillo to meet, discuss, and agree.

What separates the French, Italian, and Spanish Communist parties on the question of Europe is irremediable, namely, the choice of *levels* at which each party intends its struggle to take place. For the French Communist party, only two traditional levels continue to be operational: the world level, of course, and the national level that it considers its own and exclusive responsibility. For the Italian Communist party, even more than for the Spanish Communist party, in addition to those two traditional levels, an intermediate level consisting of two supranational regional systems is indispensable: on the one hand, the European hinterland on which the two countries border and on the other hand, the Euro-African Mediterranean region with respect to which they believe they have a mission.

This choice of privileged levels is not arbitrary. The French Communist party is the product and the obverse of the Jacobin national state. Like the great forefathers of 1792 and 1793, its leaders consider France to be the crystallization of the universal: Its interests, through a kind of preestablished harmony, could not come into conflict with the interests of the human race—in this instance, the community of European peoples. The Italian Communist party, although it has presented itself periodically as the strongest advocate of the legitimacy of a national state greatly in need of consolidation, is above all the product and the obverse of a Roman Christianity for which the Alps have never been the same as "the blue line of the Vosges." As for the Spanish Communist party, how could it forget that the only way that Spaniards have ever known of exorcising their domestic demons and imposing tolerance of nations, languages, faiths, and political convictions, every one of which claimed domination for itself, was to open themselves to the influence of the spirit emanating from the other side of the Pyrenees?

From the very beginning, the French Communist party has had no leaning toward European ideas. It experienced no pang of conscience when, following the same line according to which it condemned the Marshall Plan (1947) and the Schuman Plan (1950), it manifested hostility to the first forms of European economic cooperation. It is true that the Institute of World Economy and International Relations of the USSR Academy of Sciences, as far back as 1957 and in nineteen theses, had severely criticized the attempt at West European integration, viewing it as only "an agreement of monopolies, cartels, and trusts" and simultaneously as an "economic base for NATO" whose mission, on behalf of American imperialism, involved, first and foremost, opposition to "the socialist states and combat against communism." Incidentally, the Institute predicted failure and collapse within a short time—a prediction that justified calling a conference in Brussels of the communist parties of the six countries of the Common Market. The purpose of the conference was to "put an end to the European Iron and Steel Community (CECA) and prevent application of the Common Market" on the basis of a detailed indictment: The Common Market "intensifies exploitation of the working classes," is an obstacle "to the liberation of colonial peoples" and "to the movement of international detente and peace," worsens the living conditions of "nonmonopolistic sectors" (that is, artisans and peasants), is a "danger to democratic institutions," and, naturally, "weakens the foundations of national independence," all the more so because "one of its main objectives is the restoration of German militarism and its atomic machine."

Certainly, beginning in 1962-1963, after none of the assertions had been validated, first Khrushchev, in a *Kommunist* article (August 1962) that caused comment, then the same Institute (issuing thirty-two theses in September 1962, and, finally, a new conference of the communist parties of the six Common Market countries meeting in Brussels in March 1963 began work on a theoretical and political reevaluation of "imperialist integration in Western Europe," which, although remaining intrinsically worthy of condemnation, had nevertheless acquired such consistence that it "constitutes a fact."

A change in the global meaning of this fact was also asserted: The Common Market that had been considered only the work and the "instrument of American imperialism in Europe" was proclaimed to be "the union of Adenauer's military and clerical dictatorship with General de Gaulle's authoritarian regime," in other words, the backbone of the Franco-German alliance. Still to be discovered by Moscow and the French communists were the "positive aspects" of General de Gaulle's foreign policy that would enable them to arrive at the formula, still operational today, according to which their denunciation is focused on the Europe that is the creature of "German-American domination."

As soon as the Common Market was worthy of the status of a "fact" that no matter how regretful could no longer be overlooked, the French Communist party, through this same complicated process of political and theoretical international conferences, began progressively from 1966 onward to make known its "European" program. Although making a concession by recognizing the "reality" of the Community, to compensate for making that concession, it subjected the Community to a two-pronged attack.

First, the PCF contests the principles and the structures of the Community on the basis of which it has submitted a program that is at one and the same time a call for revision and a strategy of reform.

A call for revision: According to the PCF, the Treaty of Rome created a "Europe of monopolies"; its revision would bring about a "democratic Europe," a "Europe of workers."

The reform strategy deals with the activities of the specialized committees of the Community (European Social Fund, Economic and Social Committee, Committee for Professional Training, and others) and the democratization of institutions. The Brussels Commission, "technocratic and without allegiance to any nation," in its present status as the "superboard of directors of the European bourgeoisie" should become only an "organ of execution and study." As for the Parliament, in which a communist group was constituted only in 1973, the French Communist party that had contested the principle of electing the Parliament by universal suffrage ("a low blow against France," l'*Humanité* proclaimed after the decision taken at the summit of nine in Rome) changed its mind and yielded by accepting the position that the Italian Communist party had taken on the matter.

To this attack on the principles and structures of the Common Market the PCF has added a second and even more decisive attack: It has attacked the "closing" of the Common Market to the East and has demanded that all obstacles to the "widest possible" economic cooperation with Comecon be removed; conversely, it has attacked the Community's "opening" to the West and in so doing condemns all "broadening." The French Communist party was against the entry of Great Britain and opposes the entry of Spain, Portugal, and Greece.

The analysis of the attacks launched by the PCF clarifies what the French communists mean when they call themselves good Europeans. They are good Europeans because they no longer call for the Community's immediate disappearance.

They wish to be good Europeans in a "true Europe" that is not only freed from American ascendancy and from German domination but that requires no surrender of sovereignty.

Can we then call the French communists nationalists? Or as they themselves express it, are they guided only by France's interests as they conceive them to be? We should be prudent, for in the last analysis, in matters involving "Europe," they are faithful only to Soviet policy. Their Europe is a Europe that would be only a supply house for Comecon countries.

IV. Eurocommunism: Gestation and Substance

"It is high time for the French Communist party to consent to open its eyes," André Gide, *Afterthoughts on the USSR (Rétouchés a mon rétour d'U.R.S.S.)*. This observation was made in June 1937. Forty years afterward, the French Communist party is actually beginning to agree to do so. It has taken its time.

This fact must be kept in mind when thinking about "what can no longer go on" (Althusser) in the PCF, which controls time, duration, and moment in a manner all its own undoubtedly because the party possesses in its constitution the means to do so.

After all, a slow pace and gradualism are pedagogical obligations for a party that wants to be a "mass" party and whose sociological composition gives it weight, cohesion, and an underpinning that make tightrope walking useless and dangerous. That is the reason why those intellectuals who still believe that they are able to tolerate their heritage of horrible realities and "existing socialism" but who, in order not to feel constrained, want to proceed quickly toward an understanding of themselves and, as a result of that process, issue a revised communist version of the past have only one recourse: to leave.

That is also the reason why some commentators have made so many mistakes regarding the Eurocommunist phenomenon. At first they seized it when it was hardly out of the womb, insisting on defining it; and inasmuch as it was hardly more than an embryo, they decided either that it was not alive or that it was not interesting. Then, tired out, they decided to talk about something else. But Eurocommunism is only beginning now. A good deal of time will have to elapse before it attains a certain degree of coherence and consistency.

With the same haste, other commentators wanted to define its *usefulness,* to make it an instrument that would immediately have its part to play in the system of East-West relations. Apart from the fact that even the Sino-Soviet schism began to be instrumental only ten years after it appeared, it is an error to see in Eurocommunism a Western version of the Sino-Soviet schism. Eurocommunism should not now be categorized as a schism.

Finally, a third mistake: By stressing the prefix *Euro,* people forget the stable part of the term *communism.* Eurocommunism is communism, and everything traditional that it has not affected remains as it was. Nor is Eurocommunism any more of a heresy than it is a schism. Then what is it? Continuing the metaphor, I would suggest that Eurocommunism may develop in the direction of a new *liturgy,* like those of the national or regional churches that Rome finally recognized and that even today are special liturgies whose peculiarities go far beyond the purely "ritual."

On this basis Eurocommunism may innovate in two areas:

The first, concerning which it is already far advanced in defining its operations and its limits, is its impact on the international arena. Actually, it is maintaining intact two principles relative to dogma.

On the one hand, it upholds the necessity of viewing itself as an element, a segment of the great class struggle that at the planetary level will make history. That is the point at which it is Marxist, the boundary that prevents a Eurocommunist party from lapsing into nationalism pure and simple.

On the other hand, it maintains the no less important need to agree that in the area of the world interstate struggle (which is an aspect of the international class struggle), the very weight of the Soviet state and the system of socialist states grouped around the USSR (with a rapid "broadening" of Comecon) makes it imperative in matters of international politics for every communist party to keep the USSR's foreign policy as the inevitable point of reference. Except possibly for minor details involving their immediate environment, it is hopeless to expect the communist parties to set themselves off from the USSR in their foreign policies.

Nevertheless, the Eurocommunist parties are questioning the structure and the internal operating rules of the international communist movement. What they are rejecting is the fact that the latter has established its internal balance by delegating its power and authority to the Soviet party on the pretext that it was the first center, motor, and keystone. This is the meaning of the attempt to de-Leninize so loudly proclaimed by Santiago Carrillo. That is where the concept of autonomy (or independence) comes in. According to the communist parties, autonomy should involve commanding and governing the internal relations of the international communist movement. It is in that realm, of course, that tensions have developed with the Soviet party. Like any hegemonic center, the Communist party of the Soviet Union cannot bring itself to accept this *diminutio capitis,* although Brezhnev or possibly his successor may manage to tolerate an arrangement that would inject more flexibility and consequently more dynamism into the whole system. It is this new-found but very limited autonomy that the French Communist party intends to exercise, for instance, over its financial infrastructure. It is obvious that the drastic changes

taking place in its publishing and distribution apparatus belong in the category of measures aimed at extending in every
direction its concrete independence with respect to but within the communist system.

The second area affected by the Eurocommunist mutation
is much more delicate, and the work accomplished is much
less advanced. This area covers the enormous question of a
socialist model that is better adapted to contemporary society. The limits within which this effort can be circumscribed
are beginning to appear. First, there is no denying that "existing socialism"—found in the Soviet Union—is indeed socialism both in its essence and in its evolution. In particular, it is
essentially correct to view 1917 as the decisive break at the
world level and 1920 as the decisive break for France. This
means that any theorist who seeks a middle ground between
social democracy and communism will find his text "off limits" and its author, even if he is not "excluded," condemned
to the sidelines. Here, too, Eurocommunism remains a communism within the communist sphere of ideas.

On the other hand, although the boundaries already in
place narrow the field of research, the *substance* of the model
to replace the Soviet model in the political area is still very
unclear. It is true that a major idea that should be the keystone of the new model has been reformulated, namely, that
the crisis in the Western world is so great that a communist
revolution could in the future steal from it the weapon of
democracy, not to join in manipulating it, like a shamefaced
social democrat, but to turn it against the Western world and
make it the essential instrument of its own anticapitalist
struggle. There is nothing new here (it is an idea of the thirties), and certainly it is easier said than done. In Italy and
Spain, where democracy is fragile and threatened—although
for different reasons—such an idea can provide guidelines.
But in France for the moment, the "solution" is a bit far-
fetched. In any case, it is easy to see that the kind of

democracy about which Eurocommunist parties are debating is in no way connected with their own functioning. Any attempt at redirecting the debate from the functioning of society and the state to that of the party is for the moment being energetically fought and resisted.

The requisite condition for constructing a concrete definition of a socialist model that would be "in French colors" remains in limbo. Perhaps the first approaches to it are to be found only in Saint-Etienne or in Lorraine in the way that communist municipal political power and national capitalism can join together (in a "historic compromise") against the "multinational" and "European" sector of capitalism. With the kind of sharing that communists require when agreeing to any compromise, any agreement would mean control over their allies.

That is the point at which we have arrived. The challenge and the stakes are being measured—a challenge of such dimensions (brought about by necessity—it was that or the decline so much talked about—and correct if we agree that a very profound change, although still conforming to vital communist logic, could arrest it) that the West European communist parties have thrown themselves into an operation that could be their graveyard. Their chances of winning are indeed not as good as they would like to think. Even among their leaders there are some who would have preferred to preside over a very slow decline rather than take such risks. And the French Communist party has just had added to the basic risks of the operation the very bad luck of losing Jean Kanapa, not merely a topflight executive, as has been said so often, but one of the very few who elaborated and carried out on a day-to-day basis this risky operation of controlled change. There remains Fiterman.

It is in this framework that we must place the observations—often correct but badly focused—that have been offered here and there concerning the decline of militancy, uneasiness among the intellectuals, and the temptation to return to the ghetto because we have to admit that the French Communist party has good reason to busy itself with its own affairs.

Franco Ferrarotti

EUROCOMMUNISM, ITALIAN VERSION

There is something challenging as well as irritating about a discussion of Eurocommunism mainly because one feels that Eurocommunism is real and at the same time elusive. Eurocommunism is certainly a reality—its political, economic, and theoretical implications seem bound to become more and more important—but a clear-cut conceptualization of such a reality, at least for the time being, appears to be difficult if not impossible.

Eurocommunism is an unfolding historical phenomenon. But political expediency, emotional reactions, and practical wisdom now seem to overshadow a theoretical understanding of it. In essence, Eurocommunism is the still undefined and changing product of the gradual detachment of three major Western European communist parties—those of France, Spain, and Italy—from Soviet tutelage.[1] Eurocommunism has a general import and is capable of far-reaching consequences.

From a twofold perspective: (1) It touches the crucial theme of ideological unity that had been enforced by the Soviet monocratic leadership; (2) it is likely to upset the balance of power and the postwar division of the world into two spheres of influence—those of the United States and the Soviet Union.

The general significance of Eurocommunism cannot be doubted. Nevertheless, it is a phenomenon peculiar to Southern Europe. It is true that the British Communist party has declared its basic agreement with the three Southern European communist parties and that the Japanese Communist party has been fighting for years for its autonomous stand. But the fact remains that Eurocommunism does not even cover the whole of Europe. It is a Western European phenomenon, and within that context, it presents a marked departure from the ideologies of the left in both Eastern and Northern Europe. In fact, Eurocommunists criticize, with varying degrees of intensity, the "real socialism" of Eastern Europe and the socialist content of the Soviet model. At the same time they criticize and reject, usually in severe terms, the Northern European social democracies, which they consider structurally incapable of or unwilling to go beyond capitalism. Although they propose a new third "model," they have not developed the theoretical framework of that model.

The first question that arises is: Why France, Spain, and Italy? In each of these three countries—the core of Eurocommunism—the phenomenon takes a different shape, and the speed in elaborating an autonomous national road to socialism varies. Fast and radical in Spain, this process has suffered a series of vicissitudes. In Italy it developed first in terms of chronological order, but it is proceeding carefully and cautiously, cloaked in an almost clerical style. In France it emerged late and may prove to be not only national but perhaps, in order to capture the Gaullist vote and sentiment, nationalistic.

Thus the first point to be emphasized is that Eurocommunism is not a single, monolithic ideological scheme. It reflects the historical peculiarities of each national context and seems to have developed an original blueprint for the transition to socialism. Its existence stems from the denial of a universally valid ideological formula. On the other hand, Eurocommunism is far from being only a passing mood of dissatisfaction with Soviet leadership. When compared with the Soviet Union and most of the Eastern European countries—the only notable exception being Czechoslovakia—it becomes clear that France, Spain, and Italy are essentially different from one another, although a fundamental convergence surfaces among them from a historical point of view. Despite national differences, the three countries share a framework of civilization that originated in Graeco-Roman antiquity. That framework points to a common cultural and political heritage. Christianity, not unambiguously, began the slow movement that culminated in the recognition of the individual as a value per se. The rediscovery of classical philosophy and literature through humanism and the Renaissance perfected this value in a secularized formulation free from dogmatic church teachings. This psychologically daring mood seemed to be the prerequisite for developing a methodology for scientific discoveries and provided the stage for the emergence of modern man who "came of age," according to Kant's definition of the Enlightenment. Italian republics and French communes suggest profound historical experiences. They trace their antecedents to the Greek city-state. There can be little doubt that political democracy played a more important role in France, Spain, and Italy than it did in Eastern Europe or in Russia.

The industrialization process occurred in these countries with increasing momentum. France has been industrialized since the last century and therefore has had a strong, fairly homogeneous working class since the turn of the century.

The existence of an industrial working class may be one reason why the French Communist party has been able to count on a leadership made up of militants from the working class, whereas in Spain and especially in Italy top- and middle-echelon party executives have usually been petty bourgeois and middle-class intellectuals from urban areas.

Unlike France, Italy and Spain experienced indigenous "industrial revolutions" during the past two decades. But even in France the genuine modernization of mass-production industries through the emergence of professional managers and the relative decline of the great patrons and of family businesses is a recent experience. Beginning with the mid-fifties, Italy has had a spectacular industrial growth. Roughly in the span of one generation, the country has changed from a rural into an industrial society. To dwell on the peculiar nature of Italian capitalism is beyond the scope of this paper. But it is perhaps sufficient to remark that the traditional economic way of life has changed irreversibly. More recently, through mass tourism and close contact with the rest of the Western European economies, Spain has experienced unprecedented economic development. In all three countries both vertical and horizontal social mobility have become major phenomena. As a consequence, social realignments have taken place, and class structure has undergone considerable change.

Under present-day conditions, it seems to appear obvious to French, Spanish, and Italian communist leaders that the mechanical, dogmatic application of the Soviet model would constitute a major step backward. Especially after the 1956 "revelations" about Stalin's crimes, the importation of "real socialism" of the Soviet variety would have been, in the eyes of Eurocommunist leaders, a tragic political error. They evidently believe that formal bourgeois democracy can be superior and more conducive to substantive social progress than would any form of bureaucratic and authoritarian socialism.

Moreover, leaving aside the beliefs and the preferences of communist leaders, it is doubtful that Frenchmen, Spaniards, and Italians would ever spontaneously give up the democratic political freedoms and human rights associated with the Western political tradition. These democratic freedoms were won the hard way in Italy—despite fascism—and in Spain against Franco's dictatorship. In France they have been enshrined since the days of the revolution and the proclamation of the "immortal principles" of 1789.

The Russian political scenario developed differently. Before the revolution of 1917, the state was practically everything, and democracy in its Western parliamentary form was relatively unknown. In this connection perhaps the notion of "civil society" developed by Adam Ferguson and elaborated by Antonio Gramsci can be analytically useful. "Civil society" hardly exists in the Soviet Union. Despite the heroic efforts of the populists and early social democrats, there is no tradition of democratic freedoms. By comparison, present-day France, Spain, and Italy are highly developed economically. Their complex class structures, their democratically differentiated political systems, and their attachments to democratic values and freedoms will not allow the mechanical imposition of a political regime, such as the Soviet one, to alter their political and historical traditions. To the communist leaders of these countries, the search for some way to achieve socialism independent of the Soviet Union and its Eastern European dependencies amounts to a pure and simple necessity lest their parties, although powerful and effectively organized, be confronted with growing political irrelevance and eventual emargination. Cultural heritage and political and economic development, however, do not by themselves explain the phenomenon of Eurocommunism.

The second set of answers to the main question of why Eurocommunism developed in France, Spain, and Italy relates to the economic and political systems of the Soviet

Union—especially during Stalin's rule—and the validity of the claim that the Soviet experience represents the model for constructing socialism. From this perspective, Khrushchev's report to the twentieth congress of the Communist party of the Soviet Union in 1956 can be regarded as the birth certificate of Eurocommunism. The term was coined by Enrico Berlinguer, general secretary of the Italian Communist party, at a rally held in Paris in June 1976 that was sponsored by Georges Marchais, general secretary of the French Communist party. The word *Eurocommunism* in the text of Berlinguer's speech is in quotation marks. Santiago Carrillo, general secretary of the Spanish Communist party, declared flatly that he did not like the expression, that the term is not accepted by Spanish communists, that there is no such thing as Eurocommunism, and that what does exist is the problem, common to various communist parties, of how to move toward socialism in advanced capitalist countries.

Although the inauguration of Eurocommunism was difficult and tentative, the repercussions of Khrushchev's report can hardly be exaggerated. During the Second World War the myth of Stalin as socialist hero par excellence and of the Soviet Union as the socialist fatherland for communist militants all over the world grew and reached its epic climax at the time of the Stalingrad resistance against the Nazi attack. ("Stalin's grad—Hitler's grab," as a popular saying characterized the event.) The so-called personality cult was not a purely Russian invention. It was undoubtedly nurtured by the worshipping attitude of communist party members in various countries, including France and Italy and to a lesser degree, because of the experience during the civil war, in Spain.

Khrushchev's report, although shattering the myth of Stalin, failed to provide a Marxist explanation of the degeneration that had taken place in the land of the first proletarian revolution. Khrushchev seemed to consider Stalinism the result of pathological personality traits. He failed to understand it as the structural consequence of a system in which all the energies and power of the society emanate from a single party controlled by one man—the absolute dictator—and his loyal entourage. In the name of the dictatorship of the proletariat that had overthrown the dictatorship of the bourgeoisie according to the formula expounded by Lenin in *State and Revolution,* a very small elite under the command of Stalin exercised dictatorial power over the working class.

It is interesting to observe how the communist parties of France, Spain, and Italy reacted to Khrushchev's report, especially to the denunciation of Stalin's crimes. The shock and dismay were enormous. The Italian Communist party was the first to grasp the general meaning and import of Khrushchev's revelations. It is true that Palmiro Togliatti had been for years a prominent figure in the Comintern and that after the war he had diplomatically, if not shrewdly, refrained from defending Tito when the Yugoslav leader was "excommunicated" by the Cominform. In fact, reviewing the bleakest years of the Moscow trials, Togliatti can be regarded as co-responsible for some of Stalin's crimes. He was too much in the center of power, at the very heart of things in Moscow, not to know what was going on. But he was also a "good historicist" and was aware that history has its own capricious ways of developing. If those ways do not coincide with one's principles or ethical biases, *tant pis* for the principles. As a *realpolitiker,* Togliatti was able to survive in Moscow during Stalin's reign of terror.

On the other hand, as soon as Togliatti returned to Italy in 1943, he shaped and promoted the new policy of antifascist unity, enlisting the support of communists as well as monarchists. With the famous "Salerno turn," he bypassed the ideological trenches of socialists and "actionists" who were paralyzed by fear of political contamination associated with accepting any help or cooperation from right-wing forces. Later, on the occasion of the inclusion in the Italian constitution of the Lateran Pact signed in 1929 by the Vatican and Mussolini, Togliatti gave ample evidence of his pragmatic and seemingly unprincipled approach to issues of ideological importance.

At the fifth PCI congress, December 1945-January 1946, he engineered the "partito nuovo"—a new communist party, open to all people, Marxists and non-Marxists, believers and atheists alike, provided that they would accept the party's middle-range platform for a relentless fight against fascism and for what he called progressive democracy. In 1948 Togliatti and the PCI sided with the Soviet Union, but long before Stalin's death and especially after Khrushchev's report, Togliatti elaborated on the relationship of "via italiana" to socialism. This "via" was to be "peaceful," that is, nonviolent. The concept of the dictatorship of the proletariat was neither set aside nor declared obsolete; it was blurred with a characteristic historicist twist. The Soviet revolution, it was often pointed out, took place within the framework of special historical conditions. "At least since 1934," Togliatti observed, "it became increasingly evident that it was both impossible and absurd to think that a single decision center could provide a general direction."[2] Although cautiously and indirectly, the prerogatives of Moscow were seriously challenged.

In his interview with *Nuovi argomenti* after Khrushchev's report, Togliatti developed his conception of the "via italiana" and for the first time used the term *polycentrism* to describe relationships among various communist parties. Polycentrism was presented in a more detailed manner in his political testament, "Yalta Memorandum," which was in fact a draft consisting of notes meant as guidelines for a private conversation with Khrushchev. "Yalta Memorandum" was published by Luigi Longo immediately after Togliatti's death.

The new doctrine was couched in very careful terms. Togliatti's prudence recalls the indirect style of a Catholic prelate. But the political consequences of Togliatti's position became visible after his death when younger cadres took over the party: Berlinguer's generation that had not been exiled during fascism, had not lived through the complicated Comintern evolution under Stalin, and could not speak Russian. This younger group was active in Italy during the resistance against fascism and nazism and had deep roots in the national reality. Thus it is no wonder that the PCI refused to go along with the Soviet Union in condemning Mao's China. The PCI did, however, condemn the invasion of Czechoslovakia carried out by the armies of the Warsaw Pact.

Although Santiago Carrillo and Georges Marchais were conspicuously absent from the twenty-fifth congress of the Communist party of the Soviet Union on February 25, 1976, Enrico Berlinguer attended and reasserted firmly and with great dignity the right of each communist party to institute an autonomous, national search for a better way to reach and implement socialism in its own historical context. In a subsequent interview Berlinguer asserted that NATO was no barrier to the accomplishment of this purpose. He maintained that it would be easier to be autonomous and to implement socialism behind the shield, or under the umbrella, of NATO than to struggle to achieve socialism in a neutral position.

The ideological and political stand of the French Communist party (PCF) suggests a different approach. It did not have to face a twenty-year period of fascist dictatorship as did the PCI. (At the time that Gramsci was dying in a fascist jail and most of the Italian communist militants were in the underground or exiled, the PCF was riding the crest of power with the Front Populaire of 1936.) The French Communist party was slow in developing a Eurocommunist approach and only reluctantly gave up the Stalinist myth of socialism based on the absolute rule of a single party controlled by one man. The claim to be independent of the Soviet Union was voiced as late as 1964 when Maurice Thorez, "fils du peuple," died in July. His successor, Waldeck-Rochet, encouraged the conceptualization of a democratic transition to socialism. Georges Marchais brought to the office of secretary general the enthusiasm of the younger generation. The PCF did not understand at first the uprisings of May 1968, and the student and youth protest movement was kept separate from the trade unions and the organized working class. The PCF joined the PCI in condemning the invasion of Czechoslovakia, but in general its acceptance of democratic principles seemed to be slow and uneven. For instance, Marchais accused Berlinguer of electoral opportunism in criticizing the extreme dogmatic positions taken by the Portuguese communist party and its secretary Alvaro Cunhal. (The Portuguese communists had tried to prevent Christian Democrats from participating in general elections.) Marchais went so far as to insinuate that Berlinguer's criticism was based on the need to gain votes in the Italian elections by showing his *bona fide* democratic allegiance, that his criticism was motivated not by principle but by pure and simple "electoralism."

The rift between the PCI and the PCF cannot last very long. Berlinguer and Carrillo have developed such a close relationship that Marchais cannot afford to be excluded. Carrillo and Berlinguer signed a joint declaration asserting that the Spanish and Italian Communist parties were determined to follow "a democratic road to socialism with freedom." According to the leaders of both parties, this determination represents a "historical decision" rather than a "tactical move," a decision that emerged from the critical examination of the historical conditions of each country and of the political situation of Western Europe.

The PCF was late in renouncing the principle of the "dictatorship of the proletariat." This renunciation was announced only on the eve of the French general elections of 1978 and reflected a kind of suspect "bureaucratic unanimity." Seldom has a dictatorial principle been abolished in such a dictatorial way.

The reasons for the late development of an autonomous stand by the PCF should perhaps be traced to the nature of the French political system. For years the Communist party was isolated and had to compete with a strong democratic socialist party on basic national issues, such as Gaullism and Algeria. Moreover, the French left has a strong tradition of *ouvrierisme*. Many PCF leaders have been workers from working-class backgrounds. Intellectuals, such as Sartre or Camus, might have been fellow travelers, but the party leadership never rested in their hands.

The most drastic and coherent stand in favor of an autonomous road to socialism, implying a complete detachment from Moscow, has come from the Spanish Communist party. Santiago Carrillo remains the most vocal proponent of Eurocommunism, even though he does not like the term. His attitude toward the Soviet Union and its leaders is critical to the point of being defiant. He has gone further than Berlinguer, perhaps because he is the last traditional communist leader; he worked with Togliatti for the Comintern and knew Stalin personally. His attack against Soviet hegemony is total and comprehensive. He has criticized both the party and the state. In opposition to the French communists and in agreement with Berlinguer, Carrillo has asserted that a united Europe can be an important factor in effecting revolutionary change vis-à-vis the present division of the world into two major areas of influence. In this respect he perceives Yugoslavia and China as forerunners. "Their strength," he says, "lies in the fact that they have made their own revolution and so they are their own bosses."

In examining the conditions that could facilitate the development of Eurocommunism, it should be stated that the first set of conditions depends on the three communist parties that subscribe to Eurocommunism. It consists of a *theoretical renewal* that should lead these parties beyond the Jacobin model and Lenin's model. It is not an easy task. The Italian

Communist party has revitalized the teachings of Antonio Gramsci.[3] The concept of "social hegemony" has been used to counter the idea of the "dictatorship of the proletariat." Relations between "civil society" and the state apparatus have been explored in order to find appropriate ways of representing class interests. But problems relating to the functioning of the market, of private property, and of the basic freedoms of choice that define political democracy are still wide open and need further consideration. Moreover, what is the function of a pluralist parliament in a socialist society? Can one abolish all interest groups without risking an overall bureaucratization of the social process? Will majority rule, whatever its nature, be respected? In other words, will the communists, once in power, leave if they find themselves in a minority position? It is true that in many European countries state industry is huge, but what will be the future of private enterprise under Eurocommunism?

The French Communist party has never had a Gramsci. It has Louis Althusser. The Spanish communists are too busy reorganizing their party after forty years of clandestine existence to engage in refined ideological debates. These problems, however, are real, and the future of Eurocommunism to a certain extent depends on their resolution.

Other important factors that may affect Eurocommunism are not completely in the hands of the parties involved. As far as the direction (political and ideological) of the world communist movement is concerned, the fundamental components of Eurocommunism are *pluralism* and *polycentrism*, and therefore the right of each communist party to decide in autonomy and to map its specific road to socialism within its national context must be recognized. The continuation of *detente* between the Soviet Union and the United States seems to be the prerequisite for the growth of Eurocommunism.

The basic contradiction of Eurocommunism revolves

around detente. Detente is endangered by the diplomatic offensive of China (the visit to Ceausescu, Tito, and Carter, among others) and by the campaign for human rights launched by the Carter administration. But the most serious threat to detente comes precisely from Eurocommunism. In the long run Eurocommunism is likely to upset the delicate balance between East and West on which detente rests. Some Eurocommunist leaders are well aware of this contradiction. This awareness explains the fact that Berlinguer has gone to great pains to pacify his Soviet colleagues by reasserting his agreement with their view of the international situation. Moreover, he cannot help stating that in some Western countries socialism is no longer a project for the future but is a problem for today. The contradiction is real, and no sophistry can dismiss it. Eurocommunism is a potentially revolutionary movement that is bound to clash with the conservative attitudes of both the Soviet Union and the United States.

The disruptive effect of Eurocommunism could be greatly reduced if the Southern European communist parties, which constitute the core of Eurocommunism, were willing to develop their theoretical (ideological) platforms and adjust their political practices accordingly. Undoubtedly, these changes would pose problems for "praxis parties," that is, political organizations that claim to act on their *unmediated* political experiences rather than be guided (abstractly) by ideological principles.

In the devaluation of the role of theory per se there is also a psychological overtone of insecurity that should be made explicit. The ghost of traditional Marxist "revisionism," especially Eduard Bernstein's version that underplayed class struggle, is haunting Eurocommunist leaders and is probably responsible for their occasional paying of lipservice to Marxism-Leninism. But revisionism is not called into question. The problem does not concern classical revisionism or revolutionary "maximalism"—the famous dilemma on which rests the history of the world socialist movement and which accounts for most of its uncertainties and paralysis. Traditional revisionism consisted of listing a series of facts and social situations that seemed to contradict basic Marxist predictions: All peasants do not disappear; the middle classes do not sink; economic depressions do not necessarily grow worse; poverty and proletarian "slavery" (Marx insisted time and again that the industrial worker replaced the "slave" of antiquity) are not increasing. On the contrary, the "increase" has occurred in precisely that aspect of government that Marx did not foresee: large-scale bureaucracy, which Max Weber described as an essential feature of any industrially developed society, be it capitalist or socialist; feelings of dependence and of insecurity, economic, cultural, and psychological; the eroding of the authority of the "eternal yesterday"; increasing socialization of the production process as the effect of a perfected social division of labor, or of what Herbert Spencer called functional correlation; a growing gap between the actual power of legal owners and functional controllers.

In terms of recognizing the relatively obsolete character of Marxism, the most outspoken Eurocommunist leader is certainly Santiago Carrillo. In his book, *Eurocommunism and the State,* Carrillo touched on what is perhaps the weakest point of Marxist theory: the concept of the state and its organization vis-à-vis the growing economic potentates and their functions in advanced capitalist society. Despite his more refined approach to issues of political theory compared with other Marxist thinkers of his day, not even Antonio Gramsci was able to come to grips with the social and economic functions of the state. This failure can perhaps be attributed to his lack of familiarity with economic analysis, a common inadequacy of Mediterranean Marxism. Gramsci's educational background and orientation, shared by all major PCI leaders, belong to the traditional Italian literary and historicist school of thought, which is typical of professors of humanities and is based on a profound knowledge of philosophy, history, and philology and little, if any, systematic exposure to economic theory and analysis.

It should not come as a surprise, therefore, as has been aptly remarked, that in Gramsci's *Prison Notebooks* the "prince-party," as a party of struggle and irrespective of actual economic conditions, foreshadows those instances of hegemony and of dictatorship that must find their complements in the proletariat state. It is consistent with Gramsci's exposition of the character of the "prince-party" and with its nature of anticipating the new state that he was able to develop the general political principle according to which "there can and must be a political hegemony also prior to the advent of the government," that is, if the "prince-party" does not conceive of itself as able, even within the old order, to form and direct a social bloc adequate to the tasks of both the state and to the alternative of social management, the conquest of power becomes unrealistic or else rests on insufficient bases. Therefore, in Gramsci's terms, reinforced through a careful reading of his text, the struggle for hegemony and the struggle for the formation and the consolidation of a strong and articulate social revolutionary bloc mean establishing a theoretical and a political equivalence. It should not be forgotten, however, that especially during the period of the "Ordine Nuovo," Gramsci held a definitely anti-Jacobin conception of the party according to which it was assigned the task of being the critical conscience of the mass of producers organized in factory councils. This conception has been blurred all too easily by most contemporary commentators. In the *Prison Notebooks* it is possible to find a typology of revolutionary forces drawn from European history and derived from illuminating connections between Machiavelli's *Prince,* the Jacobins, the Leninist Bolshevik party, and what Gramsci regarded as the essence of a Western communist party. Each has an element in common. They all represent the "total negation" of the old order and the struggle to achieve a new order. This struggle involves the elaboration of a new *Weltanschaung* and the construction of state institutions that would transform existing ones—in other words, the mobilization of forces relevant to a revolutionary project. In this sense it is correct to maintain that the Italian prince of Machiavelli, the French Jacobin party, and the Russian Bolshevik party are the three sources of inspiration that guide the construction of the Gramscian Communist party.

Special attention was given by Gramsci to the Jacobins. In fact, according to him, the Jacobins represent the two basic requirements of every modern revolutionary force, that is, "separation," and "social recomposition," dictatorial rule and authoritative hegemony. "The Jacobins," Gramsci asserted, "constitute the only revolutionary party inasmuch as they understand not only the immediate interests of the surviving members of the French bourgeoisie but also envision the future interests, not restricted to bona fide members but extended to other social strata of the third state which tomorrow will become the bourgeoisie. . . ." According to some commentators, the Jacobins correspond to the engineers who constructed "rule" and "hegemony," as envisaged by Gramsci, that is, (a) they "destroyed the adversary class or at least reduced it to impotency; they negated the possibility of a counterrevolution"; (b) they "broadened the interests of the bourgeoisie, discerning the common interests between the bourgeoisie and the other strata of the third state, by inaugurating and promoting the movement of those strata, by leading them in the struggle. . . . The Jacobins made of the bourgeoisie the managing, hegemonic class, that is, they gave a permanent base to the state." Thus, according to Gramsci, the Jacobins achieved the historical feat of giving an expansive base to the dictatorship in the sense that in destroying the adversary class, they gave a hegemonic foundation to the new state. It is evident that without the dictatorship, the Jacobins, as a revolutionary force, would not have been able to enact and implement the politics of hegemony. The study of hegemony without dictatorship is a project of Girondinian social democrats, a reductive view of the Gramsci model.

Gramsci's idea of the revolutionary party as the "new prince" in Machiavelli's sense is taken, in my judgment, a little too literally. Undoubtedly, the modern prince, as envisioned by Gramsci, can only be "an organism" in which collective will is centralized. The first characteristic of such an organism is "totality," that is, the ability to mediate among different local or sectorial wills and aspirations in order to fuse them into a unified, more or less homogeneous, will, "effective and total." The second feature relates to the historical subject of this total will—the proletariat. The third feature concerns the party as the instrument through which the social, political, and moral transformation of existing society is finally accomplished. The modern prince is thus the modern political form that fuses "the partial collective wills, which tend to become universal and total."

It is difficult to resist the temptation to accept the assertion that Gramsci should be listed among those neoidealist thinkers who, especially under the influence of Giovanni Gentile, ended their careers by asserting their belief in the absolute "ethical state." I think, however, that exploiting the category of "totality" in order to place Gramsci elbow to elbow with Lenin, on one side, and with Gentile, on the other, is a stroke of polemical legerdemain used as political ammunition against the PCI in particular and against the Eurocommunist parties in general. I do not think that it is legitimate to use purely theoretical arguments in order to wage a purely political and contingent battle in terms of internal competition within the left in Southern Europe, especially between the PCI and the PSI in Italy. Norberto Bobbio, Massimo L. Salvadori, and other less well-known commentators have gone to great pains to demonstrate that Lenin and Gramsci were essentially species of the same political genus who thought along the same lines. It is surprising that in attempting to prove this assertion, polemicists have completely forgotten about the rift between Amadeo Bordiga and Gramsci, while trying, in a rather desperate anti-Marxian attempt, to revamp the ideas of Pierre-Joseph Proudhon. According to Massimo L. Salvadori, "Jacobinism is thus [for Gramsci] an exemplary model, a model that Gramsci sees retaken, actualized, and developed by the Russian Bolsheviks, the real inheritors of the first revolutionaries of the modern epoch. The great historical and revolutionary merit of the followers of Lenin was to have elaborated a scheme of dictatorship-hegemony, adapted to time and place, as an emergency from all the pores of the society which required transformation, that is, alliance between two classes (the proletariat and the peasants) with the hegemony of the urban class as the frame of the system of the dictatorship of the proletariat. It is therefore a substantial conclusion that Gramsci finds in Lenin he who has furnished "the maximum theoretical contribution" to Marxism itself as he constructed and realized the "theoretical-practical principle of hegemony."[5]

This reconstruction of Gramsci's thinking and political goals seems to me to be uncritically sweeping and in the end misleading and untenable. I think that Gramsci's model of the party, metaphorically termed the modern prince, cannot be equated with the Jacobin model or with the Marxist-Leninist model. The Jacobin model is too elitist to be compatible with Gramsci's notion of a state based on grass-roots workers' councils. The Jacobin model, perhaps revised to include some of the ideas of Blanqui, implies Lenin's notion of the revolution as a "value" brought to the working class from the outside by the bourgeois revolutionary intellectuals. This notion does not fit well with Gramsci's concept of "social hegemony" resulting from a "moral and cultural reform of the whole society to be transformed."

It is possible to show, on the other hand, that Gramsci's notion of the state is not compatible with the classical Marxist-Leninist model of the state. Opposing itself on principle to all bourgeois theorizings on the state, which are dismissed as expressions of the "common good" or as realizations of an idea that is "universally human," "ethical," "divine," or ahistorical, that is, located above and beyond social classes, Marxist-Leninist theory posits the constant association between a society that is divided into classes and the state. According to this theory, it can be demonstrated that the state, originating in the division of society into classes, represents a necessary manifestation of every class-conscious society and contains the key to deriving the essence of power that has revealed and developed itself in history. The scientific analysis and critique of the state thus acquire fundamental importance in a capitalist class-based society. The discovery of the historical, nonmetaphysical nature of the state contributes to demonstrating the necessity of destroying the imperialist bourgeois state in order to end the exploitation of man by man. The comprehension of the historical nature of the state in a society characterized by class antagonisms enables one to perceive the irreconcilability of the state of the exploiters and the socialist state. It also shows the alleged superiority of the socialist state as a completely new social manifestation. It seems obvious that Marxist-Leninist theory postulates a unitary state, a postulate that cannot be validated by any factual analysis. Within the sphere of the bourgeois state there exist important and evident differences between the state that characterized the period of premonopolistic capitalism, that is, the laissez-faire state, and the state that characterized the imperialist phase of capitalism in which the state acted as the supreme economic balancer and "crisis shock absorber," as it were.

Antonio Gramsci was not in a position to detect the shortcomings of Marxist-Leninist theory, including Lenin's formulation of "imperialism," for he did not live to analyze the new economic role of the modern state.

The analysis of this new state role emerges quite clearly in Santiago Carrillo's book. The leader of the Spanish Communist party was well aware that his book might shock orthodox militants. Nevertheless, he stated his aim explicitly: "It is necessary to recognize that the way in which the problem of the state is approached today departs from the practices implicit in the theses put forward by Lenin in 1917 and in 1918; these were at the time applicable to Russia and, at least theoretically, to the whole world; today they are not applicable because they are obsolete, at least for the developed capitalistic countries of Europe. What has made them inapplicable is the change of economic structures and the objective gains of progressive social forces, the development of productive forces, the progress of socialism, decolonization, and the defeat of fascism in the Second World War. To some it might sound blasphemous to hear that Lenin's theses are bypassed. . . ."[6]

The first dogma that Carrillo squarely faced and demolished is the principle of the dictatorship of the proletariat. His insistence on this point was so strong and in his judgment so important that he returned to the subject in the last chapter of his book. "Even if Marx and Engels used publicly the phrase *dictatorship of the proletariat* on a few occasions," he wrote, "one certainly cannot share the reformistic view that this was a mere misprint. . . . It is interesting to recall that Marx suggested the idea of a *true democracy.* . . . The experience of fascism—and we, as Spaniards, have long suffered it in our very flesh—reveals the extreme, most intolerable, and most repugnant aspect of the state. . . . By living through this sinister experience we have perhaps understood more fully that *democracy is not a historical creation of the bourgeoisie,* as we used to think in those moments during which our principal aim was to unmask bourgeois democraticism and to assert against it the position and the ideological stand of the working class."[7]

Carrillo argued that Lenin's error, especially in *State and Revolution*, derived from the fact that he equated democracy with the state: "Lenin identified *democracy* with the *state*.... I submit that the concept of democracy, as it was understood by Lenin, that is, the equivalence between democracy and the "state," and also the idea that the subordination of the minority to the majority amounts to the exercise of systematic violence by one section of the population against the other, is a reductionistic conception of democracy which is derived from the strong polemic against the defenders of the pseudodemocratic character of the bourgeois state."[8]

This argument led Carrillo to discuss the role of violence in history. He did not deny the revolutionary function of violence as the midwife of the new society to be born from the old one. What he denied is the generalization about the use of violence that, he maintained, is strictly tied to specific historical conditions. Achieving the goal of "socialism with democracy," according to Carrillo, does not require the use of violence even though historical experience suggests that violence has played a crucial role not only in socialist revolutions but in capitalist, democratic, bourgeois transformations of society. What makes the old notion of violent transition from capitalism to socialism obsolete for Carrillo is the new role and function of the modern state. Marx and Lenin were confronted with a bourgeois state that could be defined as the "business committee" of the dominant bourgeois interests. At the present time the state has assumed new, public-oriented functions that can neither be reduced nor understood merely as protective devices used by vested interests. The new factors are large-scale technology and science both as directly productive forces and as public procedures. Marx, Engels, and Lenin correctly underlined the coercive nature of the state. What they did not foresee were the ideological functions of the present-day state, those "ideological apparatuses" that were explored by Antonio Gramsci and Louis Althusser. But these additions to the classical Marxist theory of the state, important and necessary as they continue to be, are no longer sufficient. Something else must be taken into consideration. "It is necessary to add a new dimension," Carrillo wrote, " ... the *control of economic development which brings under state control all the major economic activities*. . . . The development of technology calls into question the very principle of the private firm."[9] In other words, capital becomes more and more socialized; the state acquires the power of intervention that is decisive in the development of the economic life of a country. The use of this power has an obvious consequence for Western European communist parties: The state is no longer an enemy to be confronted and eventually overcome by violent means. It is an instrument to be reoriented, set in the right direction, endowed with a public function, and made functional in order to be effectively used for social purposes, not only for narrow private interests.

From this perspective what becomes of paramount importance for Eurocommunist parties is not so much the waging of a struggle against the bourgeois state, but rather the gaining of as much electoral support as possible for left-wing political organizations. Morton A. Kaplan remarked that "the communist parties of Western Europe (perhaps with the single exception of the Portuguese party) are attempting to extend the strength of the entire left, including the moderate left. Nationalism has become a signal aspect of the parties' programs. . . . The internal organization of the party has become noncellular in Spain and Italy and is closer to normal political organization. . . . The parties, again with the exception of the Portuguese, also appear to be European oriented rather than merely nationalistic, although there are individual differences among them."[10]

In this sense, one feels that Eurocommunism emerged from a genuine political and ideological crisis of the communist movement, although the crisis has been difficult to detect. What kind of economic and social system will emerge from this crisis, and what would be the practical political result if the communists finally reach ministerial responsibilities in countries such as Italy and France? One thing is already clear. The sectarian view of Eurocommunism set forth by Ernest Mandel in his book, *From Stalinism to Eurocommunism—the Bitter Fruits of "Socialism in One Country,"*[1] seems to be too narrow in focus and conspiratorial in tone to be tenable. Presenting Eurocommunism as a case of corruption involving specific communist parties hardly fits Marxian methodology or terminology. Instead of looking into the actual economic and political conditions of the Mediterranean countries in which the phenomenon originated, Mandel indulged in a moralistic dissertation concerning "the progressive disappearance of the whole communist generation trained in the year prior to 1935" and the "virtually permanent installation of the apparatuses of the communist parties within the machinery of the bourgeois democratic state."[2]

The "project of theses," which the PCI published in connection with its party convention held in March 1979, is worth considering as further evidence of the critical search on the part of Eurocommunists for a "third way" to socialism, that is, for a political and an ideological project that will be qualitatively different from the Soviet model and from the prevailing pattern of the Northern European social democratic regimes. A sincere effort seems to have been made in this "project" to tackle major theoretical issues, not only matters of political expediency. On the other hand, in 1978 the president of the Chamber of Deputies, Pietro Ingrao, a well-known leader of the PCI, published a long interview "Crisis and the Third Way."[3] Ingrao insisted, in the same vein as Carrillo, that the crisis of the state is real and that although the Soviet model and the regimes of the so-called countries of real socialism are not practicable, it would be futile to seek a solution along the lines of a neoliberal approach. Instead, he favored what he called a third way that would provide a solution equally distant from the Soviet model and from the social democratic pattern. Ingrao was careful to make explicit the difference between his position and other interpretations of the state crisis, especially O'Connor's "fiscal crisis": "The present-day state crisis cannot be reduced to a functional defect or to a waste of resources. . . . What has been termed the fiscal crisis does exist, but it is only one aspect of the general crisis. The difficulty does not concern only an irrationality of a quantitative kind, as it were. It goes deeper.[14]

According to Ingrao, the crisis of the laissez-faire state was cured through the "welfare state." But it is the welfare state that is in deep, structural crisis. The attempt to mitigate the pure and simple market mechanism through the allocation of funds destined to satisfy needs emerging from the society has failed. New contradictions are surfacing. People make larger and larger demands on the state and at the same time they resent state intervention. More and more deeply, people feel that they face social problems that they cannot solve by themselves; at the same time, people resent and fear a trend toward big government and total bureaucratization. The "social" and the "political" are two categories that do not seem to combine easily. During the past fifty years, there has been a strong drive toward state intervention in social affairs in Italy and elsewhere: An elite society has evolved into a mass society. But a state-dominated society is not necessarily a more socialized society. This realization is the historical lesson to be derived from Stalinism and fascism, according to Eurocommunist leaders. They seem to accept the notion of a "state legitimation crisis" in the sense that this phrase has been appropriated by the epigones of the "Frankfurt school," notably by Jürgen Habermas and Claus Offe. However, they object to the idea that the crisis is a consequence of the advanced capitalist state. It seems that the political and social forces, capable of acting as dialectical antagonists in the crisis in order to ensure a positive solution, are missing from such analyses. Habermas wrote, in a quasi-Heideggerian vein, about the mysterious path of "truth"; Offe referred to the highly mobile emergence of opposition nuclei and small groups, to a proliferation of grass-roots counterpowers and countercultural cells, not dissimilar to the ones described by Michel Foucault in his "Microphysique du pouvoir." It is obvious, however, that in such a phenomenology of the legitimation crisis of advanced capitalism, the state crisis appears to be self-induced, and the notion of class struggle is blurred, if not altogether eliminated.

Can the state then be considered the guardian, if not the supreme builder, of the "common good"? Can political activity express the humanity of man? Did civil society precede the political system, and is the individual bound to serve the needs of the social structure and derive from such service the essential meaning of his life? What is the basis of the state's legitimacy, and what limitation can be imposed against government planning activity? What about the functioning and the role of the "free market"? Is private property necessarily linked, as Marx and Engels thought, with the workings of the market and conceived as a contrivance in the hands of the prevailing interests, or is the market to be understood as detached from property relations, that is, as a sounding board for people's needs and aspirations?

Any one of these questions would be sufficient to shake Leninist orthodoxy. The importance of the "PCI Theses"[15] lies precisely in the fact that first, tentative answers were given concerning the internal life of the party and the organization of the state.

The opening paragraph of the "PCI Theses" confirms the allegiance of the party to the constitution of the Italian Republic. This formal declaration of allegiance does not mean much because the Italian constitution is ambiguous. What seems important is the overall approach to the question of social and political development. This approach is problematic and experimental rather than dogmatic and doctrinaire. For instance, it is clearly recognized and admitted that state industry, that is, public ownership and control of the means of production, is not in itself good. In fact it can give rise to clientele groups and sectorial, "corporative" interests that may prove to be more negative in their economic and political effects than those connected with private industry. In other words, whether an industrial organization of production is "good" or "bad" cannot be decided on the basis of a doctrinaire evaluative criterion but only on the basis of actual, empirically-testable, performance.

Moreover, and more interestingly, the structure of the party was called into question. In the first place, the Stalinist equation of the party with the state, which led historically to the construction of a *state party* characterized by dogmatism and monolithic bureaucracy, was flatly denounced and rejected. "It must be very clear," it is asserted, "that the party is *part* of the society and of the state. In the first place, the party is intended to be a direct and organized expression of the working class and of all the popular strata, a mass and struggle party *(partito di massa e di lotta)*, an autonomous force for the transformation of society, capable of expressing a conscious government function. In such a pluralist dimension, the party must remain a part; it is not meant to extend itself into the state." This insight has characterized the development of Togliatti's thinking since 1944: "a national, democratic road to socialism; a party of a new type."[16]

This general declaration was followed by the exposition of two basic proposals: an explicit proposal regarding the abolition of Article 5 of the party statute that makes it compulsory for members of the PCI to accept the principles of Marxism-Leninism: "We do not conceive," it is asserted, "of the thought of Marx, Engels, and Lenin as a doctrinaire system; for this reason we have felt for a long time that the formula 'Marxism-Leninism' does not express the whole wealth of our theoretical and ideal heritage."[17] Second, it was proposed that the religious phenomenon be reexplored not only as a residual superstitious belief system but as positivistic rationalism, as paleo-Marxism would have it. Religion must be reanalyzed on the basis of a more mature approach that is capable of understanding the permanent function in history of religious values not only as an alienating force and mystifying system of beliefs but also as a positive progressive force—hence the attempt on the part of PCI to find a way to cooperate with the "Catholic world" in Italy. For this purpose Italian communists are trying to redefine religion in a more sophisticated way than did the paleopositivists and rationalists of the nineteenth century: "For the present and for the future, the PCI reasserts the principle of respect for religion and for the central role of safeguarding religious peace in order to ensure the continuation and the development of democracy and to strengthen the unity of the working masses. The Italian communists are engaged in a permanent effort to search for an agreement with the Christian and Catholic world in order to save mankind from nuclear war and to promote justice and human progress."[18] To achieve such goals the Italian communists underline the importance of "dialogue," that is, a "reciprocal recognition of values." It seems that the PCI is not so much eager to change its platform and to revise its theoretical frame of referrence as it is to be accepted as a *legitimate* political force in the democratic arena.

However, as far as the internal life of the PCI is concerned, no major change seems imminent. The Leninist principle of democratic centralism, it has been asserted, will neither be revised nor abolished. It seems that the "PCI Theses" proclaim the abiding value of this principle: "The method of democratic centralism corresponds to the goals of a political party which intends to transform the basis and the class structure of society and of the state." At least from this organizational point of view—although one should consider the fear of PCI leaders that their party could become a victim of, and therefore ruined by, sectarian struggles and power games—Eurocommunism has not given birth to anything new or inspiring.

From an international point of view, it is necessary to take notice of the PCI's explicit claim that it favors the construction of a federated and united Europe and of its intention of elaborating a new communist platform, something still mysterious but usually called a third way, that would be completely different from the Soviet and Eastern European model, on the one hand, and from the social democratic North European model, on the other. Not much can be discerned from official declarations. What seems to have emerged is the realization that the "struggle for socialism" can no longer be based on a "universally valid model" or on "exlusive worldwide centers of political decisions." As far as the political nature of the future Europe is concerned, there is an insistence that it should not be the "Europe of large-scale monopolies and multinational corporations." As far as a positive program is concerned, there has been formulated nothing beyond general declarations of intent, such as, "We do not want more nationalizations of industries; we want socialization." But the difference between "nationalization" and "socialization," at least in terms of the practical organization of work and decision-making authority, remains unspecified. Eurocommunism is a reality in the making. Although its development should be followed carefully, it seems unwise to speculate dogmatically, and therefore uncritically, about its final outcome.

NOTES

1. For a more detailed examination, see Franco Ferrarotti, "The Italian Communist Party and Eurocommunism" in *The Many Faces of Communism,* ed. Morton A. Kaplan (New York, 1978), pp. 30-71.

2. See P. T. in *Rinascita,* 7-8, 1959.

3. See also F. Ferrarotti, "Legitimacy, Hegemony, and Domination: Gramsci—with and versus Lenin" in *Legitimation and Delegitimation of Regimes,* ed. B. Denitch (New York, 1978).

4. Original title: *Eurocomunismo y Estado* (Madrid, 1977); quotations are from the Italian translation (Rome, 1977).

5. See M. L. Salvadori, *Eurocomunismo e socialismo sovietico* (Turin, 1978), p. 50.

6. Carrillo, *op. cit.,* pp. 6-7.

7. *Ibid.,* pp. 174-180, italics in the text.

8. *Ibid.,* pp. 108-109, italics in the text.

9. *Ibid.,* pp. 20-21, italics added.

10. Morton A. Kaplan, "Introduction: What is Communism?" in *The Many Faces of Communism, op. cit.,* p. 27.

11. London, 1978.

12. *Ibid.,* p. 21.

13. Rome, 1978.

14. *Ibid.,* p. 75.

15. Published on December 10, 1978.

16. *Ibid.,* p. 3; italics in the text.

17. *Ibid.,* p. 3.

18. *Ibid.*

Eusebio M. Mujal-León

EUROCOMMUNISM, SPANISH VERSION

There are two approaches available to someone interested in dealing with the ideological and political foundations of Eurocommunism in Spain. One would be to focus on policy changes implemented by the Spanish communists in the course of the last two and a half decades, with a view to describing, analyzing, and measuring the substance of the PCE evolution. The other approach would deal with the issue from a more historical perspective. It would accept as given a description that emphasized the changed position of the Spanish party and would turn instead to a more distant set of experiences, with a view to identifying those elements that may have affected or favored the subsequent evolution of the PCE.

Both approaches have merit, and in a book-length analysis of the PCE, both have a place.[1] Space constraints do not permit their incorporation into this chapter, however. Forced to choose and aware of few efforts in the literature to establish or discuss the possible roots of contemporary Spanish Eurocommunism, I have opted for the latter approach.

Interest in the affairs of a still relatively small and, until recently, clandestine party stems from the roles that the PCE and its secretary general, Santiago Carrillo, have played in the emergence and the development of what came in the late 1970s to be called Eurocommunism. The Spanish communists have been in the public eye for almost a decade because of their insistent calls for a pluralist socialist society and because of their trenchant criticisms of Soviet and East European domestic and foreign policies. The publication in early 1977 of *"Eurocomunismo" y Estado* by Carrillo marked the most important effort that West European communists had made to persuade the potential voter of their desire to combine socialism and democracy on the Continent.[2] In the book, Carrillo also discussed the nature of the Soviet system, how it differed from socialism, and the prospects for change in the Soviet Union. Arguing that the October 1917 revolution had laid the structural foundations for socialism in the U.S.S.R., Carrillo contended that in the ensuing years a *capa burocratica,* which prevented the democratization of political life in the country, had emerged. To assert that the Soviet Union was not a socialist society was a major heresy, but Carrillo did not stop there. He discussed the prospects for change in the U.S.S.R. and explicitly linked the transformation of the Soviet state "into a democratic workers' (one)" to the example set by West European communists when they entered government in their respective countries.

This chapter will explore some of those aspects or elements of the Spanish communist past that have led the PCE to become one of the most vociferous proponents of Eurocommunism and to adopt positions that either matched or outpaced those of their more publicized French and Italian counterparts.

I

Like other communist parties, the PCE appeared on the political horizon in the wake of the October 1917 revolution and the upsurge of revolutionary fervor that shook Europe following the Bolshevik seizure of power in Russia. Unlike their French, German, and Czechoslovak counterparts, however, the Spanish communists developed only a precarious presence in their country during the first decade in which they were active. Membership in the party never rose above the 5,000 mark,[3] and the communists remained locked into their position as a reduced, sectarian *groupuscule* until the Comintern shift to the Popular-Front strategy brought about the cessation of attacks on the socialists and others on the left. The reorientation of communist strategy became official in July 1935, but the shift was only the pro forma ratification of an initiative articulated in rough form more than a year before. The driving force behind the change appears to have been the German-Polish nonaggression pact of January 1934, which led Stalin to conclude that Hitler and Nazi Germany posed a threat to Soviet security. This realization led to a Russian *rapprochement* with the French government and then to the proposal (first voiced publicly in May 1934 in *Pravda* and republished shortly thereafter in *l'Humanité*) for antifascist unity among the forces of the left.[4] In Spain, the first formal steps in this direction came during the summer of 1934, and finally, in September of that year, the communists entered into the *Alianza Obrera* with the PSOE.

The shift toward a Popular-Front strategy marked an important turning point for the PCE and its fortunes, ushering in the period during which the influence of the communists grew tremendously. It is a period to which contemporary Spanish communists harken as they trace the roots of their present orientation. There are divergent interpretations about when and why the Spanish communists changed to Popular-Front tactics. Dolores Ibarruri claims, for example, that despite "severe criticism" from the Comintern, the PCE began to pursue a policy of fostering closer ties with the socialists a year before Stalin sanctioned such an initiative. Most of the historiographers of the Popular-Front period reject that argument. However, Victor Alba stresses that during 1933 and early 1934, the communists responded to all socialist suggestions for unity of action with vituperative scorn.[5] With the new line, the communists experienced a notable increase in their influence on the left. The first major test of the anti-fascist bloc, known as the *Alianza Obrera,* was the aborted Asturias revolt in October 1934. Although the PCE role was not nearly so important as the party subsequently claimed, it emerged from that insurrection, which the government put down with much bloodshed, with its profile raised and its alliance with the PSOE (Partido Socialista Obrero Español) consolidated. Of equal importance for the PCE, the socialists experienced a deep radicalization after the Asturias revolt, and its left wing, rallying around Largo Caballero and the *Juventudes Socialistas,* became the dominent force in party affairs.[6]

Largo Caballero had once been considered a moderate, earning the enmity of the anarchists for accepting the quasi-official post of *consejero del trabajo* during the Primo de Rivera dictatorship in an effort to build UGT (Unión General de Trabajadores) influence *vis-à-vis* the CNT (Confederación Nacional del Trabajo), but after 1934, he gravitated leftward. For approximately two and a half years thereafter, the communists lavished praise on him, building a cult around him as the second Lenin. Members of the *Caballerista* wing of the PSOE—individuals such as Julio Alvarez del Vayo, Margarita Nelken, and the secretary of the *Juventudes Socialistas,* Santiago Carrillo—developed close ties with the PCE during this period. They played leading roles in the merger of the socialist and communist youth movements (April 1936) and encouraged further talks aimed at bringing about the unification of the PCE and the PSOE. Although the socialists retained a numerical advantage over the communists in the months preceding the civil war—one perceptive observer argued that the communist claim of 20,000 members in early 1936 had been exaggerated perhaps sevenfold—the PCE developed a very important psychological edge on the PSOE, exerting enormous influence on the latter's left wing. To those socialists, the PCE and the Russian Revolution became a point of reference, a kind of magnet toward which they were inexorably attracted.

The dynamic of socialist-communist unity led to the creation of the Popular-Front bloc—composed of two republican parties and the Catalan *Esquerra*, in addition to the PSOE and the PCE—that contested and won the February 1936 parliamentary election. In its aftermath, the republicans formed a new government, but the climate of instability and polarization sweeping Spain numbered the days of constitutional rule. After several months characterized by a sharply deteriorating political situation, conservatives in the military made their move: Francisco Franco led a rebellion against the Second Republic. The fratricidal conflict lasted for three years, involving three European powers—Italy, Germany, and the Soviet Union. It was in many ways a dress rehearsal for World War II.

II

Much has been written about the Spanish communist role during the civil war, and it is not my intention to add to that extensive literature. Obviously, what the communists did in those years cannot be ignored. In this section, however, attention will be focused on the impact that those actions might have had on the PCE political style, on the perception that the communists developed of other parties and groups, and on the way that many of those on the noncommunist left viewed the PCE after 1939.

During the Spanish civil war, the PCE distinguished itself by advocating moderate policies and stretching out its hand to a beleaguered middle class. Against anarchists, left-wing socialists, and Trotskyites who argued for social revolution in the short term, the communists counterposed the slogan "First win the war, then proceed to revolutionary changes." This approach struck a favorable chord among moderates and middle of the roaders in the republican camp, but those who stood to the communists' left became convinced that "the communists were working . . . not to postpone the Spanish Revolution but to make sure it never happened."[7]

Such a judgment sounded harsh, but it was not without foundation. In the first place, the kind of revolution that the PCE favored was certainly not that which others on the left had in mind. When the PCE talked about eventual socialism, they meant change patterned after the Russian revolution and accomplished under the aegis and the direction of the Communist party. Because other groups would be relegated, with lesser or greater dispatch, to the dustbin of history, it is no wonder that the scenario did not find much favor among the communists' erstwhile allies on the left. More moderate groups (and the radical factions in the Socialist party, for example) did not necessarily trust the PCE, but they obviously thought that given the alternative of revolution and terror now or revolution and terror later, they would take their chances with the latter sequence.

It was not a conversion to evolutionary or democratic socialism that caused the PCE in 1936 to put the Spanish revolution on the back burner. Instead, the principal communist aim was to keep matters under control in Spain in order not to damage Soviet efforts to effect a *rapprochement* with Great Britain and France. It was this Soviet foreign-policy imperative that led the communists to issue repeated appeals for moderation and restraint and to adopt programs (such as the one issued in December 1936) emphasizing organization, production, and efficiency above all else.

Whether the policy made sense—and there are those who say it did not, that it reflected a profound misunderstanding of the social and political dynamics of revolution, and that this conceptual disability affects the PCE to this day—the Spanish communists distinguished themselves as loyal and obedient servants of Moscow. They did not hesitate to move against individuals or groups considered by Stalin to be his and the Soviet Union's enemies. The communists precipitated the ouster of Largo Caballero from his post as premier in May 1937 because he was not sufficiently malleable to communist pressure.[8] Although his ouster did not result in his imprisonment or death, others were less lucky. Such a fate did befall leaders of the quasi-Trotskyite *Partido Obrero de Unificación Marxista* (POUM). Thus the KGB kidnapped Andreu Nin and murdered him in the Soviet Union.[9] Meanwhile, the Spanish communists, whose official role in the Nin affair might have been largely indirect and passive,[10] sarcastically answered queries about his whereabouts by insisting that he was a fascist agent and as such likely to be in Berlin or Rome.

During this period, the PCE never had more than 2 out of 9 ministers in the cabinet, and its parliamentary representation was 17 out of approximately 280 Popular-Front deputies. Nevertheless, the influence that the communists exerted on the republican side was not that of a weak party. To what can the expansion of communist influence during the civil war be attributed?

First, the communists may be said to have derived an important psychological advantage from the fascination and fixation that many PSOE left wingers developed for the Soviet Union and the Russian revolution. Some individuals—Largo Caballero is a good example—had lost their enthusiasm for the communist cause by early 1937, but others, particularly those who subscribed to a more moderate political approach, took their place as the civil war wore on. Not only did they consider the PCE a bulwark of opposition to the radicals on the left, but they viewed the Soviet Union with increasing favor. It was the only major power openly willing to help the republican government by sending military advisers to Spain and helping constitute the international brigades.[11] These measures helped raise the prestige of the Soviet Union among broad sectors of the population and undoubtedly also worked to the benefit of the PCE. But the Spanish communists did not receive merely a psychological boost from Soviet aid. As Spanish agents of the Kremlin, they were responsible for the distribution of arms and supplies shipped from the Soviet Union. [The anarchists and the POUM—whom the Soviet Union considered enemies—did not receive much in the way of assistance. During his stay at the Aragon front, where anarchist militias were holding an important position against insurgent nationalists, George Orwell noted only one Soviet-made weapon in the anarchist arsenal, a submachine gun.][12]

The role played by the Soviet Union during the civil war undoubtedly helped the PCE to expand its influence, but it was not the only factor working in favor of the Spanish communists. They demonstrated consummate political abilities during the conflict. Obviously, the ruthlessness shown by the communists in disposing of no longer convenient allies and exploiting the presence of fellow travelers in the PSOE can be criticized. But there can be little doubt that the PCE was the best organized and effective component on the republican side during the civil war.

At a time when most members of the Popular Front had fallen to quarreling among themselves and blaming each other for failures in the prosecution of the war, when bitter factional struggles were renting the PSOE, and when the anarchists seemed unable to resolve the contradictions between their utopian theories and the realities imposed by the civil war, the communists became the party of order and organization. One prominent analyst and critic of the communist role during the civil war referred to the PCE as the *partido militar* of the Republic, a description that is not far off the mark.[13] The communists spared no effort in trying to set up a command structure and in reestablishing discipline within the armed forces. They also took advantage of the opportunity presented in October 1936, when the government established the posts of political commissars for the armed forces. As a result, the communists installed party members in perhaps 90 percent of those positions.[14]

The expansion of communist influence in the Popular-Front bloc and the assistance provided by the Soviet Union to the republican government did not avert the defeat of the Second Spanish Republic. The war ended in April 1939 amid recriminations and countercharges. Many on the left blamed the PCE and Stalin for the loss. They argued that in frustrating the early efforts to link war and revolution in Spain, the Soviet Union and the PCE laid the groundwork for the republican defeat. They insisted, moreover, that in the last year of the war, when all hope for a military victory had realistically dissipated, Stalin ordered the communists to prosecute the conflict as long as possible—at reprehensible costs in human life and suffering—with a view to strengthening the Soviet hand in negotiations that were either under way with Hitler or soon would be. These are serious charges, but no clear-cut judgment can be rendered on either of them because interpretations reflect the political persuasions of individuals. What cannot be denied is that secret negotiations between Berlin and Moscow had begun, perhaps as early as 1938, and eventually led to the signing of the German-Soviet Nonaggression Pact in 1939.[15]

III

The civil war had a profound impact, both in an immediate and in a longer-term sense, on the PCE. Perhaps its most important consequence was its adverse effect on communist relations with other parties on the left. Some of the resentment that these groups felt toward the PCE undoubtedly sprang from jealousy over the efficiency and organizational cohesion of the Communist party. But there was also the total Spanish communist identification with and defense of Soviet objectives. Outrage over the ruthlessness with which the communists swept away opposition led many on the left—not to mention on the right, on the Francoist side, who considered communism an antinational virus and the most hideous manifestation of all that was wrong with the twentieth century—to ostracize the PCE. The civil war thus left a deep impression on CNT and PSOE leaders, rendering the communists suspect and unwelcome as political allies. The communists participated in the republican government-in-exile between early 1946 and mid-1947 but otherwise experienced the phenomenon that Ignacio Fernández de Castro perceptively described as an *exilio dentro del exilio.*[16] That isolation was not to be overcome formally until nearly thirty years later (1976), when the PCE finally joined most other opposition groups, including the PSOE, in a coalition named the *Plataforma de Convergencia.*

Anticommunism in Spain became a matter of principle not only on the right but on the left. The obstacles that this hostility placed in the way of the communists only began to disappear when the torch of resistance to Franco passed from the exile leaders to the new generation living in Spain who had not directly experienced the civil war. Although progress on this issue was slower than the communists expected, their isolation in the exile community also had a more felicitous side: It led the party to devote more of its efforts to clandestine activity inside Spain. The isolation of the Spanish communists with respect to other opposition groups and the virulently anticommunist line proclaimed by the Franco regime also meant that in the 1960s and 1970s, as the PCE tried to break out of the ghetto into which it had been cast after the civil war, the party had to move more vigorously than its French and Italian counterparts. Those parties might also have felt the effects of an instinctive anticommunism, but because of the relatively open environments in which they operated, those parties had greater maneuvering room.

The civil war also exerted influence on the communists by setting—not in a fixed way but in terms of giving direction to—what, for want of a better term, may be called the Spanish communist political style. That style, emphasizing broad alliances and moderate policies, aimed at assuaging the fears of the middle class in Spain. Obviously, the adoption of Popular-Front policies by the PCE in the years after 1934 had a good deal to do with Stalin and the Comintern. But it is equally true that the policy, at least in its antifascist dimension, made excellent sense, particularly because the CNT and left-wing socialists made little effort to reassure the middle classes. Whatever the reasons for the adoption of those policies, the point is that they worked (at least in contributing to the growth of the influence of the PCE and its membership strength) and demonstrated that the party did not need to fear alliances with others. In this respect, the communist performance during the civil war came very close to fitting the category of "worldly success" that Robert Tucker posited as one of the more important causal factors explaining the deradicalization of a revolutionary party.[17]

The adoption of Popular-Front policies also exerted an influence on the recruitment patterns of the PCE. At one level, it meant that many people from middle-class backgrounds entered the party during the civil-war years.[18] What political implications this *embourgeoisement* had for the communists need not overly concern us here. What is noteworthy is that after 1939, when the Franco regime destroyed the remnants of the communist organization in Spain, the PCE stopped looking for ways to attract the middle class to its ranks.

The organizational expansion of the PCE during the civil war affected the Spanish communists at the elite level as well. A new generation of leaders entered the party in those years. They saw the PCE as a rising star, the vehicle through which the Spanish working class would be led to socialism. These recruits—whether motivated by opportunism or conviction— would probably have joined the CNT or the PSOE in the 1920s or early 1930s, but it was symptomatic of the growth of communist influence that they turned to the PCE banner. Many socialist youth leaders, who joined the PCE in 1936, were in their late teens or early twenties at the end of the civil war and consequently did not enter the highest policy-making bodies of the party until at least a decade later. In the 1950s some of them—specifically, Santiago Carrillo—reacted against the idea in which the older leaders seemed almost to revel. The PCE should remain a reduced sectarian group, proudly isolated on the left. Various circumstances to be considered later in this chapter helped exacerbate latent generational and attitudinal conflicts and provoked changes in leadership and policies that led to the emergence of Euro-communism in Spain.

A final consequence of the civil war for the communists related to the development of the view that the Franco regime was illegitimate and that its replacement was the *sine qua non* for the establishment of democracy in Spain. This attitude remained at the core of communist thinking for four decades, but during those years, the physiognomy of Spain, if not the attitudes of Spaniards, changed dramatically. The communists did show flexibility, of course. Hoping to take advantage of the increasingly generalized sentiment that the quarrels that engendered the civil war should be put aside, Carrillo and the PCE issued a call for national reconciliation in 1956. By the end of the Franco era, moreover, the party had begun to use the term *ruptura pactada* to describe the agreement between the opposition and reformers within the regime for an orderly transition. Nevertheless, the PCE invariably regarded individuals or groups aligned with the regime or the solutions proposed by them as somehow fundamentally illegitimate. In rendering this judgment, they failed to understand that most Spaniards had given at least tacit assent to the Franco regime. This blinder handicapped the party in the mid-1970s, making it difficult for the communists to understand (and thus to counteract) the popular assent given to King Juan Carlos and Premier Adolfo Suárez as they assumed responsibility for leading Spain in its transition to democracy.

For the most part, the one exception being its isolation *vis-à-vis* others on the left, the PCE did not immediately feel the impact of the consequences that have been sketched. The communist presence began to be felt only in the mid-1950s when a crisis, which coincided with de-Stalinization in the international communist movement and with the reappearance of worker and student strikes in Spain, erupted in the party. That crisis, which will be discussed in the concluding part of this chapter, turned the tide within the PCE in favor of those who wanted the party to adopt more flexible and activist policies. Before turning to an analysis of those circumstances, however, it is necessary to discuss what happened to the PCE in the decade and a half after the end of the civil war. A consideration of the isolation that the party experienced during that period and of its failure to foment the overthrow of the Franco regime will help explain why in 1956 and subsequent years some PCE leaders believed that the party would have to take bold steps to break out of the ghetto into which it had been cast.

IV

The PCE entered the postcivil-war era with its organization shattered and its leaders dispersed in France and, after the

German invasion and occupation of that country, throughout North and South America, the Soviet Union, and the unoccupied parts of Europe.[19] Whatever efforts the party undertook in Spain in those years were focused primarily on organizing the jails and camps set up by the regime. Those efforts were carried out almost instinctively and certainly without direction. Contact between communists outside and inside Spain was virtually impossible. (Even in 1946 and 1947, all Central-Committee members sent in to organize the party fell into the hands of the police, and most were executed.) Among the exiles in France, the party devoted most of its energies to setting up guerrilla contingents that fought as part of the French resistance movement.

As noted above, after 1939, Spanish communist relations with their erstwhile Popular-Front partners were poor.[20] PCE leaders continued to emphasize broad-front tactics—calling, first, in 1939-1940, for a *unión democrática popular* and, after the German invasion of the Soviet Union, for a *unión nacional*—but important sectors of the anarchist and socialist movements refused to have anything to do with the PCE. The *Junta de Unión Nacional* (JUN), set up by the communists in late 1943, was a more or less phantom organization that attracted only slight support from noncommunist elements. Some anarchists and socialists joined, but they formed distinct minorities in their own groups. The majoritarian factions in the PSOE and CNT sponsored their own coalitions, the *Junta Española de Liberación*, which was mostly a creation of the exile community in Mexico, and the more serious effort known as the *Alianza Nacional de Fuerzas Democráticas* (ANFD) in late 1944. Having failed to rally support for the JUN and its fighting arm, the *Agrupación de Guerrilleros Españoles*, the communists eventually forsook the JUN. After negotiations with the socialists, they entered the ANFD in July 1945.

The communist decision to join the ANFD and

subsequently the republican government-in-exile (the party proposed that a *govierno de concentración nacional* should follow Franco—a notion to be resurrected in the post-Franco era)[21] as well as socialist acquiescence in those moves should be understood in the context of the euphoria with which republican exiles greeted the liberation of Europe. Opponents of Franco became convinced that his regime was the logical next target for the victorious allies. Events—among them the division of the allied coalition along ideological lines and the consolidation of the Franco regime—conspired to frustrate the desires of the anti-Franco opposition. In the wake of that failure and parallel to the escalation of the cold war, the quarrels among communists and noncommunist elements, never far below the surface, came to the fore once again. The communist minister withdrew from the republican government-in-exile in August 1947.

If it can be said that at the end of the civil war, the Spanish communists had difficulty developing ties with other opposition groups, their isolation became virtually complete in the years after 1947. The party withdrew more and more into itself, becoming a small, almost incestuous organization whose leaders conducted periodic purges to find various (mostly imagined) traitors. As soon as the party leaders returned to France in 1944 and 1945, they took measures to root out "fascist agents of the POUM" and "Falangist provocateurs."[22] Paranoia led to the setting up of commissions—reminiscent not only of the ones set up in the Soviet Union to process prisoners of war who had been captured by the German armies but of the subsequent show trials in Eastern Europe against veterans of the international brigades—to investigate the behavior and the loyalties of those who had survived the concentration-camp experience.

Internal conflicts and conspiracies consumed much of the party leaders' time after 1939. The exile community became bitterly divided by the struggle between Jesús Hernández and

Dolores Ibárruri for succession to the post of secretary general after the death of José Díaz in 1942. Hernández lost and subsequently broke with the party. His *La Grande Trahison* gives a most unattractive view of life in the Spanish communist exile community.[23] His objectivity is open to question, but he is cited here in the absence of more direct evidence (party leaders prefer not to discuss the matter) about the excesses that occurred during this period. That there were excesses, however, there is little doubt, as the following extract from Dolores Ibárruri's statement in April 1956 makes clear:

Our "war communism" led by Anton [one of the top leaders in the party who had risen in the PCE largely because he was Ibárruri's lover but by 1951 had committed too many outrages to avoid criticism] with a selective, policy-oriented criterion, which was not only his but of the entire party leadership, to hateful arbitrarinesses, to massive expulsion of those who were not considered faithful. . . . If during that period, we did not lose the party, it was because, despite the poorness of our work, the base was healthy.[24]

It was not simply within the exile community that Anton and other leaders of the party acted with impunity. Party oligarchs, as discussed elsewhere,[25] used heavy-handed methods, occasionally resorting to assassinations and turning in people to the Francoist police, to reassert control over the communist organization in Spain. For several years after 1939, contact between the exile leadership and party members operating in Spain or even in France was difficult, and leaders who emerged in both countries had free reign in directing party policies. People such as Heriberto Quiñones and Jesús Monzón led the party in Spain without heeding the exile leadership. Until the end of World War II, there was not much that the exiled leaders could do about such behavior. But after the invasion of Normandy, representatives of the Political Bureau returned to France and reasserted control.

Quiñonismo and *Monzonismo* (the police arrested and executed Quiñones in 1942) became heresies to be extirpated. Even more outrageous were the "physical eliminations ordered by the PCE secretariat against dissident communists such as Gabriel León Trilla, Antonio Beltrán, and Joan Comorera. Even the erstwhile war hero Enrique Líster—who left the party in 1970 and created a pro-Soviet faction—did not escape the tarring brush, being mentioned at one point in the late 1940s as a participant in a plot to murder Dolores Ibárruri.

Reduced to squabbling among themselves, the Spanish communists fell victim to the machinations of Soviet espionage and intelligence services, a fate that befalls almost all exile communities. But the Stalinist reality in the late 1940s and the cooperation that individual members of the party (if not the entire leadership) gave the Soviet secret services during the civil war aggravated the situation. Alluding to those machinations, former Executive-Committee member Jorge Semprún charged that Eduardo García, who subsequently became organizational secretary, had been an agent of the KGB.[26] Blackmail and the settling of old political and personal accounts, to which Líster alluded in his book *Basta!*,[27] undoubtedly helped make this one of the most distasteful periods in Spanish communist history. Little has been written about it, but the experiences that some individuals—such as Fernando Claudín, who ran the PCE organization in Moscow from the late 1940s until 1954—had with the Soviet system might well have laid the groundwork for their subsequent break with Stalinism. For others, such as Carrillo, whose ideological evolution took longer, that background probably spurred the development of nationalist resentment against the Soviet Union.

Throughout this period, the Spanish communists did their best to present a brave front, and their public statements never lost that bravado for which small and increasingly irrelevant exile groups are noted. They exuded a *triunfalismo* that was false and misplaced, particularly when many of the strikes for which the party took credit had been led by other groups or were spontaneous phenomena for which no one group was responsible. Important strikes did take place in the Basque country (1947) and Barcelona (1951), but the former was the last gasp of the civil war and the latter, although creating possibilities for organization and participation by opposition groups, was only a first step in that direction. Exhaustion was the dominant feeling in the late 1940s, and it did not dissipate for another decade. The regime, on the other hand, consolidated itself. The signing of a base agreement with the United States and the concordat with the Vatican in 1953 served to confirm its stability.

V

PCE fortunes stood at their lowest ebb in the early 1950s. Under these circumstances, it would not have been surprising had the Spanish communists retreated more and more into their shell, reveling in their isolation. That this did not happen stemmed in large measure from a confluence of events and circumstances that led not only to a change of leadership but to a shift toward more adaptive policies.

Competition among the ruling oligarchs had been evident in the PCE since the end of the civil war and particularly after the death of Secretary General José Díaz in 1942. There was in this sense nothing new about the struggles that began to manifest themselves in the early 1950s. On one side was what may be termed the old guard in the party, such people as Dolores Ibárruri, Vicente Uribe, and Francisco Anton, who had been important figures in the PCE during the civil war and owed their positions to the roles that they had played. Eventually lining up on the other side and increasingly identifying himself as a spokesman for change was another member of the Political Bureau, Santiago Carrillo. He had been a member of the party's inner circle since 1944, when he returned to liberated France and established the *comisión del interior*, the instrument used to reassert control over the party organization in Spain.

Carrillo had been the secretary general of the Socialist Youth, presiding over the fusion of that organization with the communist one, becoming a member of the PCE in 1936, and attaining membership in the Central Committee shortly thereafter. Carrillo had been part of that activist wave (alluded to earlier, when the consequences of the civil war were discussed), whose entry into the Communist party reflected the conviction that the PCE was the most efficient and effective political instrument in Spain. To prove his loyalty to the party, Carrillo even wrote a public letter to his socialist father in 1939, breaking off all ties because the senior Carrillo had supported a *junta* that seized control of Madrid in the last days of the war and negotiated with Franco the surrender of the capital.[28] Despite such a demonstration of fidelity (whether motivated by conviction or opportunism or both) to the cause of communism, Carrillo apparently remained a relative outsider in the party oligarchy.[29] Older members doubtless held against him his relative youth, his Trotskyite leanings before entering the PCE—in 1935 he proposed to Andreu Nin and Joaquin Maurin that they join the PSOE and help the Socialist Youth "bolshevize" the PSOE from within—[30] and perhaps even his role during the 1933 parliamentary campaign, when he either coined or encouraged the widespread use of the phrase, "If you want to liberate Spain from Marxism, vote communist."[31]

Carrillo spent only a few months (early in World War II) in the Soviet Union and then left that country, spending the rest of the war in Latin America, the United States, and Portugal. He returned in late 1944 to France as the representative of the Political Bureau. It was there that he established the *comisión del interior* and began to develop a base of power. By the late 1940s, he became one of the four or five most important leaders of Spanish communism, participating as such in an October 1948 meeting with Stalin. His participation in some of the excesses of the period—the murder of Gabriel León Trilla and the campaign against Jesús Monzón—seems probable, and it is unlikely that remorse led him to engage in open conflict with his fellow oligarchs in the 1950s. The search for an explanation of his behavior would probably have to focus more on personal rivalries than anything else. Anton was not the most engaging of individuals, and resentment against him and his imperiousness was strong.[32] Carrillo probably couched in general terms his support of moves to discipline and strip power from Anton (he received a reprimand in 1952 and then in July 1953 came his ouster from the Political Bureau), arguing that his removal would restore party confidence in its leaders and permit the PCE to overcome the failures of earlier years.

With Anton eliminated from the inner councils, a *troika* composed of Ibárruri, Uribe, and Carrillo ran the party. The last two did not square off until the mid-1950s. Meanwhile, the death of Stalin in March 1953 injected a new element into the discussions under way in the Spanish Communist party. What had been a battle between and over personalities became a struggle among contending political approaches and attitudes, between those who thought things were going well and others who were dissatisfied with the course of events since 1939. A partial renovation of the Spanish communist leadership occurred at the fifth congress in 1954 with the entry of some activists from Spain and the revision of party statutes. Despite those developments, Carrillo made no move to articulate a clear challenge designed to enable him to take control of the party.

That move came in late 1955, during a crisis precipitated by Spanish admission to the United Nations. A majority of the Political Bureau—some of whose members, Uribe, Antonio Mije, Ignacio Gallego, and Líster, had gone to Bucharest for the birthday of *La Pasionaria*—issued a statement, broadcast over *Radio España Independiente*,[33] calling for a massive international campaign and condemning the event as another instance of the betrayal of the antifascist and republican cause. Apparently unaware of what had been decided in Bucharest, Carrillo and three other members of the Political Bureau who had stayed in Paris penned an article for *Mundo Obrero* in which they praised Spanish entry as "a logical continuation of the policy of coexistence" and "a new blow against the Francoist war policy."[34] When Ibárruri found out about this document, which had in the meantime been sent to the printers, she grew livid and threatened to have Carrillo expelled for factional activity and indiscipline. In a conciliatory effort, Carrillo sent Jorge Semprún to Bucharest to argue that the position adopted by the majority made little sense because in the existing situation, any international campaign undertaken against Franco was destined to fail.[35] Semprún apparently did not convince Ibárruri that Carrillo was right, but he did manage to have her agree not to take any measures against Carrillo until a plenary session of the Political Bureau met in April 1956. In the meantime, however, she and others in the majority tried to rally support against Carrillo. To that end, they invited Fernando Claudín, one of the Political-Bureau members who had joined Carrillo in drafting the *Mundo Obrero* article, to join the Spanish communist delegation attending the twentieth CPSU congress in February.[36]

In early 1956 Carrillo stood on the verge of expulsion from the party. The fortuitous coincidence of two events— the condemnation of Stalin by Khrushchev at the twentieth CPSU congress and the first widespread political strikes that erupted in Spain since the end of the civil war—helped him avoid that fate. Dolores Ibárruri saw which way the wind was blowing in the international communist movement, and, probably still resentful of Vicente Uribe's all too eager acquiescence several years before in the defenestration of Anton, she shifted her support to Carrillo. The official change came at a tumultuous and marathon Political-Bureau meeting that lasted from early April until the second week of May. Carrillo further consolidated his position at the Central-Committee plenum in August, coopting six members into the Political Bureau. Delivering a report on "The Situation in the Leadership of the Party and the Problems of Reinforcing It," Carrillo used the revelations about Stalin as a foil with which to attack his opponents, accusing them of succumbing to the cult of personality and other deviations. Ibárruri was not the target of much criticism. Neither was the disgraced Anton, whom Carrillo attacked almost in passing. Instead, it was Uribe, the Political-Bureau leader responsible for the day-to-day operation of party affairs, who felt the brunt of the criticism. Carrillo described him sweepingly as one who "opposed collective leadership, [who] did not accept criticism and self-criticism, was prone to self-satisfaction, tended to rely on personalist methods, inclined toward *practicismo,* and underestimated the importance of ideological work."[37]

Carrillo made good political use of the condemnation that Khrushchev made of Stalin at the twentieth CPSU congress, but his victory cannot be understood simply in those terms. For one thing, although he used the Stalinist phenomenon, Carrillo did not go very far in analyzing the issue. His (and Khrushchev's) argument that Stalinism was an aberration in an otherwise healthy system contrasted with the views expressed by PCI Secretary General Palmiro Togliatti in *Nuovi Argumenti* and with the judgment articulated within the leadership but not publicly by Fernando Claudín that the problem had an institutional root.[38] Moreover, when Claudín and Semprún moved in the early 1960s to formulate a global critique of Spanish policies (anticipating many of the positions of what has come to be termed Eurocommunism, they argued for greater internal democracy, for independence from the Soviet Union, for a thorough and scientific investigation of the influence that Stalinism had exerted on communist attitudes and policies), Carrillo moved against them and engineered their expulsion.

Certainly more important than the de-Stalinization issue in explaining his victory within the party were the proposals that Carrillo made for revitalizing communist strategy and organization. What began as a largely personal quarrel with Uribe, Anton, and others in the old guard shifted to a political argument over what, if anything, might be done to increase the influence of the Spanish Communist party. The older members of the leadership, it may be surmised, were more satisfied with the *status quo* than was this young Turk, who saw his political talents being wasted in what was rapidly becoming a sectarian and limited nucleus of activists. In an effort to invigorate the party (and probably also outflank the older leaders), Carrillo argued for the inclusion of activists working inside Spain. In 1956 he seized on the first mass anti-Franco demonstrations involving students and workers to argue that the PCE could decisively break out of its ghetto and lead the overthrow of Franco. Others in the leadership had always talked about the inevitability of change in Spain, reiterating that Franco could not survive much longer, but they seemed reluctant to precipitate matters. The activism and optimism implicit in Carrillo's arguments rallied supporters to his side. His position on Spanish entry into the United Nations reflected the conviction that if a change in regime were to come, it would have to come from within Spain and by adapting to the emerging realities in the country.

Under Carrillo's direction, the Political Bureau approved in June 1956 a call for national reconciliation. Although the appeal paralleled previous PCE efforts to galvanize broad fronts against the Franco regime, it nevertheless represented an important break with the past. Coming on the twentieth anniversary of the outbreak of the civil war, the call signified the desire of the communists to take the first step toward overcoming the division of Spain into two camps—a division, according to Carrillo, that not only permitted Franco to consolidate his power but contributed to the perpetuation of communist isolation as well. Convinced that the regime had an extremely narrow base of support and would soon fall under the weight of its contradictions, Carrillo persuaded others in the leadership to call for mass action (in May 1958 and June 1959) to mobilize broad strata of the Spanish population, including groups that had once supported the regime. The PCE exhorted communist militants and sympathizers throughout Spain to prepare for the imminent *huelga nacional* that would overthrow the regime.

Life, as Marxists are fond of saying, rendered its judgment on this matter. The regime did not fall, and in retrospect it is evident that Carrillo seriously misjudged the depth of the economic and social crisis of the late 1950s and early 1960s and the extent to which it could be overcome by the government's stabilization plan of 1959. He never admitted his erroneous assessment, holding to the notion that there was no way in which the regime could reform itself, that it was destined to fall by means of a general strike. As a result of that miscalculation, the party leadership and Carrillo had to spend a great deal of time and effort over the course of the next decade explaining why their overoptimistic predictions had not materialized and fending off the attacks of assorted leftists (supporters of the various *Frente(s) de Liberación Popular,* Maoists, and Castroists) who rejected the emphasis placed on peaceful transformation and the notion of extended interclass collaboration that the party espoused after 1956.

The mistakes that Carrillo made concerning the magnitude

of the crisis facing the Franco regime also led to tensions in the highest ranks of the PCE. Accompanied by several other members of the Political Bureau, he journeyed to Eastern Europe in midsummer 1959 in an effort to convince Ibárruri that the call for a *huelga nacional pacífica* issued in June had been an enormous success and confirmed the correctness of the policies instituted since 1956.[39] Ibárruri, who remained the nominal secretary general of the PCE until its sixth congress in December 1959, when Carrillo took her place, might not have been satisfied with the explanation, but, cast more and more in the role of spectator and *grande dame,* she could hardly muster opposition to the course pursued by Carrillo.

A more significant challenge to Carrillo came, as was mentioned earlier, from Fernando Claudín and Jorge Semprún. Beginning in 1963, they openly criticized the *subjectivismo* of party policies and called for an end to all the talk about an imminent *huelga nacional.* From an analytical point of view, Claudín and Semprún were close to the mark in predicting and explaining the failure of communist efforts, but their insights into the psychology of a clandestine party were less well developed than Carrillo's. He admitted that mistakes had been made, but, comparing himself and the PCE to Lenin and the Bolsheviks, he wondered whether "[those] harm[ed] the revolutionary workers' movement or [whether] . . . on the contrary, [they] served to stimulate its faith, its confidence, its decision to fight, its inclination to make sacrifices which [were] required by the revolutionary struggle."[40] The communist cadre, operating under hazardous conditions in Spain and sacrificing so much for party and cause, reacted favorably to Carrillo's rhetoric. Forced to swallow unsavory revelations about Stalin not too long before, the average militant did not want to make another admission of defeat.

The same activist vision that helped Carrillo take control of the PCE and retain power in the face of the Claudín-Semprún challenge engendered change within the Spanish

Communist party. The belief in the inability of the regime to reform its structures and in the imminence of its downfall led the PCE leadership (preeminently, Santiago Carrillo) to consider how to achieve legitimacy and a broad base of support for the party in a democratic Spain. The results were the adaptive policies toward the labor movement and the Catholic church and its subculture, as well as the revision in the ideological, organization, and foreign-policy spheres that eventually constituted the core of Spanish Eurocommunism.

VI

Despite occasional dramatic changes in policy, the Spanish communists did not do well in the first two parliamentary elections of the post-Franco era. Eurocommunism has not yet taken root in Spanish soil. The reasons for this failure are complex. Any explanation would have to point first to the weight of the past. At one level, of course, the civil war may be said to have had a favorable impact on the PCE. Not only did that conflict serve as a catalyst for recruitment, bringing some of "the best and the brightest" young activists into the party, but it provided concrete experience on which party leaders could draw when they began to espouse policies that emphasized interclass collaboration. Although the experience of the civil war played a role in encouraging less sectarian and adaptive policies on the part of the Spanish communists, it had less salutary consequences. The experience led the PCE to view politics primarily through the Manichaean left-right prism fired during the 1930s and to insist for sometime on the illegitimacy of a gradual transition to democracy.

A second part of the explanation would focus on the ambiguities of the Spanish communist evolution and the mistrust that many Spaniards felt toward the party. In the space of several decades, it is true, the PCE moved away from Leninist and Stalinist politics, but in important ways the party retained an instrumental view of parliamentary democracy and democratic values. Many Spaniards, in any case, remained deeply skeptical about the real intentions of the party, and those fears were not assuaged by events in neighboring Portugal after April 1974.

We have pointed to two factors that are relevant in explaining the poor communist showing in the June 1977 and March 1979 elections to the Spanish Cortes. Their importance might have been minimized, however, and the fortunes of the PCE might have been different had the Spanish communists not been forced to contend with the leadership abilities of King Juan Carlos and Premier Adolfo Suarez during the transition to the post-Franco era. In this respect, the assassination of Admiral Luis Carrero Blanco in December 1973 looms as a significant political event. Carrero Blanco was the man to whom Franco intended to entrust the task of preserving his regime. Although Carrero Blanco would probably have failed in his efforts to hold the line against change, he would have tried. By so doing, he would have contributed to the polarization and radicalization of Spanish society. Under those circumstances, the communists would have been less affected by ambiguities and contradictions that have characterized their evolution. Unfortunately, from their point of view, the communists did not face an unrepentant Francoist such as Carrero Blanco during the transition period. Instead, they had to deal with younger men who had much greater stakes in the future than in the past and who accepted the inevitability of change in the political structures of the regime. The ability of King Juan Carlos and Premier Adolfo Suarez to retain the political initiative in the months after the death of Franco worked against the PCE and in favor of its less well-organized competitors on the left, such as the PSOE. That the communists nevertheless did not lapse into sterile, radical rhetoric when things did not go their way demonstrated how far the party had evolved in the two decades since the proclamation of national reconciliation and indicated the desire of the principal communist leaders to continue to work for their party's integration into Spanish political life. By its moderation, the PCE permitted others in the opposition to act with restraint, and in this sense the party made an important contribution to effecting a peaceful, nontraumatic transition from Francoism. It is on that record that the Spanish communists must build as they try to develop their influence in Spanish society.

NOTES

1. For an example, see my essay entitled "The Domestic and International Evolution of the Spanish Communist Party" in Rudolph Tökes (ed.), *Eurocommunism and Detente* (New York, 1978), pp. 204-270.

2. Santiago Carrillo, *"Eurocomunismo" y Estado* (Barcelona, 1977).

3. Branko Lazitch, *Les Partis Communistes d'Europe* (Paris, 1956), p. 183.

4. Fernando Claudín, *La Crisis del Movimiento Comunista* (Paris, 1970), pp. 134-144.

5. Dolores Ibárruri, "The Seventh Congress of the Comintern and the Spanish Experience," *World Marxist Review 8* (December 1965), pp. 43-47; Victor Alba, El Partido *Communista en España* (Barcelona, 1979), p. 140.

6. For an analysis of this process, see Andrés de Blas Guerrero, *El Socialismo Radical en la Segunda República* (Madrid, 1978).

7. George Orwell, *Homage to Catalonia* (New York, 1952), p. 67, makes the statement. For a useful compilation of communist documents sketching the PCE's position, see José Díaz, *Tres Años de Lucha* (Paris, 1970),

8. David I. Cattell, *Communism and the Spanish Civil War* (Berkeley and Los Angeles, 1957), pp. 165-168. Also Gabriel Jackson, *The Spanish Republic and the Civil War, 1931-1939* (Princeton, N.J., 1965), pp. 360-374, and Stanley Payne, *The Spanish Revolution* (New York, 1970), pp. 298-299.

9. Jackson, *The Spanish Republic, op. cit.,* pp. 403-405.

10. This is at least the claim that Carrillo made in *"Eurocomunismo" y Estado*, pp. 147-152.

11. Orwell, *op. cit.,* pp. 53-54, and Cattell, *op. cit.,* pp. 69-83.

12. Ibid., p. 34. Also Franz Borkenau, *The Spanish Cockpit* (Ann Arbor, Michigan, 1963), pp.179-180.

13. Claudín, *op. cit.*, p. 186.

14. Cattell, **op. cit.**, p. 184.

15. Claudín, *op. cit.*, pp. 195-197; Payne, *op. cit.*, p. 311; and Cattell, *op. cit.*, p. 32.

16. Ignacio Fernández de Castro, *De las Cortes de Cádiz al Plan de Desarrollo* (Paris, 1968), p. 286.

17. Robert C. Tucker, *The Marxian Revolutionary Idea* (New York, 1969), p. 186.

18. See the evidence sketched in Guy Hermet, *Los Comunistas en España* (Paris, 1972), pp. 37-39.

19. See Dolores Ibárruri *et al., Historia del Partido Comunista de España* (Warsaw, 1960), pp. 211-247 ff, for the official view on those years. For a contrast, Angel Ruiz Ayúcar, *El Partido Comunista* (Madrid, 1976), pp. 49-226.

20. A detailed account of the struggles among the exiled Popular-Front parties may be found in José Borrás, *Políticas de los Exiliados Españoles, 1944-1958* (Paris, 1976).

21. Santiago Carrillo, "Somos el Partido de la Destrucción del franquismo y también el Partido de la Reconstrucción de una España grande y democrática," *Nuestra Bandera* (January-February 1946), p. 60.

22. ___ , "La Situación de España y Nuestras Tareas despues de la Victoria de las Naciones Unidas," *Nuestra Bandera* (June 1945), pp. 18-19.

23. Jesus Hernández, *La Grande Trahison* (Paris, 1953).

24. See the text in Enrique Líster, *Basta!* (Madrid, 1978), pp. 266-268.

25. See my "Ideology and Organization in the PCE," in *Marxism in the Contemporary West*, edited by Carl Linden and Charles Elliott (Westview Press, forthcoming).

26. Jorge Semprún, *Autobiografía de Federico Sánchez* (Barcelona, 1977), pp. 38-39.

27. Líster, *op. cit.*, pp. 211-264.

28. Alba, *op. cit.*, pp. 259-261.

29. This is at least the opinion of Líster, *op. cit.*, pp. 182-183.

30. Santiago Carrillo, *Demain l'Espagne* (Paris, 1974), p. 44. Also Alba, *op. cit.*, p. 170, and forthcoming: Boulder, Colorado.

31. Alba, *op. cit.*, p. 140.

32. Líster, *op. cit.*, pp. 218-219.

33. Semprún, *op. cit.*, pp. 217-218.

34. Mundo Obrero (Paris), January 1956.

35. Semprún, *op. cit.*, pp. 219-223.

36. Carrillo apparently believes that his opponents of the time saw

Claudín as recuperable because he, unlike Carrillo, came from the Communist Youth. Maria Eugenia Yagüe, *Santiago Carrillo: Una Biografia Política* (Madrid, 1977), pp. 52-53.

37. The pamphlet of that title has no date or place of publication.

38. See Fernando Claudín, *Documentos de una Divergencia Comunista* (Barcelona, 1978), p. iii. As late as 1964, Carrillo still opposed the effort, urged by Claudín and Semprún, to analyze the Stalinist era more critically. In April of that year, he admitted that "there had been political police, concentration camps, etc.," in the Soviet Union but insisted that those institutions "were necessary and I am not sure they might not be in other socialist revolutions, even though these be realized under more favorable circumstances": from a speech in the Political Bureau, cited in Semprún, *op. cit.,* p. 280. See also pp. 277-279 for the negative reaction to a Semprún article in *Realidad* in which he asserted the need to "liquidate the institutional (Stalinist) system."

39. Claudín, *Ibid.,* pp. iv-v.

40. See the text of the speech delivered by Carrillo in April 1964, translated in *Joint Publications Research Service* (Washington, D.C.), no. 26413, September 16, 1964, p. 22. Semprún, *op. cit.,* pp. 212-215, quotes from the original speech and contrasts that version with the one later published by the PCE.

Juan J. Linz

A SOCIOLOGICAL LOOK
AT SPANISH COMMUNISM

Introduction

The Spanish Communist party has attracted considerable attention as a leading exponent of Eurocommunism, but until now its place in Spanish society has not been the object of much research.[1] This chapter will focus not on the ideology, the programs, or the recent history of the party but on its electorate: the attitudes and opinions of its voters, the social bases of the party, the appeals that it has made, and the difficulties that it has encountered in reaching the electorate.[2] We shall try to answer such questions as how do communist voters and supporters of other parties perceive

*This paper was written while the author held a fellowship awarded by the German Marshall Fund of the United States, which is gratefully acknowledged. I benefited from the help of colleagues at DATA, Madrid, and the assistance of Rocío de Terán.

the PCE and its leadership and what reasons do they cite for its successes and its failures by analyzing public-opinion surveys and electoral returns. We shall compare the party to other Southern European communist parties and to its competitors in Spain, mainly the Socialist Workers party—the PSOE—the parties on the extreme left, and leftist regional parties that have competed with the PCE. Therefore, many of the tables give information about the PCE and PSOE, even when the analysis is centered on the PCE. Because almost one of four communist voters in Spain support the Catalan affiliate of the Communist party—the Unified Socialist party of Catalonia (PSUC)—and differences in outlook are supposed to distinguish it from the statewide PCE, much of the information is comparative in nature. At other times, when comparison was not the primary objective, data pertaining to the PCE and the PSUC were combined.[3]

It may be useful to begin the analysis by highlighting a few basic facts about the PCE. In terms of electorate, the PCE is a large party that elicits the support of almost two million voters. It is the third largest communist party in Western Europe, but in terms of its share of the total vote and consequently of its parliamentary representation, it ranks behind the communist parties of Cyprus, Italy, France, Iceland, Finland, Portugal, and even, Luxembourg. (See Table 1.) Furthermore, the Spanish Communist party, unlike the PCI in Italy, is not the dominant party on the left in Spain, nor is its strength in relation to the socialists comparable to that of the French PCF or the Portuguese PCP.

In spite of its ostensible presence throughout Spain, it depends heavily for its success on Catalonia, Andalucía, and Madrid where 45.6 percent of the country's voters are concentrated. Those regions contain 62.7 percent of the communist electorate. The party's weakness in one of the most industrialized regions of Spain, the Basque country, is particularly striking. Unlike the PSOE, even when it is less

Table I. Electoral Strength of Western European Communist Parties with More Than 4 Percent of the Vote in Recent Elections. (Adapted from Neil McInnes, <u>The Communist Parties of Western Europe</u>, London, 1975, pp. 21, and other sources.)

Country	Party	Date of Election	Communist Votes	Percent of Vote	Seats Won	Total Seats
Cyprus	AKEL	July 1970	79,280	39.7	9	35
Italy	PCI	June 1976	12,614,650	34.4	228	629
France	PCF	March 1978			103	491
		First ballot	5,870,402	20.6		
		Second ballot	4,744,868	18.6		
Finland	SKDL	January 1972	438,387	17.1	37	200
Iceland	AB	June 1974	20,922	18.1	11	60
Luxembourg	CPL	December 1968	402,610	15.5	6	56
Portugal	PCP	April 1976	785,594	14.6	40	264
Greece	KKE (Ex)	November 1977	480,188	9.4	11	300
	Alliance of Progressive and Left-wing Forces (CP of the Interior and 4 other parties)		139,762	2.7	2	
Spain	PCE	June 1977	1,112,473	6.1	12	
	PSUC		531,006	3.1	8	
			1,655,744	9.2	20	350
	PCE	March 1979	1,427,104	7.7	14	
	PSUC		511,800	2.8	9	
			1,938,904	10.5	23	350
Sweden	VPK	September 1973	274,929	5.3	19	350
Holland	CPN	November 1972	329,973	4.5	7	150
Belgium	PCB	December 1979	180,088	3.3	4	212

concentrated in certain parts of the country than the PCP, the PCE must travel a long road before it can gain a significant presence in many parts of the country. Like other Spanish parties, but perhaps more so, the PCE has to compete with the regional nationalist parties of the extreme left, a situation that differentiates it from the Italian, Portuguese, and French parties.

The PCE is a working-class party but is not the party of the working class. A large proportion of workers support the PSOE and the PCE, although both parties have to share the working-class electorate with other parties. In this respect, the position of the PCE contrasts with that of the Comisiones Obreras (CCOO), the trade-union federation that is closely linked with the party. In the labor movement, CCOO occupies a stronger position than the socialist union federation—Unión General de Trabajadores (UGT).[4]

The PCE must confront parties to its left both at the state and at the regional level, whereas in other European countries the communist party is almost the only party to the left of the socialists. The PCE, therefore, must fight on two fronts rather than only against the socialists. Like other communist parties, particularly those in Italy, Portugal, and France, the PCE receives a considerable share of its vote from a rural electorate, mainly in Andalucía and south central Spain.

Neither its strength in industrial metropolitan areas nor in certain rural areas gives it a hegemonic position in any political division of the country comparable to that held by the PCI in north central Italy or the PCP in certain parts of Portugal. Even in its areas of greater strength and of dominance by the left, the PCE has to share power with the stronger PSOE.

Few data could reveal better the position that the PCE now occupies in Spain than a comparison of the maximum votes received by the various parties in the fifty Spanish electoral districts with the votes received by comparable parties in the districts of electoral strength in Portugal and Italy in recent elections. (See Table 2.) In both 1977 and 1979, the PCE and, in Catalonia, the PSUC were not able to get over 20 percent in any district. In 1977 only in eight districts did the PCE get over 10 percent. In Portugal, in three of the twenty-two districts, the PCP managed to obtain over 40 percent, and in another two, including the capital Lisbon, it obtained over 20 percent. In the three districts of Setubal, Beja, and Evora, a red belt that crosses the country south of Lisbon, the communist party enjoyed what could be considered a hegemonic position at the provincial level, and in most of the municipalities, it achieved the largest plurality. There is no area of Spain in which the PCE has obtained such a hegemonic position. In Italy, even several decades ago, the PCI has been able to obtain over 40 percent in two districts, Tuscany and Emilia-Romagna, and over 30 percent in four other districts compared to its national average of 27 percent. In the 1978 elections in France, the PCF managed to obtain pluralities of over 40 percent in eight departments and over 30 percent in many others. As long ago as 1946, the first postwar election, the communists in Italy were able to obtain over 30 percent of the vote in the districts of Firenze-Pistoia and Emilia-Romagna.

The Regional Strength of the Communist Party

The two legislative elections and the more recent municipal elections pinpoint the party's strength and weakness.[5] Undoubtedly resistance to the communist appeal is strongest in those parts of rural Spain where small- and medium-sized landowners dominate and the voters retain their Catholic tradition, such as Old Castile, the only exception being Valladolid—the largest and most industrial city in the region. It had a relatively strong socialist tradition before the civil war, and fascist violence during the first days of the conflict

Table 2. Maximum and Minimum Vote for Selected Parties in Spain (1977 and 1979), Portugal (1976), and Italy (1976).

	Maximum	Minimum
Communists		
Spain 1977	20.0 Barcelona	1.6 Orense
1979	18.9 Córdoba	1.5 Lugo
Portugal	44.3 Setubal	1.5 Island Districts
Italy	50.4 Firenze-Pistoia	23.1 Brescia-Bergamo
Socialists		
Spain 1977	40.0 Málaga	12.2 Lugo
1979	41.9 Jaén	14.5 Las Palmas
Portugal	44.7 Faro	22.6 Braganca
Italy (PSI)	13.5 Mantova-Cremona	7.6 Roma-Viterbo Latina-Frosinone
Center-right		
Spain (UCD) 1977	67.5 Avila	14.9 Barcelona
1979	65.0 Avila	15.1 Guipúzcoa
Portugal		
PPD	57.0 Horta (Açores)	8.2 Beja
CDS	32.1 Guarda	4.2 Beja
Italy (DC)	55.5 Verona, Padova Vicenza, Rovigo	25.8 Bologna, Ferrara Ravenna, Forli

Spain   50 provinces, 1977, 1979.
Portugal: 22 districts, 1976.
Italy: 32 constituencies, 1976.

was particularly strong. Valladolid is the only province in Castile-León in which the party gained slightly more than 5 percent of the vote in 1977. Its success in some mining communities in the province of León enabled the party to obtain an even greater margin of support in 1979, as it did in the relatively industrialized province formerly linked with Castile but now manifesting a separate regional identity in the province of Santander.

Another area of considerable weakness in the primarily rural interior provinces is Galicia, in spite of the dominant role played by the communists in catalyzing labor unrest under Franco, the success of Comisiones Obreras in trade-union elections, and the presence of communist leaders of considerable prestige in the labor movement.

Even though there can be little doubt that the minifundia owners in the countryside continue to resist the PCE, the lists of communist candidates presented at the municipal level in the 1979 local elections show that the party has a weak infrastructure. Migration has drained the region of the most politically-active younger population who would most probably be susceptible to the appeals of the party. To these difficulties and the influence of local notables and cacique structures should be added the competition posed by the extreme left nationalist Marxist revolutionary movement, the Bloque Nacional-Popular Galego, in appealing to the more radical students, intellectuals, and working-class electorate in the region.[6]

The Canary Islands, despite the relatively low standard of living in the area, the oligarchic structures of the society, the inequalities in land ownership, and considerable discontent, is another area of persistent communist weakness,[7] which can be attributed to the competitiveness of a splinter group that severed its connection to the communist party. In the form of an extremist, nationalist, independence movement with terrorist tendencies (the Movimiento para la Autodeterminación e Independencia del Archipiélago Canario, MPAIAC), its electoral expression—Coalición Unión del Pueblo Canario—managed to elect one deputy in 1979 and gained 13.4 percent of the vote in Las Palmas and 8.4 in Santa Cruz de Tenerife, compared to 2.8 and 4.6 percent of the vote obtained by the communist party in those provinces.

The most striking case of successful competition waged by nationalist revolutionary Marxist-Leninist parties can be found in the Basque country—one of the two most industrialized regions of Spain.[8] Only in Vizcaya was the communist vote slightly over 5 percent of the poll, whereas in Guipúzcoa it was 3.6 percent in 1977 and even less than that in 1979. In this region leftist parties such as the MC-OIC have posed significant challenges to the PCE. The Basque country is also a region in which the socialist tradition and the hold of the PSOE over a large portion of the immigrant Castilian-speaking working class represent a serious barrier to the progress of the PCE. The PSOE has also suffered from nationalist competition for the working-class left vote.

The situation in the other industrialized region, in which the most distinctive national identity, strong aspirations toward autonomy, and bilingualism are apparent, is different inasmuch as it is favorable to the PCE. The communist advantage in Catalonia derives from the support gained in the four Catalan provinces, particularly in Barcelona and its metropolitan area, by the PSUC—the Catalan federate party. In 1977 Barcelona was the province in which the party reached its highest vote, 19.9 percent of the votes cast and slightly more of the valid votes, a record that in 1979 was surpassed by a few decimal points in Andalucía in the largely rural province of Córdoba. In the other Catalan provinces, the party in 1977 held close to or exceeded the national average. In 1979, for reasons hard to explain, in three of the Catalan provinces, the PSUC suffered slight losses. Nevertheless, of all industrial regions of Spain, Catalonia is the one in which the communists are strongest.

Their strength can be traced to the fact that before the civil war, the PSOE, at least electorally and organizationally, was virtually nonexistent and since the early decades of the century, the UGT had lost the working class to the anarcho-syndicalist CNT and therefore could not rely on a party- or trade-union tradition, as it could in Madrid, the Basque country, Asturias, and even the cities of Old Castile.[9] This part of the country was for a considerable period of the civil war on the republican revolutionary side, and therefore the party had gained influence during the war. Thanks to the international support that it enjoyed, the party was able to build a cadre of supporters. The historic crisis of anarchosyndicalism, its lack of international reference points, and the post-Franco weakness of the CNT have undoubtedly benefited the PSUC and the CCOO trade-union federation.[10] In addition, during the Franco period, the communists, inspired by the position taken by the communist movements and the Soviet Union on the nationalities question, espoused autonomy and self-determination in Catalonia, a stand that facilitated their penetration of the native Catalan-speaking electorate.

The electoral map reveals that the party is appreciably stronger in the east and in the south of Spain. [Perhaps the fact that the south-center of Spain and the País Valencià fell into Franco's hands at the end of the civil war allowed the party to build an organization that it did not have before and, with its moderation dictated by Stalin, appeal to segments of the population that were afraid of the social revolution that was taking place.] This is the region in which the PCE made significant progress between the two legislative elections. The role played by the party during the civil war, as well as the relative weakness of the socialists in the thirties, stemming from the eminent place occupied by the CNT in the labor movement, considerable secularization, and even anticlericalism, may account for the somewhat surprising strength of the party in Valencià province, even in rural communities where landownership is relatively widespread. Another factor is the importance of the cooperatives in which the communists seem to have placed capable activists. Valencia is perhaps the most interesting case of discontinuity in political orientation: It has shifted from left-bourgeois republicanism to strong support for the PSOE and even the PCE.[11] It is also a bilingual region, but, as in Catalonia, extreme left nationalist groups have not emerged in some areas or failed in their appeals to the electorate in other areas, in contrast to the multiplicity of political groups that contend in the Basque country and to a lesser extent in Galicia and the Canary Islands.

Latifundia Spain, the provinces south of Madrid and particularly the Guadalquivir Valley, constitutes one of the areas of PCE strength—an area analogous to that of latifundia Portugal, a stronghold of the PCP.[12] However, despite the PCE's considerable progress between the two elections, its strength does not extend to all the latifundia provinces. In Badajoz, one of the two provinces of Extremadura that have sustained traditions of radical socialist rural protest, the PSOE has succeeded in holding its own. Despite the PCE's recent progress in the areas in which the PSOE was implanted before the civil war, areas such as the provinces of Jaén and Granada are still strongholds of the PSOE, whereas in the more industrial and urbanized western Andalucian provinces, Córdoba and Sevilla, the PCE occupies a dominant position in a number of communities.[13] A more detailed analysis would show to what extent the centers of communist strength coincide with those in which the anarchosyndicalist movement had been most successful before the civil war.

The party has a long history in the south. At the Andalucian regional conference in March 1932 there were 98 delegates, 75 from Sevilla—the strongest organization in the country, with 1,600 members—8 from the villages of the province, 7 from Córdoba, 2 from Málaga, 2 from Jaén, 2 from

Granada—representing 5,750 members in Andalucía, of which 1,800 came from Córdoba and 1,600 from Sevilla. José Díaz, then secretary general of the organization in Sevilla, eventually became secretary general of the party. Approximately 10,000 members were represented at the fourth congress as well as 4,000 or 5,000 from the youth organization. Even though those figures are debated, party membership ranged from 8,547 to 11,874. In any case, one-half of the membership appears to have been Andalucian.

The red belt around Madrid, a city that became a major industrial center in the Franco era and attracted masses of immigrants who did not share the socialist-party and trade-union tradition of the native working class of the city, is one of the strongholds of the party. It produced 14 percent of the vote in 1979. The communist vote in Madrid was less than in Lisbon and some of its metropolitan districts. Whereas the maximum vote of the PCE in any of the 18 districts of Madrid city in 1977 was 22.9 percent and 29 percent in the municipalities surrounding the city, in 5 communities around Lisbon—particularly south of the Tejo River where emigrants from the communist countryside constitute an important segment of the electorate—the PCP managed to gain over 50 percent of the votes. In the city of Lisbon, the party achieved 23.5 percent in the 1975 elections in one of the 53 districts into which it was divided.[14]

As will become apparent from the analysis of party competition, the presence of parties to the left of the PCE in several provinces of Spain accounts for the communists' relative weakness. The social structure of those areas, in terms of industrialization and patterns of rural property ownership, does not explain the party's electoral performance, which is a function of a number of factors: the nature of the existing social structure, the strength of political traditions, for example, there are indications that the areas in which the CNT used to be strong may be more susceptible to communist appeal, the competition mounted by the Marxist-Leninist revolutionary nationalist movements, and the presence of parties to the left of the PCE, which, for a variety of reasons, splintered from it or emerged during the struggle waged against the Franco regime. These factors have conduced to the advantage of the PCE in only a few provinces. Undoubtedly communist competition with the PSOE, which, in part, is a function of the historical strength of the socialists in certain parts of Spain, is a major but by no means the only factor accounting for the relative strength of the two major working-class parties. One area in which competition between the two major parties proceeds without challenge from the other leftist parties is Asturias, where the UGT and the socialists built a strong organization relatively early. In the recent elections, the PCE reinforced its strong presence in many of the mining communities in the area. The PSOE has held onto its dominant position by winning 37 percent of the vote, compared to 14 percent for the PCE.

Progress or Stagnation: The Dynamics of the Left Vote Between 1977 and 1979

Analyzing changes in support for the parties, which should be discernible in the second legislative election held on March 1, 1979, is complicated because of the simultaneous increase in the size of the electorate and a large decrease in participation, which, at the national level, was almost equivalent to the number of voters in 1977 and led to a decrease in the absolute number of voters in some of the provinces, making it very difficult to determine which party lost or gained votes from others and how many of the losses can be attributed to the increase in abstentions and to the vote of the 18-21 year olds who were enfranchised after 1977, whereas others, illegal and competing either under fronts or advocating abstention in 1977, appeared on the ballot in 1979. (See Table 3.)

Table 3. Gains and Losses of the PCE-PSUC and PSOE in the 52 Electoral Districts Between 1977 and 1979.

Provinces of Disproportionate PCE Gains

	Changes in: PCE Vote	PSOE Vote	PSP/US Vote 1977
Albacete	4.44	6.25	—
Valencia	4.19	.42	5.18
Jaén	3.50	2.79	2.05
Madrid	3.31	3.15	9.08
Asturias	3.28	5.66	7.13
Granada	2.88	-3.39	3.58
Zaragoza	2.79	.99	10.53
Sevilla	2.78	-7.07	4.78
Toledo	2.65	.64	1.56
Badajoz	2.43	3.28	1.70
Almería	2.02	9.77	2.96
Alicante	2.01	.43	3.88

Provinces of Moderate PCE Gains

	Changes in: PCE Vote	PSOE Vote	PSP/US Vote 1977
Cuenca	1.97	8.87	1.52
Cáceres	1.91	10.01	1.99
Pontevedra	1.82	.47	4.80
Segovia	1.69	1.87	6.16
Huelva	1.56	1.80	2.52
Guadalajara	1.53	2.54	2.52
Ciudad Real	1.49	7.43	5.44
Burgos	1.43	-0.58	3.12
Valladolid	1.40	-0.35	2.48
Castellón	1.34	6.19	2.67
Murcia	1.33	4.35	5.02
Avila	1.29	5.65	1.67
León	1.25	3.68	3.34
Santander	1.14	4.07	2.57
Salamanca	1.12	3.50	5.69
Córdoba	1.11	-3.68	3.62
Huesca	1.08	6.89	11.00

Provinces of PCE or PSUC Losses

	Changes in: PCE or PSUC Vote	PSOE Vote	PSP/US Vote 1977
Tarragona	-1.66	.31	—
Lérida	-1.58	9.81	—
Barcelona	-1.22	-.78	1.55
Melilla	-.58	-5.72	—
Gerona	-.94	2.99	.69
Guipúzcoa	-.61	-5.60	1.45
Lugo	-.18	5.16	5.47

Provinces of Small or No Advance for the PCE

	Changes in: PCE Vote	PSOE Vote	PSP/US Vote 1977
Coruña	.96	.57	5.17
Orense	.96	3.17	1.44
Palencia	.87	.71	2.97
Soria	.76	7.42	4.75
Zamora	.71	2.16	2.08
Málaga	.67	-3.01	1.31
Balearic Is.	.65	6.89	4.98
Teruel	.63	9.32	3.58
Logroño	.59	2.85	2.28
Cádiz	.48	-6.37	9.57
Vizcaya	.47	-5.70	2.06
St. Cruz de Tenerife	.45	2.06	5.41
Navarra	.22	.63	2.45
Las Palmas	.20	5.33	2.46
Alava	.01	-6.17	1.32
Ceuta	—	2.82	11.24

Data from *El País,* May 2 and 3, 1979, and D. G. de Política Interior, Ministerio de la Gobernación.

In this respect, it is important to know that in 1977 the Partido Socialista Popular (PSP), under the leadership of Enrique Tierno, competed under the label PSP/US, Partido Socialista Popular/Unidad Socialista, grouping a series of regional parties with a left socialist outlook, but did not appear on the ballot in 1979.[15] The PSP fused with the PSOE, its leader becoming the honorary president of the PSOE. A number of its candidates ran on the PSOE ticket, giving the socialists considerable hope that the vote for the PSP would be transferred to the PSOE in the election. However, many of those voting for the PSP/US were really voting for the regional socialist parties that had joined in coalition with the PSP and continued on the ballot as separate parties, particularly the Partido Socialista de Andalucía (PSA). A major change in the 1979 election was the appearance on the ballot of Herri Batasuna, an extreme left nationalist Basque party coalition of the abertzale (patriotic) left. Its voters were primarily those who abstained in 1977 or supported Euskadiko Ezkerra and the newly-enfranchised youth.

All these factors have to be considered when comparing progress made between the two elections by the two nationwide leftist parties: the PCE-PSUC and the PSOE. The dynamics of those two parties is central to understanding the future of the Spanish party system and the PCE. Without some hypotheses about PCE-PSUC and PSOE trends and the outcome of their competition for the support of the electorate, we would be unable to ascertain whether Spain is moving in the direction followed by Italy over the last thirty years (during which period the PSI split and in successive elections was reduced to its present minority status to the relative advantage of the PCI) or whether it is following the French model, according to which the communist advance has been checked, and the socialists have regained and retained a strong position on the left. The results of one election cannot provide a definitive answer. The complexity of the returns makes even tentative conclusions difficult. Public-opinion data are of limited help, and a thorough ecological analysis at the municipal level, both for the whole of Spain and for the regions that present quite different patterns, has not yet been carried out. Nevertheless, we can point to some tentative conclusions on the basis of the returns at the provincial level that constitutes the Spanish election district.

The national returns suggest that the PCE has made an advance that fell below its expectations. The PSUC, so important within the PCE-PSUC bloc, however, suffered significant losses in three of the Catalan provinces, in contrast to the PCE that lost votes in only two provinces and in the district of Melilla (an enclave on the northern Moroccan coast). In this analysis we used the difference in the percentage of votes received in 1977 and 1979 (both calculated on the basis of the total number of voters, including void and blank votes because the latter might have political significance in some regions, particularly in the Basque country). If those invalid votes had been ignored, the percentages would be slightly larger for the parties, but the patterns would not be different.

The gains made by the PCE in most provinces were quite small. In 15 of the 52 districts, they were less than 1 percent, and only in one, Ceuta—an enclave on the southern shore of the Strait of Gibraltar—the PCE did not present a candidate. In 17 districts, its progress was less than 2 percent, and in 12, it exceeded 2 percent, with a maximum of 4.4 percent. Many of the areas in which the PCE made no progress are the less populated provinces of the Spanish interior, provincial areas that have retained strong conservative orientations. Success was achieved in provinces that contain large populations and in a number of very important metropolitan and urban centers. Even so, PCE leaders cannot ignore the fact that in some areas of traditional party strength, such as Málaga and Cádiz, that include large urban and important industrial centers, progress was small. The same result was recorded in Córdoba, an Andalucian province in which the PCE should have demonstrated its greatest strength but gained only 1.11 percent over 1977.

The 1979 returns confirm the fundamental weakness of the PCE in the second most industrial region of Spain, the Basque country: It made absolutely no progress in Alava, minimal progress in Vizcaya, lost some of the few votes that it had obtained in Guipúzcoa in 1977, and merely held its own in Navarra. Certainly, it proved more adept in holding onto its few votes in that region than did the PSOE, which suffered losses above 5 percent in Alava, Vizcaya, and Guipúzcoa. The PCE was unable to stem the wave of support for the left-wing Basque nationalists. With the exception of the province of Pontevedra, the PCE has been unable to overcome its weakness in Galicia, where the gains achieved by the left in the election of 1979 belong to the Bloque Nacional Popular Galego (BNPG). Minimal communist gains in the Canary Islands once more show that the competition of radical nationalist movements limits the progress of the PCE.

In the more favorable returns, the success of the party in Valencia, Madrid, Asturias, Zaragoza, and three Andalucian provinces—Jaén, Granada, and Sevilla—stands out. Those provinces are comprised of some of the largest metropolitan areas of Spain, and some are important industrial centers. In all of them except Asturias, the PCE's progress has exceeded that of the PSOE, which, in two Andalucian provinces, suffered losses because of the performance of the Partido Socialista de Andalucía. Signs in the more successful districts and in those where the PCE made moderate gains suggest that southern and central-southern Spain, which in part coincide with the old latifundia areas, constitute the most promising field for the party. Despite the promising outlook in those areas, in the two provinces of Extremadura that have long traditions of socialist rural protest, the PSOE's gains have been larger than those of the PCE.

The 1979 gains do not represent any breakthrough in areas where the party was weak in 1977. Nor did the party achieve success in such areas as the Basque country and some of the industrial centers of Galicia, the social structures of which should conduce to the advantage of the PCE. One of the positive results of the election for the PCE was that it sustained its momentum in Valencia and Alicante, two districts in which the strong showing of the party in the 1977 election had not been predicted. Perhaps the only surprise was the PCE's modest gains in the industrializing provinces of the Castilian heartland, Burgos and Valladolid. In the latter province, which has a socialist tradition, the PSOE experienced light losses.

The overall picture that emerges from these trends is that with the exception of Catalonia, the PCE has been inching ahead in most of Spain. It made significant gains in a few industrialized areas, Andalucía and some south-central agrarian provinces.

How does the picture look for the PCE's main competitor, the PSOE?[16] If we compare the votes for the party ticket in 1977 and 1979, the PSOE, too, made progress in most of Spain but experienced losses in 10 of the 52 districts. Those losses were heavy in the Basque country and Andalucía, where it made progress in only 3 of the 8 provinces but not in the most populated urban and industrial ones. In contrast to the PCE, the PSOE made some gains in Galicia and in the Canary Islands, two areas in which it had been relatively weak. In the Castilian heartland, where the more urban and industrial working class has a socialist tradition, the PSOE's progress was significant. But given the number of seats allocated to those largely depopulated provinces and the strength of the UCD, those gains are not significant. Only in Aragón were they important but not in the metropolitan center of Zaragoza, which includes most of the population in the region. In contrast to the PSUC, the PSC-PSOE made progress in two of the Catalan provinces, even though it experienced a slight loss in the giant metropolitan area of Barcelona. Certainly, in one of the key areas of competition between the communists and the socialists—the great industrial region of Catalonia—the PSC-PSOE achieved a better performance. The heavy losses of the PSOE in Andalucía seem to have benefited the regional socialist party, the PSA. In this crucial area of Spain, the future strength of the PCE and the PSOE depends on the capacity of that new party, which primarily gathered protest votes, to hold onto its electorate. A comparison of the 1977 and 1979 vote was heartening to the socialists, but heavy losses in areas of traditional strength, such as the Basque country and parts of Andalucía, were perceived as a serious defeat.

The optimistic evaluation of the changes between the two elections for the PSOE would be tempered if we consider the expectations generated by the fusion between the PSP and the PSOE. It is hard to say to what extent expectations that the PSP vote would be transferred to the PSOE were justifiable, particularly considering the fact that the PSP/US lists in 1977 reflected a coalition between the PSP and regional socialist parties, some of which retained their identity in 1979. But there can be little doubt that in areas of PSP electoral strength, one could have expected that vote to strengthen the unified socialist party. If the PSP/US votes in 1977 are subtracted from the gains made by the PSOE in 1979, the PSP's strength in a significant number of districts was larger than the gains made by the PSOE between the two elections. This means that a number of PSP voters must have gone to other parties—perhaps in some cases to the communists—or abstained.

The inclusion of the PSP in our analysis certainly makes the gains of the PSOE look much more modest in many parts of Spain. Let us take one particularly important case, Madrid. Under the leadership of Tierno, who is now the PSOE mayor of Madrid, the PSP won 9.08 percent of the vote in 1977. But in 1979 the PSOE gained only 3.15 percent more votes, whereas the communists gained 3.31 percent. There certainly must have been considerable shifts in the votes for the major parties of the left. Inasmuch as the parties of the extreme left, ORT and PTE, experienced no losses and some gains, the strengthening of the PCE cannot be attributed to them. To what extent 9 percent of voters of the PSP divided their votes between the PSOE and the PCE and perhaps the center-right parties or abstained is almost impossible to estimate without a detailed analysis. Only a careful ecological analysis of the PSP vote, taking into account the presence of former PSP leaders on the lists of the PSOE and the distinctive identity of the regional parties within the PSP/US coalition, could enable us to ascertain where the vote of this third nationwide party of the left went in the 1979 legislative election.

Although the challenge presented by the regional extreme left in the Basque country limited the expansion of the communist electorate and the presence of regional extreme left parties in Galicia and the Canary Islands represented competition for scarce votes on the left end of the political spectrum, given the social structure and the political culture of those areas, the numerous communist parties to the left of the PCE appear to be insignificant at the nationwide level. The fractionalization of the extreme left manifest in the presence on the ballot of nine communist parties and one syndicalist party and the electoral law that discriminates against small parties and allocates fewer seats to the large urban concentrations can lead one to ignore their impact. But it would be a mistake to dismiss the Marxist parties to the left of the PCE, for they won 552,302 votes, that is, 3.08 percent of the vote, in 1979, compared to the almost 2 million votes, or 10.8 percent, won by the PCE-PSUC. (See Table 4.) Those dispersed votes represent 22 percent of the total of 2,491,206 votes cast in 1979 for all communist parties and, therefore, a significant loss of potential PCE voters.

Table 4. Vote for Parties or Candidates to the Left of the PCE in 1979 and 1977.

Vote in 1979	Votes	Percent of Vote
PTE Partido del Trabajo de España	192,440	1.07
ORT Organización Revolucionaria de Trabajadores	138,634	.77
MC-OIC Movimiento Comunista-Organización de Izquierda Comunista	84,505	.47
PC de T Partido Comunista de los Trabajadores	47,828	.27
LCR Liga Comunista Revolucionaria	36,818	.21
LC Liga Comunista	3,365	.02
OCE-BR Organización Comunista de España-Bandera Roja	23,258	.13
OCE-BR-UCE	1,832	.011
OCE-UCE	922	.013
UCE Unificación Comunista de España	20,386	.11
POC Partido Obrero y Campesino	2,314	.005
Total Marxist parties to the left of the PCE-PSUC	552,302	3.08
Partido Sindicalista	9,743	.05
PCE-PSUC	1,938,904	10.80
Vote in 1977		
FDI Frente Democrático de Izquierdas (Standing for PTE) outside Catalonia*	155,881	.85
AET Agrupación Electoral de los Trabajadores (Standing for ORT)	80,121	.44
FUT Frente para la Unidad de los Trabajadores	37,992	.21
Total	273,994	1.50
PCE-PSUC	1,655,744	9.08

*FDI formed joint lists with Esquerra Republicana de Catalunya, obtaining 103,959 votes and one seat for Esquerra.

This table does not include the regional-nationalist extreme left parties nor 1977 isolated candidatures.

Probably in no other European country does the communist party encounter such strong competition from assorted Maoist, Trotzkyite, and other dissident groups. Certainly, the ratio of such extreme left groups to the PCI in Italy is completely different. In addition, some of the extreme left parties in Spain have considerable strength in some districts, including important industrial centers such as Navarra where the vote exceeds that of the PCE. Some have trade-union federations that have done quite well in some places. The militancy, enthusiasm, and considerable campaign resources of those parties cannot be ignored. It is tempting to attribute the presence of those parties to the Eurocommunist line of the PCE, but in Portugal, where the PCP has taken a hard, anti-Eurocommunist line, their impact is not at all negligible.

The presence of this left should be linked to the historical context in which the Spanish party system evolved, the polycentrism and fractionalization of the communist movement after Stalin, and the new radicalism that emerged after the events in France in May 1968. A comparison of the returns of 1977, when those parties appeared under other names and were illegal, and 1979 shows that in a number of places they have made progress. Their presence on the political scene can catalyze the centripetal potential of the Spanish party system and may prove to be a source of social and political tension. By using the symbols of communism, the left could arouse the suspicions of some voters about the PCE. Their presence at the local level and in the factories can be a source of tension for the PCE and the CCOO, as happened recently in Navarra.

It remains to be seen whether the fusion of the two largest Marxist-Leninist parties that have roots in a number of districts—the Partido del Trabajo de España (PTE) and the Organización Revolucionaria de Trabajadores (ORT)—that won, respectively, 138,634 and 84,505 votes, or 1.24 percent of the total vote, will endure. Despite their initial radicalism, their doctrinaire positions, and their positions on the Moncloa Pacts, these two parties have experienced centripetal pressures, as reflected in their positions toward the constitution and the autonomy statute of Euskadi. Whether their search for respectability will make it easier for them to compete with the PCE or will propel their supporters to shift to the weak but much more extremist groups to their left remains to be seen. Should the union succeed, the PCE will not be able to discount the significance of the united PTE-ORT, even if it decides to continue its strategy of ignoring revolutionary parties in its pronouncements.

Stable or Unstable Electorates?

One of the most intriguing questions about an emerging electorate and party system is how stable are party identifications likely to be. Some of the data that we have analyzed about changes between the two elections indicate considerable stability in the electorate of the major parties, except on the right, within the Basque country and to some extent in Andalucía, where the PSA has competed successfully with the PSOE.[17]

The most important question, however, is how will competition develop between the communists and the socialists and between the UCD and the PSOE. To explore these questions, a survey conducted in the summer of 1978, that is, in a period between elections, posed questions designed to elicit from the potential supporters of each party their second choices if, for one reason or another, they could not vote for their first choices. When confronted with that situation, 62 percent of the potential communist voters chose the PSOE, 16 percent chose the PTE, and 11 percent chose the ORT. Almost all the remaining 11 percent were either undecided or stated that they would abstain. The PSOE supporters divided almost equally between those prepared to give their second-choice votes to the PCE—37 percent—and to the UCD—40 percent. A minority of 5 percent preferred the parties to the left of the communists to the PCE, and a significant minority of 13 percent declared that they were ready to abstain. The same dichotomy of choice was found in the electorate of the UCD, 44 percent preferring the PSOE as a second choice and 31 percent the AP.

To determine the leanings of the voters, we went one step further and divided the constituencies of the different parties not only by that second choice but by the proximity of the respondent's ideological position to that of the party of his or her second choice. In this way we defined as leaning toward one or another party those who selected it as a second choice and felt very or fairly close to the ideological position that they perceived to be espoused by the party of their second choice. By using these two criteria, we found that 57 percent of the PCE supporters had a leaning toward the PSOE. Among socialist voters, 33 percent can be defined as leaning toward the PCE and 29 percent as leaning toward the UCD, with 37 percent not fitting the definition to be classified as leaning in neither direction. In the UCD electorate, we found a similar potential or shift toward neighboring parties, with approximately 35 percent leaning toward the PSOE, about 25 percent toward the AP, and 40 percent without any leaning in either direction. These data suggest considerable room for turnover between the parties, which would be reflected in a panel study but not necessarily in the electoral returns.

For our purposes, the most interesting questions are what are the characteristics of those who have specific leanings, and how close are those who have tendencies toward other parties to the positions of those parties.

If we turn to the figures relating to self-placement on the left-right scale (see Table 5), there is relatively little difference between PCE-PSUC supporters with no leaning toward

Table 5. Self-Placement on the Left-Right Dimension of Potential PCE-PSUC, PSOE, and UCD Voters with Different Leanings.

	PCE-PSUC		PSOE			UCD	
	With No PSOE Leaning	PSOE Leaning	PCE-PSUC Leaning	With No Leaning	UCD Leaning	PSOE Leaning	No Leaning
Scale							
1	10	7	3	2	1	—	—
2	22	20	9	5	1	—	—
3	35	41	33	26	16	2	2
4	19	19	37	30	32	9	6
5	4	3	9	20	25	40	34
in the middle	2	1	1	4	6	7	9
6	3	1	1	5	8	28	23
7-10	1	1	1	1	9	9	17
n.a.	4	6	6	4	1	5	9
	(259)	(340)	(628)	(703)	(548)	(555)	(629)

the PSOE and those who have been classified as potentially leaning toward the PSOE. Their positions on this scale and their attitudes on a number of issues are still quite far from those of the PSOE electorate, even of the left wing of the PSOE. Considering this pattern, it seems unlikely that the socialists can make many inroads into the communist electorate. If we turn to the PSOE voters, we find considerable differences in placement and attitudes between the one-third leaning toward the PCE and the somewhat less than one-third leaning toward the UCD, showing the heterogeneity of the socialist electorate. Among those with leanings toward the PCE, 12 percent placed themselves on points one and two of the scale, and another 33 percent placed themselves on point 3. Among those leaning toward the UCD, the proportions were 2 and 16 percent, respectively. Even so, the PSOE voters with leanings toward the UCD were considerably to the left—on the scale—of the UCD voters with leanings toward the PSOE. One-half of the socialist voters with a leaning toward the UCD placed themselves on or below four on the left-right scale, compared to only 12 percent of the UCD supporters with a leaning toward the PSOE. This finding confirms that even on the borderlines between the parties, party preferences are congruent with the ideological orientations of the voters and that the room that would ensure party competition for those less committed voters is not that great.

If we turn to ideological positions (see Table 6), it is evident that on central issues, such as Marxism, the monarchy, attitudes toward the United States, and religious issues, particularly aid for private schools, the communist electorate is homogeneous. Even those with leanings toward the socialists hold positions quite different from the left wing of the PSOE electorate.

This relative homogeneity of the supporters of the PCE-PSUC contrasts with the heterogeneity of those of the PSOE. Almost one-half of those with leanings toward the com-

Table 6. Response to Political Alternatives by Potential Voters of the PCE-PSUC, PSOE, and UCD of Different Leanings (1978).

	PCE-PSUC		PSOE			UCD
	With No Leaning to PSOE	Leaning to PSOE	Leaning to PCE-PSUC	With No Leaning	Leaning to UCD	Leaning to PSOE
Preferences:						
Marxism	66	75	48	28	14	6
No Marxism	24	17	31	48	59	68
Monarchy	16	21	30	33	69	77
Republic	68	66	54	47	22	8
Friendship with:						
the United States	9	8	9	20	22	31
the Soviet Union	19	29	16	8	5	2
Both	53	49	56	49	54	53
Neither	13	10	13	12	11	6
Anticlericalism	65	68	50	45	28	10
Clericalism	24	17	31	48	59	68
No aid to private education	78	80	67	56	47	38
Aid to private education	25	16	25	36	42	52
Order	13	15	16	23	36	42
Freedom	40	38	34	32	14	11
Both	48	47	49	45	50	47
	(259)	(340)	(628)	(703)	(548)	(555)

The difference between those expressing an opinion and 100% recorded for each of the alternatives is comprised of those who rejected both alternatives, did not answer, or said "both," seeing positive and negative sides to the alternatives offered.

munists express preference for Marxism, whereas over one-half of those with leanings toward the UCD prefer "no Marxism." The monarchy is accepted by fewer than one-third of PSOE supporters with leanings toward the communists, compared to 69 percent with leanings toward the UCD who favor that institution.

There are similar differences on religious issues and on attitudes toward foreign affairs. Three times as many socialists with leanings toward the communists express a preference for friendship with the Soviet Union as do socialists who lean in the direction of the government party, whereas more than two times as many socialists with a UCD inclination as socialists with a pro-PCE leaning favor friendship with the United States. Significantly, those having no inclination toward the left or the right among socialist voters occupy an intermediate position that places them closer to the left on some issues and closer to the right on other issues. Their republicanism brings them closer to the left, but they are considerably less sympathetic to Marxism and appreciably more favorable to the United States than those on the left within the party. In terms of overall self-placement on the left-right scale, however, they are slightly closer to the left than to the right within the party, suggesting that they share some of the doctrinaire attitudes of the left, as their antipathy toward the monarchy and their preference for freedom rather than order show, but on some specific issues, they seem to be closer to social democratic positions.

However, there is not much affinity between PSOE supporters who lean toward the UCD and UCD supporters who lean toward the PSOE. Both groups would have to change their positions on a number of issues before they could vote for the other party, confirming our general impression that despite some temptations to shift sides before the 1979 election, most voters would ratify their original choices. It is hard to say how many votes would be lost or gained by the PSOE if it shifted in either direction. Certainly, maintaining its

ideological positions and some of its policies would not contribute toward making inroads into the UCD electorate, even
among those who do not reject the possibility of voting for
the PSOE. On the other hand, the more decided shift in a
right direction to gain UCD votes would consolidate PSOE
support among voters with some leanings toward the UCD
but would probably alienate a significant number of voters
who lean toward the PCE. These data suggest that the initial
ambivalence and ambiguity of PSOE positions have created
heterogeneous outlooks on the part of the party's electorate
or reflect that heterogeneity. For reasons too complex to be
explained here, we believe that in its formative stages after
the death of Franco and during the first year of democratization, the party contributed to that heterogeneity and made
possible the affinity expressed by a significant segment of the
socialist electorate for the positions of the PCE.

The data not only seem to suggest that the PCE does not
have much to fear from PSOE competition but that the socialists have an exposed left flank. Consequently, their
chances of making any deep inroad into the UCD electorate
are not favorable unless the UCD moves considerably toward
the right—a mistake that it may well make. The socialist
leadership may have to maintain ambiguous and ambivalent
positions in order to retain the party's electorate—positions
that would limit their capacity to expand in the short run,
would probably ensure the loyalty of those who lean toward
the PCE, and would probably lead to contradictions that
would have to be resolved if the party shared governmental
power. Those contradictions have made a segment of its constituency susceptible to appeals by the PCE whose moderate
position may bring it closer to the PSOE. Unfortunately, the
number of cases examined does not allow a similar analysis of
communist voters who lean toward the Marxist parties to the
left of the PCE. But their number is not large, and although
the PCE cannot neglect them, the threat of extreme left

competition is perceived to be not great and may explain the communist leaders' professed ignorance of that competition.

An analysis of the social composition of the segments within the socialist and communist electorates (see Table 7) reveals that in terms of subjective class identification, communist voters defining themselves as working class have greater leanings toward the PSOE, whereas socialist voters identifying themselves as working class are slightly more likely to lean toward the PCE. The differences among age groups are insignificant, except that relatively few of the socialist voters leaning toward the communists can be found among the young.

The Image of the PCE-PSUC

There is great disagreement between the image that communist supporters and those of the other parties hold of the PCE. Naturally, differences are greatest among them and the supporters of the right, Alianza Popular. But they are also significant in the case of the UCD and even of the PSOE. An overwhelming number of PCE-PSUC supporters consider their party to be democratic, whereas close to one-third of PSOE supporters question that characteristic. UCD voters expressing an opinion are almost equally divided, and more than one-third of the electorate expressing an opinion deny that the PCE possesses that quality. In this respect, the image of the PCE is more favorable than that of the PCI, for in Italy only 47 percent of socialist voters consider the party democratic, compared to 30 percent who deny that it possesses that quality. Only 20 percent of Christian Democratic voters (a party that would be equivalent to the UCD in the Italian political spectrum) granted it that quality, whereas 15 percent denied it in 1975.[18] The image of the PSOE in this respect is quite different: Only 12 percent of the electorate question its democratic character, and even 62 percent of

Table 7. Social Characteristics of Potential Voters of the PCE-PSUC and PSOE in 1978 with Different Leanings.

	PCE-PSUC		PSOE		
	Without PSOE Leanings	With PSOE Leanings	With PCE-PSUC Leanings	With No Leaning	With UCD Leanings
Male	69	60	56	53	46
Age:					
18-20	9	7	8	9	4
21-24	18	12	13	11	7
25-34	27	22	26	25	24
35-44	18	22	21	21	27
45-54	14	18	16	15	16
55-64	9	7	10	10	10
65 and over	4	11	7	8	11
Subjective Class:					
Upper	1	—	—	—	—
Upper Middle	9	8	13	13	15
Lower Middle	32	27	35	37	40
Working	56	63	51	47	43
n.a.	2	, 2	2	4	2

those who vote for its main opponents, the UCD, consider it democratic. There is no major difference in the republican images of the two major parties of the left. In fact the communists, whose party, after its legalization in 1977, recognized the monarchy under the condition that it be democratic, perceive their party as less republican than do the socialists who, during the constitutional debates, made a formal statement affirming their republican faith even when they voted to institute a monarchical constitution. The communists consider themselves members of a Marxist party and so do the electorate who express an opinion. Only a small minority thinks that the party is not Marxist. The PSOE, which declared itself Marxist after its twenty-seventh congress and has been debating the Marxism question at its congresses since then, finally approved a platform that leaves room for both Marxists and non-Marxists in the party. The PSOE is perceived by more than one-third of the electorate expressing opinions as non-Marxist, an opinion shared by 37 percent of its voters. Marxism is therefore one of the issues that heighten as well as blur the difference between the two parties of the left.

Surprisingly, perhaps because many of the respondents do not know its meaning but value positively the term democratic, a significant proportion of the PCE-PSUC voters—37 percent—defined their party as social democratic, whereas much fewer of the PSOE supporters thought that the expression characterized the PCE-PSUC. Communist supporters overwhelmingly perceived the PSOE as a social democratic party, reiterating all the negative attitudes that they and, to a large extent, even the PSOE supporters attach to that term. In fact, fewer PSOE supporters than communist supporters are willing to call their party social democratic. Among the UCD supporters, however, the images of the two parties were reversed. Only one-third was willing to call the PCE social democratic, whereas 71 percent of those who expressed opinions considered the PSOE social democratic, ignoring its disclaimers and the unwillingness of a large number of its supporters to be so identified, despite the PSOE's linkages with the social democratic parties of northern and central Europe from which the PSOE has received support. (See Table 8.)

Developments within the PSOE in 1979 suggest that the perceptions of the communists and the electorate in general in 1978 were more accurate than the self-perceptions or self-definitions of the socialist voters. The ideological ambiguities of the socialist party in the early stages of its growth, after the restoration of democracy, will render it vulnerable to criticism and competition by the PCE should it redefine itself as social democratic.[19] The PSOE faces the situation that confronted the German SPD at the time of the debate between Bernstein and Kautsky, a schism that proved to be so costly after World War I inasmuch as it resulted in a split between the USPD and the SPD and made the USPD a way-station for the KPD. Few communists identify themselves as revolutionaries. There is no national sample that would enable us to ascertain how many Spaniards consider the party a revolutionary movement, but we have some information from a sample of Madrid voters. In the fall of 1977, 53 percent of the respondents perceived it as revolutionary, and 29 percent disagreed.[20] Among the PCE voters, 51 percent considered their party revolutionary, and 44 percent did not. The corresponding opinions among PSOE voters were 53 and 35 percent. The contrast with the socialists was quite marked: Only 23 percent of the electorate considered the PSOE revolutionary, including only 24 percent of its own supporters, despite the image that some of its leaders tried to project at that time. In the highly politically-conscious electorate of Madrid, 63 percent of UCD voters perceived the PCE as a revolutionary party, and 49 percent perceived the PCE as a defender of freedom, whereas 29 percent denied that it subscribed to that commitment.

Table 8. Image of the PCE-PSUC and PSOE Among Their Own Voters and Those of Other Parties.

		Image of the PCE-PSUC Among Voters of:				Image of the PSOE Among Voters of:			
		PCE-PSUC	PSOE	UCD	Electorate	PCE-PSUC	PSOE	UCD	Electorate
Democratic	yes	84	60	38	49	87	81	62	67
	no	9	26	36	29	7	6	14	12
Republican	yes	77	63	57	59	70	61	54	56
	no	15	21	15	18	22	24	19	22
Not Marxist	yes	13	16	13	14	30	31	25	27
	no	79	67	58	62	62	53	47	49
Social Democratic	yes	37	29	21	25	71	62	47	53
	no	51	51	44	46	18	20	19	19
Capable of avoiding political confrontation between Spaniards	yes	77	49	21	36	69	72	40	51
	no	15	36	52	40	22	13	33	25
Capable of solving the regional and nationalities problem	yes	79	53	31	41	72	73	48	55
	no	12	30	39	33	18	11	23	21
Defender of Christian values	yes	20	15	11	13	29	32	26	26
	no	70	67	63	64	60	49	49	50
In favor of subsidies to private education	yes	10	9	11	9	12	13	19	14
	no	82	74	57	65	79	70	52	61
Defender of the workers	yes	90	78	56	65	84	85	68	71
	no	4	10	19	14	9	3	10	9
Defender of the employers	yes	12	12	12	12	29	17	18	20
	no	81	74	62	66	64	68	56	58
		(599)	(1842)	(1573)	(5898)	(599)	(1842)	(1573)	(5898)

PSOE voters seem to be closer to the opinions of the electorate—respectively, 47 and 28 percent—than were communist voters who expressed the almost unanimous belief that their party was the defender of freedom. One of the great handicaps of communist parties in many countries is their perceived link with the Soviet Union and the CPSU, but in the Spanish case the perception has been neutralized primarily because of the more visible links between the European social democrats and the PSOE and in 1977 the Christian Democrats and the Equipo de la Democracia Cristiana. It is therefore not surprising that in the Madrid electorate, 68 percent perceived the PCE as linked with foreign parties. Fifty-eight percent of PCE voters agreed with 76 percent of PSOE voters. The perceptions of the PSOE's foreign connections were similar in magnitude: 72 percent of the electorate perceived it to be linked with foreign parties, as did 73 percent of its own supporters and 84 percent of those of the PCE.

One interesting difference between the perceptions of the parties of the left that the 1977 study revealed is that the PCE was perceived as slightly less favorable to self-management of enterprises than the PSOE. Sixty-four percent of PCE supporters believed that their party stood for that position, and 22 percent denied it. The proportions among PSOE supporters were 43 and 33 percent. On the other hand, an almost equal proportion of PCE and PSOE supporters believed that the PSOE stood for self-management: 56 and 58 percent.

One of the significant differences between the images held of the PCE and the PSOE is that one-half of the electorate in 1978 perceived the socialists as capable of avoiding a political confrontation between Spaniards, and only 25 percent believed that they possessed no such skill. In the case of the PCE, the proportions were 36 and 40 percent.[21] On this fundamental question, PSOE supporters were divided, 49 percent positive and 36 percent negative, whereas among the electorate, those expressing negative judgments had a slight edge—40 versus 30 percent. As far as confidence in their parties' capacities to do so was concerned, the supporters of both parties of the left did not differ. Regarding the capacity to handle the regional problem and those associated with the existence of peripheral nationalist groups, the electorate expressed more favorable opinions of the PSOE, and socialist voters expressed significantly more favorable judgments, although 30 percent of socialist respondents did not feel that the PSOE could handle that difficult problem.

As to the capacity to avoid a political confrontation between Spaniards, communist voters were more optimistic about the capacity of their party than were socialist supporters about the PSOE.

It should not be surprising that only a small number of voters considered the communist party a defender of Christian values—13 percent—and among party voters, despite efforts to identify social justice and progress with the Christian struggle against injustice and the support given by progressive Catholics to the communist party, only 20 percent of party supporters characterized the party as a defender of Christian values. The PSOE's electorate, especially its militants, cannot be identified with the church; on numerous issues the party has taken positions leading to conflict with the church, and its leaders have made less effort to "stretch out their hands" to Catholics than the PCE has made. Nevertheless, twice as many voters perceived the Socialist party as a defender of Christian values—26 percent—than voters who held corresponding perceptions of the communist party, and among supporters, 32 percent agreed with such an image of their party. There is little difference between the two parties in terms of the attitudes that their supporters perceived them to hold toward subsidies to private education, which, to a large extent, mean subsidies to church-run educational institutions: The PSOE was perceived as slightly more favorable.

Both communists and socialists considered themselves supporters of the working-class parties, and both parties were perceived as such by the electorate. But the PSOE's image was stronger largely because of disagreement expressed by a small minority of UCD and even PSOE supporters. Obviously, both the supporters of the communists and the socialists were almost unanimous in perceiving their parties as defenders of the workers, but more communists were willing to grant that position to the PSOE than socialists were willing to accord to the PCE. Congruent with their programmatic positions, neither of the two parties was perceived to define itself as a defender of the interests of employers, although a small number of the electorate and even supporters of the PSOE perceived the socialists as defending the interests of employers. Obviously, some communists—29 percent—perceived the PSOE in that light, probably reflections of their overall assessments of the party.

For whatever reason, communist supporters tended to have relatively positive images of the PSOE, a response that is not always reciprocated by PSOE supporters who, on some dimensions, positioned themselves closer to the mean attitude of the electorate and halfway between the self-image of the communists and that held of the PCE by UCD voters.

Who Are the PCE-PSUC Voters?

The communist electorate in Spain shows some of the same characteristics as those of other communist parties in Western and Southern Europe.[22] (See Table 9). It contains more males than do the parties of the center right and the PSOE. One of the factors accounting for the party's different rate of success among men and women is undoubtedly the greater religiosity of women.

In terms of subjective class identification, a large majority—60 percent of the PCE-PSUC voters and 55 percent of

Table 9. Social Characteristics of Potential PCE-PSUC and PSOE Voters.

			Potential Voters of:			
	PCE-PSUC	PCE	PSUC	PSOE	PSOE Except Catalonia	PSC-PSOE
SEX:						
Male	60	60	59	53	53	54
OCCUPATIONAL STATUS:						
Salaried	40	37	54	37	37	41
Self-employed	14	15	8	10	10	10
Retired, salaried	8	9	4	8	8	9
Retired, self-employed	2	2	1	2	2	1
Unemployed	6	6	7	3	3	4
Student	9	9	7	7	7	4
Housewife	21	21	21	32	32	31
SUBJECTIVE CLASS OF FAMILY:						
Upper and Middle	8	10	8	10	11	5
Lower-middle	32	31	34	32	31	36
Working	60	60	55	57	57	55
n.a.	1		3	2	1	3
RELIGIOSITY:						
Very good Catholic	3	3	3	5	6	1
Practicing	8	9	4	17	18	9
Seldom practicing	22	22	24	30	31	26
Not practicing	36	33	47	29	25	48
Indifferent	21	23	13	14	15	10
Atheist	9	10	8	3	3	3
Other religion						
n.a.	1	1	1	1	1	3
	(394)	(318)	(76)	(1300)	(1071)	(229)

the Catalan wing—identify themselves as working class. The remaining voters—32 percent—tend to be overwhelmingly lower-middle class. Very few identify themselves as upper or upper-middle class. However, subjective class identification does not differentiate the communist from the socialist electorate, either in Spain as a whole or in Catalonia.

Analysis reveals that the fundamental socioeconomic characteristic of the PCE-PSUC relates to the fact that the PCE-PSUC is composed mainly (40 percent) of salaried personnel, either workers or employees. In the electorate of the PSUC, workers and employees are even more important because of the industrial character of Catalonia. Because of the presence of small farmers in its electorate, the PCE has more self-employed voters. However, salaried status does not distinguish the communist electorate from the socialist electorate, although in Catalonia numerical differences distinguish the salaried constituencies of the PSUC and the PSOE-PSC. If the number of retired salaried and unemployed is considered, a majority of the communist and close to a majority of the socialist electorate consist of those who are now or in the past were salaried. In both parties, the number of self-employed is small but, surprisingly, somewhat larger in the PCE perhaps because of the incidence of rural communist supporters. Congruent with the larger number of women voting for the PSOE, the proportion of housewives distinguishes both parties—21 percent among the PCE-PSUC electorate and 32 percent among that of the PSOE. There are slight indications that the PCE-PSUC has been more successful in generating support among students, but the difference is not striking. Somewhat more noteworthy is the larger number of unemployed among the communist electorate, but, again, the difference is not great. Certainly, the two parties cannot be differentiated according to the occupational status of their supporters. There are, however, differences in the success rate achieved by the parties in generating support among blue-collar and white-collar workers.

The Leadership of Santiago Carrillo and Felipe González

Neither communist nor socialist voters based their party choices on the appeals of the leaders to the same extent as did UCD voters, 42 percent of whom mentioned in first or second place the personal appeal of Prime Minister Suárez as their motive for voting for the party. More communist voters—58 percent—than those of any other party mentioned ideology as their primary motive, and 11 percent cited it as their second motive. Among PSOE voters the responses totaled 35 and 16 percent. Similar numbers of both electorates mentioned the party program in first place, but among communists, a larger number, 28 versus 19 percent, mentioned it in second place. Communists were more likely than socialists to mention the organization and the strength of the party as motives for their choices. Very few communist voters cited as the first reason the appeal of the leader—only 5 percent, compared to 17 percent of PSOE voters. If the number of first and second choices are added, leadership was a consideration for only 13 percent of the PCE-PSUC voters, compared to 32 percent of the PSOE. There can be little question that in terms of attractive personality, Felipe González has an edge over Santiago Carrillo.

The patterns that we have described have also been found in other West European electorates for whose support the communists compete with other parties and are congruent with the more ideological character of the communist movement. It is probable that the pattern in Spain is magnified because of the appealing personality of the young socialist leader and the success achieved in projecting a favorable image of him during the 1977 campaign.

To supplement the information gleaned about the importance of the personality of the leaders, we asked to what extent and with what intensity the followers of both parties approve of the actions of their leaders. A majority—64 percent—of the PCE-PSUC voters approved of the actions of the secretary general of the PCE, whereas 14 percent expressed doubt or were critical, and approximately 16 percent disapproved. The attitudes of PSUC supporters toward Carrillo's leadership were considerably less supportive than those of PCE supporters. Only 13 percent expressed total approval, compared to 33 percent among PCE supporters. Twenty-eight percent thought that he had acted fairly well, compared to 26 percent of PCE supporters. Criticism reached 27 percent among the PSUC, compared to 13 percent among the PCE. The electorate of the PSOE-PSC was slightly less enthusiastic about Felipe Gonzalez than were socialists in the rest of Spain. No such clear difference could be discerned within socialist ranks in the disapproval. The electorates of both the communist and socialist parties stood behind their respective leaders in 1978.

Asymmetry was found between the judgments made by communist voters about the performance of the leader of the PSOE and those made by socialist supporters about Carrillo's performance. Communist supporters, perhaps inspired by the idea of the unity of the left, tended to give considerable approval to the socialist leader, in contrast to the approval rating given to Carrillo by the supporters of the PSOE. Although only 6 percent of the potential PCE-PSUC supporters totally disapproved of the actions of Felipe González, 18 percent of the potential PSOE voters totally disapproved of Santiago Carrillo. Although 43 percent of the communists accorded approval to some of the actions of Felipe González, only 25 percent of socialists accorded a similar level of approval to the actions of Santiago Carrillo. There can be little doubt that however proximate the two electorates may be, the political actions and the personality of Carrillo have little attraction for the voters of the PSOE. (See Table 10.)

An analysis of the judgments made by communist and socialist supporters of their respective leaders reveals that most communists are sure of the political ability of their leader, primarily the result of the image of experience that

Table 10, Attitudes Toward Santiago Carrillo and Felipe González Among Voters of the PCE-PSUC and the PSOE.

	Approval of Carrillo Among Voters of:			Approval of González Among Voters of:		
	PCE PSUC	PCE	PSUC	PSOE	PSOE Except Catalonia	PSC- PSOE
a.	29	33	13	25	26	23
b.	35	36	28	37	38	31
c.	14	13	21	18	17	23
d.	9	8	14	7	7	11
e.	7	5	13	5	5	4
f.	3	3	5	5	5	4
g.	3	2	7	3	3	3

	Approval of González Among Voters of:			Approval of Carrillo Among Voters of:		
	PCE- PSUC	PCE	PSUC	PSOE	PSOE Except Catalonia	PSC- PSOE
a.	10	10	11	4	4	5
b.	33	35	24	21	19	26
c.	28	29	26	26	27	24
d.	17	16	20	13	14	12
e.	6	5	11	18	18	15
f.	3	3	3	13	13	12
g.	3	2	5	4	4	4
	(394)	(318)	(76)	(1300)	(1071)	(229)

The alternatives given were: (a) I approve of his actions totally. (b) In general, he has acted quite well. (c) His actions have been mediocre but without too many errors. (d) He has committed many errors that could have been avoided. (e) I disapprove totally. (f) Don't know. (g) No answer.

almost half a century in politics has given the secretary general of the party. Fifty-five percent of the electorate consider Carrillo an experienced politician, compared to 23 percent who attribute that quality to González and 38 percent to Suárez. The communist voters tend to give Carrillo a favorable rating on the entire list of qualities, whereas the socialists tend to see their own leader in a less favorable light. Only on two dimensions did the socialists rate their leader more favorably than the communists judged Carrillo. Although 15 percent perceive Carrillo as authoritarian, only 9 percent of socialists believe that González can be so characterized. The main difference is that 33 percent of the communists perceive Carrillo as "simpático," compared to 54 percent of socialists who attribute that quality to González. Except for experience and smartness or craftiness, the electorate tends to perceive González in a considerably more favorable light than it perceives Carrillo, even when both are ranked equally in terms of political ability. Congruent with the image of the party, Carrillo is perceived as more authoritarian by the electorate in general and by the electorate of the PSOE.

In view of the generally higher approval rating given to González by communist voters than to Carrillo by socialist voters, the general image held by communist supporters of González is more favorable than that held by the socialists of Carrillo. What is particularly weak is the socialist voters' perceptions of his sincerity, honesty, and sympathy. If no other consideration entered into their choice, it is not likely that socialist voters would be attracted to the PCE by the personality of its secretary general. To give one example: Whereas 55 percent of the communists consider González "simpático," only 16 percent of the PSOE think of Carrillo in those terms. Only in experience and craftiness do the socialists consider him ahead of their own leader, whereas among the communists, González is not ahead of their secretary general in any quality listed. One of the great weaknesses of Carrillo derives from the fact that a small number of Spaniards (13 percent of the electorate and 15 percent of socialists) consider him sincere. (See Table 11.)

Supporters and Critics of Santiago Carrillo in the PCE-PSUC Electorate

The 1978 survey showed clearly that whereas the secretary general of the party enjoyed the approval of a large majority of the PCE-PSUC electorate and a larger and more enthusiastic approval of PCE voters, a minority was more or less critical of his actions: somewhat less than one-third of the joint electorate and 48 percent of the PSUC's potential voters. This finding raises an interesting question: Who are the critics of Carrillo within the party? Undoubtedly, both critics and supporters have different motives for their positions. There are indications that some of the most supportive communists hold opinions that do not coincide with the Eurocommunist stance taken by the secretary general and that, unlike their disagreements with him about many issues, a number of his critics, particularly in the PSUC, seem to be close to his ideological position. In the case of the former, the explanation may be entrenched loyalty to the man who has led the party for many years and party discipline. In the case of the latter, perhaps agreement on ideological positions is not enough to justify overcoming their reservations about his personality and record, which may constitute for those Eurocommunist voters an embarrassing memory, a reminder of the disavowed past. There are obvious difficulties involved in analyzing these different and, to some extent, contradictory tendencies within the communist electorate. Further research would have to be conducted to determine whether they have been sustained. Nevertheless, it may be worthwhile to present some of the data characterizing both supporters and critics of the party leader and their attitudes on a number of issues.

Table 11. Assessment of Santiago Carrillo and Felipe González by the Potential Voters of Different Parties in 1978.

	Santiago Carrillo Supporters of:				Felipe González Supporters of:			
	PCE-PSUC	PSOE	UCD	Electorate	PCE-PSUC	PSOE	UCD	Electorate
Political ability	87	63	48	55	59	71	51	54
Responsible	70	34	16	28	44	54	30	36
Honest	51	18	10	17	35	45	24	28
Understanding	47	20	8	17	31	40	19	25
Sincere	41	15	5	13	26	39	18	23
"Simpático"	33	16	9	14	55	54	45	46
Experienced	78	63	48	55	28	31	23	23
Smart (Hábil)	69	53	42	48	47	47	37	40
Authoritarian	15	23	25	22	6	9	11	10
Demagogic	15	23	28	25	22	15	22	21
Excitable	6	9	13	10	9	6	8	7
d.k.	2	9	19	16	4	6	16	14
	(599)	(1842)	(1573)	(5898)	(599)	(1842)	(1573)	(5898)

There is little doubt that Carrillo's supporters place themselves much farther to the left than do his critics. Among the supporters, 45 percent placed themselves on points one and two of the scale, compared to 28 percent of his critics. Even more surprising in view of the criticism expressed by Carrillo of the Soviet Union is that 8 percent more of his supporters than his critics advocate friendship with the Soviet Union and that the pro-American minority is slightly stronger among the latter. The commitment to the party, as indicated by having voted in 1977 for the PCE or for the PSUC rather than for other parties or not voting at all, is stronger among his supporters. One factor that may reduce the significance of that finding is that a number of his critics were not old enough to vote in 1977. (See Table 12.)

In terms of social background, family, and subjective class, the supporters of Carrillo identify with the working class—63 percent, compared to 48 percent of his critics. Among his critics are those who identify with the upper and middle-middle classes—13 percent, compared to 7 percent among his supporters. Significantly more of Carrillo's supporters are farm laborers or unskilled workers, whereas skilled workers and white-collar groups seem to be disproportionately represented among his critics.

Table 12. Ideological Position of Those Approving or Disapproving of Santiago Carrillo Among 1979 Voters of the PCE-PSUC.

Self-placement on the left-right scale.

	Approve	Disapprove		Approve	Disapprove
Left 1	19	9	Monarchy	18	21
2	26	19	Republic	65	61
3	30	41	Ambivalent	10	8
4	19	16	n.a.	7	11
5-6	3	6			
Other		7			
n.a.		3			
	(251)	(120)			

	Approve	Disapprove	Spain should join Common Market	Approve	Disapprove
Favor friendship with:			Yes	87	70
the United States	4	8	No	6	21
			Undecided		4
the Soviet Union	35	27	n.a.	7	7
Both	44	37			
Neither	9	15	Spain should join NATO		
			Yes	27	28
n.a.	9	13	No	52	50
			Undecided	5	1
			n.a.	16	20

Voted 1977	Approve	Disapprove	Approval of Suárez	Approve	Disapprove
PCE/PSUC	82	59			
PSOE	6	12	Approve totally	2	3
UCD	3	4	Acted quite well	9	8
Other		5	Mediocre	33	16
None	1	5	Many errors	32	44
Not old enough	7	15	Disapprove totally	24	30
n.a.	1	1	d.k.	1	
				(251)	(120)

NOTES

1. For the history of and the ideological debates within the PCE, the reader is referred to the contribution by Eusebio M. Mujal-León and the bibliography cited as well as to the basic sources on Eurocommunism. On the complex process of legalizing the party, see Francisco Rubio and Manuel Aragón, "La legalización del P.C.E. y su incidencia en el estatuto jurídico de los partidos políticos en España," in Pedro de Vega, ed., *Teoría y práctica de los partidos políticos.* Madrid, 1977, pp. 219-237; Richard S. Fisher, "The Spanish Left: Resurgence After Four Decades of Franco," *Occasional Papers, Western Societies Program,* Cornell University, 1978, which provides a useful overview. An outstanding sociological monograph contributing toward an understanding of the Spanish left based on interviews with working class and student leaders is José Maravall, *Dictatorship and Political Dissent. Workers and Students in Franco's Spain,* London, 1978, and his "Spain. Eurocommunism and Socialism," *Political Studies,* June 1979. Useful for the "genealogy" of the splits within the communist camp is Antonio Sala and Eduardo Durán, *Crítica de la izquierda autoritaria en Cataluña, 1967-1974,* 1975, p. XIII.

2. Juan J. Linz in collaboration with DATA, "The New Spanish Party System," in Richard Rose, ed., *Electoral Participation,* London, 1980.

3. PSUC, with introduction by Gregori López Raimundo, *PSUC: Per Catalunya, la democràcia i el socialisme,* Barcelona, 1976; Pere Ardiaca, ed., *PSUC: Una proposta democràtica i socialista per a Catalunya,* Barcelona, 1976.

4. For the history and programmatic positions of the main trade-union federations, see José Luis Guinea, *Los movimientos obreros y sindicales en España. De 1833 a 1978,* Madrid, 1978; Fernando Almendros Morcillo et al., *El sindicalismo de clase en España (1939-1977),* Barcelona, 1978; Marco Calamai, *Storia del movimento operaio spagnolo dal 1960 at 1975, con un saggio introduttivo di Nicolas Sartorius,* Bari, 1975; Colectivo Sindicalista de la UGT, *UGT. Unión General de Trabajadores,* Barcelona, 1976; Julián Ariza, *CCOO Comisiones Obreras,* Barcelona, 1976; Reyes Mate, *Una interpretación histórica de la USO (por un socialismo autogestionario),* Madrid, 1977, a very interesting collection of historical and ideological documents; Jose María Zufiaur, *USO. Unión Sindical Obrera,* Barcelona, 1976; Benjamin Martin, "Labor and Politics in Spain Today," *Relations Industrielles,* 34, 1, 1979, pp. 108-121.

On trade-union elections and political elections, see José M. Maravall, "Spain: Eurocommunism and Socialism," *Political Studies*, 27, 2 1979; Juan J. Linz, "Il sistema partitico. . ." *op. cit.*, and research by Robert Fishman (forthcoming). Víctor M. Pérez-Díaz, "Elecciones sindicales, afiliación y vida sindical de los obreros españoles hoy," *Revista Española de Investigaciones Sociológicas*, 6, 1979.

5. In the absence of an official publication containing the electoral returns for all parties and provinces, the standard source used is the newspaper *El País*, May 2 and 3, 1979. *El País* gives only national totals for eligible voters, valid voters, blank and void voters (but the sum of the three is not identical to the figure of votes cast, which was used to calculate abstentions) and the vote for parties with representation. The only possibility for all other parties is to add their returns in each electoral district. This is the calculation that we have used. Adding the vote for the represented parties in the same way does not yield the same result as the national totals given by *El País*, May 3, p. 17 (apparently announced for information purposes by the Junta Central del Censo). The difference results in part from the exclusion of lists running on a different label (in the case of CD) and to inconsistencies in the additions. Jorge de Esteban, Luis López Guerra, eds., *Las elecciones legislativas del 1 de Marzo de 1979*, Madrid, 1979, is a monumental work that includes a wealth of information on electoral legislation, the electorate, the parties, their platforms, their strategies, the candidates, public-opinion polls published at the time of the election, and returns by districts. The data used are derived from a variety of sources (not always specified), including the Junta Electoral Central and the Juntas Electorales Provinciales (that should but do not coincide), *El País* (which we have used), and the research staff of the PCE. The variety of sources used accounts for the differences between their data and ours. The table on pp. 303-305 gives the vote for each party (except the PRE), but that table *should be corrected*, using the data on p. 447 based on corrected returns for Pontevedra and Teruel (included without explicit reference on pp. 303-305). Other tables, such as those by region and party, in the text do not take into account the corrections on page 447. The addition of data reported at the municipal level (often hand written) being done by DATA and placed on computer tape to elaborate electoral maps at the municipal level is likely to differ somewhat from those published here and by Jorge Esteban et al., *op. cit.*, pp. 303-305, 447, and by province and region, pp. 335-442. None of the data will be "official" and wholly consistent or accurate. The differences in percentages are small and do not change the allocation of seats. This fact probably explains the low interest of the major parties in obtaining a more accurate report of the returns.

6. Although there is a growing literature on Galician society and politics before 1936, there is a dearth of scholarly monographs on the present. For an informative overview, see José Luis Prada Fernández, "El sistema de partidos políticos en Galicia. Una aproximación descriptiva," in Pedro de Vega, ed., *Teoría y práctica de los partidos políticos,* Madrid, 1977, pp. 193-218, which deals mainly with the efforts of the parties to coordinate their activities as the opposition at the regional level during the transition. Also see Manuel Rivas and X. Taibo, *Os partidos políticos no Galiza,* La Coruña, 1977. César Díaz is writing a study of elections, parties, and political elites in Galicia.

7. Oscar Bergasa, "Canarias, región marginal," *Argumentos,* January 1979, pp. 40-44. Lurra, *Canarias otro volcán,* Donostia (San Sebastián), 1978, is a partisan account of the M.P.A.I.A.C., its platform, and documents on its international activities. See pp. 161-171 on its relations with and position toward the communist parties as well as the Soviet Union. See also Oscar Bergasa and Antonio González Vietez, *Desarrollo y subdesarrollo en la economía canaria,* Madrid, 1969. José A. Alemán, *Canarias hoy. Apuntes a un proceso histórico,* Madrid, 1977.

8. Juan J. Linz, "The Basques in Spain: Nationalism and Political Conflict in a New Democracy," in Phillips Davison and Leon Gordenker, eds., *Resolving Nationality Conflicts,* New York, 1978, presents an overview using electoral and survey data with bibliographic references. Of the growing literature on Basque politics and society, we will mention only Stanley G. Payne, *Basque Nationalism,* Reno, Nevada, 1975; the survey of Basque parties by Alberto Pérez Calvo, *Los partidos políticos en el País Vasco. (Aproximación a su estudio),* San Sebastián-Madrid, 1977; the synthesis on the socioeconomic structure of the region by Luis C. Núñez, *Clases sociales en Euskadi,* San Sebastián, 1977; and Carlos Alonso Zaldívar, "Primeras reflexiones sobre el resultado de las elecciones de Euskadi," *Nuestra Bandera,* 87, pp. 13-18.

9. José M. Maravall, "The Socialist Alternative. Politics and the Electorate." in H. Penniman, ed., *The Polls in Spain,* Washington, D.C., forthcoming, provides interesting data on the socialist family background of delegates to the 28th PSOE congress. For correlations between the vote in 1936 and 1977 in Spain and Guipúzcoa, see Juan J. Linz, "Il sistema partitico spagnolo," *Revista Italiana di Scienza Politica,* 3, 1978, pp. 363-414, Table 1, p. 367.

10. On the anarchosyndicalist CNT strength by province, which tends to support our conclusion, see Antonio Elorza, *La utopía anarquista bajo la segunda república española, precedido de otros trabajos,* Madrid, 1973; tables and maps in appendix.

11. For the parties of the País Valencià and the statewide parties in Valencia, see Amadeu Fabregat, *Partits polítics al País Valencià*, 1976, based on a questionnaire addressed to the leaders of each party and brief biographies.

12. On the Portuguese party system and elections, see the excellent ecological-statistical study and factorial analysis of party language by Jorge Gaspar and Nuno Vitorino, *As Eleições de 25 de Abril, Geografia e Imagem dos Partidos*, Lisboa, 1976; Instituto Superior Económico e Social, "Eleições 1976. Assembleia da República," *Economia e Sociologia (Estudos Eborenses)*, 21-22, 1976; *Eleições '75 (Primeras Eleições Livres). O Programa do M.F.A. e dos Partidos Políticos*, Lisbon, 1975; Maria Emilia Arroz et al., *Eleições Legislativas—algunos aspectos regionais*, Lisbon, 1977.

Preliminary evidence for the much closer competition in terms of the geographical location of their respective electorates in Spain than in Portugal of communists and socialists can be adduced from the fact that the correlation between the PS and the PCP vote was only .40 (in 1976) and that between the PSOE and the PCE vote at the provincial level (in 1977) was .55. For the Portuguese data, see Gaspar and Vitorino, *op. cit.*, p. 62. On the PCP vote, see pp. 44-46 and the map on p. 32 showing the large and contiguous area south of the Tejo in which the PCP obtained the largest or second largest plurality. On the vote in the Lisbon metropolitan area, see p. 158 and the map on p. 157; for the vote in the city of Lisbon, see pp. 174-175. The tables on pp. 267-308 give the data for districts, *concelhos*, and urban centers.

13. The vote of the PCE, the PSOE, and the parties to their left in Andalucía, particularly in the countryside, deserves careful analysis: relating the vote to different kinds of property structure, the presence of farm laborers, rural unemployment, areas of influence in the large cities, and political traditions. It would be specious to link the PCE vote to the presence of latifundia, the large agrotowns, the rural landless proletariat, and so forth without careful analysis. For example, most of the large agrotowns with latifundia in the province of Sevilla are strongholds of the PSOE, whereas the Cordobese campiña that contains many small holders is a PCE stronghold. On the Córdoba PCE stronghold, see Juan Trías Vejarano, "Resultados electorales en la provincia de Córdoba," *Nuestra Bandera*, 87, 1977, pp. 29-33, and on social structure, see Antonio López Ontiveros, *Emigración, propiedad y paisaje agrario en la Campiña de Córdoba*, Esplugues de Llobregat, 1974; Francisco Ortega Alba, *El Sur de Córdoba. Estudio de Geografía Agraria*, Córdoba, 1975, 2 vols. On voting in Sevilla, see Enrique Soria Medina, *Sevilla: elecciones 1936 y 1977*, Sevilla, 1978, p. 186, map on p. 195.

On social structure, see Michel Drain, *Les campagnes de la province de Sevilla*, Paris, 1977, 2 vols.

14. Jorge Gaspar and Nuno Vitorino, *As eleicões de 25 de abril. Geografía e imagen dos partidos*, Lisbon, 1976.

15. On the PSP, see the numerous writings of its leader, the distinguished intellectual, Enrique Tierno Galván, and the little book by Francisco Bobillo, *PSP. Partido Socialista Popular*, Barcelona, 1976. This series on parties is informative. See also the biographies of Tierno Galván and Raúl Morodo.

16. For an analysis of the electoral changes, 1977-1979, that does not coincide with ours given the different sources used for the election returns, see José Félix Tezanos, "Análisis sociopolítico del voto socialista en las elecciones de 1979," *Sistema*, 31, July 1979, pp. 113-117, including data on Madrid by neighborhoods and suburban municipalities.

17. The changes between the two legislative elections are discussed by José Félix Tezanos, "El espacio político y sociológico del socialismo español," *Sistema*, 32, 1979, pp. 66-73. See table 7, p. 70.

18. Giacomo Sani, "Mass Support for Italian Communism: Trends and Prospects," in Austin Ranney and Giovanni Sartori, ed., *Eurocommunism: The Italian Case*, Washington, D.C., 1978, pp. 67-69, Table 7, p. 82.

19. On the PSOE, see Fundación Pablo Iglesias, *Cien años de Socialismo en España (Bibliografía)*, Madrid, 1979; Felipe González et al., *Socialismo es Libertad. Escuela de Verano del P.S.O.E. 1976*, Madrid, 1976; Francisco Bustelo, Gregorio Peces-Barba, Ciriaco de Vicente, and Virgilio Zapatero, *PSOE. Partido Socialista Obrero Español*, Barcelona, 1976. Most interesting for the history of Spanish socialism in the underground is Elías Díaz, "Sobre los orígenes de la fragmentación actual del socialismo español (Autocrítica para la unidad)," *Sistema* 15, 1976, pp. 125-137. For a bibliography of recent studies on Spanish socialism, the reissue of classic works, magazines, and so on, see Enrique Moral, "Estudios sobre el socialismo en España," *Sistema*, 15, 1976, pp. 139-197 (with bibliography for the period 1951-1976), pp. 150-156, and Fundación Pablo Iglesias, *100 años de socialismo en España (Bibliografía)*, Madrid, 1979. For the ideological positions on the left of the party, the "sector crítico," see Francisco Bustelo, *Introducción al socialismo marxista*, Madrid, 1979; Pablo Castellano, *Sobre el Partido Obrero*, Hospitalet de Llo-regat: El Viejo Topo, 1970; Luis Gómez Llorente, Enrique Gomaríz, Joaquín Leguina, and Fernando Claudín, *Teoría socialista del Estado*, Madrid, 1978.

20. The random area survey of 493 interviews was planned and executed by DATA in the fall of 1977. The sample was a panel study of those interviewed in January-February of 1977.

21. The 1978 survey that we have referred to repeatedly was planned and executed by DATA under the direction of Manuel Gómez Reino, Darío Vila, Francisco Andrés Orizo, and the author for the Fundación Democracia y Humanismo in July of that year and was replicated in July 1979 with the support of the Centro de Investigaciones Sociológicas (CIS). The 1979 data that we quoted come from this study. DATA plans to publish a detailed analysis of these and other political surveys with the support of the FOESSA Foundation. I acknowledge with gratitude the support of the Fundación Democracia y Humanismo and the CIS.

22. On the social background of PCE voters and studies on the PSOE electorate, see J. M. Maravall, "The Socialist Alternative," in H. Penniman, ed., *op. cit.* José Félix Tezanos, "El espacio político y sociológico del socialismo español," *Sistema,* 32, September 1979, pp. 41-75, based on a January 1979 survey, gives data on the social background of voters and attitudes toward Marxism, images of the party, first and second choice, and reasons for voting, as well as the social background of delegates to the 28th congress; Mónica Threlfall, "El Socialismo y el electorado femenino," *Sistema,* 32, September 1979, pp. 19-33.

Kenneth Maxwell

PORTUGUESE COMMUNISM

1.

The Portuguese revolution occurred at an inopportune moment for the superpowers. The height of the crisis in Portugal was sandwiched between the summits at Vladivostok (November 24, 1974) and at Helsinki (August 1, 1975), and although both East and West meddled in the internal affairs of Portugal, each superpower was ultimately restrained by the mutual desire to protect more important bilateral arrangements with one another. Nonetheless, the collapse of the dictatorship in 1974 and Portugal's inability to hold onto its African territories meant that there were advantages to be gained, especially by the Soviet Union. The West was challenged where its hegemony had been unquestioned for decades, and in consequence the response of Western governments throughout the crisis tended to be defensive.

On the other hand, the movement to the left in Portugal, which seemed categorical in 1975, failed to sustain itself. Moreover, the key political element in that reversal had more to do with the dynamics of Portuguese politics and society than with outside interference. The failure of the left to consolidate the broad base of social support for the transformation of Portuguese society was caused primarily by the bitter split that developed between the Portuguese socialists and the communists. Throughout the spring and summer of 1975, the two major parties of the left developed the perception that the other was the principal enemy. Blame for the split has been debated and apportioned. Perhaps the split was inevitable, even desirable. The behavior of the Portuguese communists, however, was central to the left's failure in Portugal. It was sufficiently ambivalent to alienate both the radical left and the democratic socialists, forcing the former into a futile putsch in November 1975 and the latter into a de facto alliance with a reemergent right, weakening and isolating the forces of radical change and allowing the forces of moderation (or reaction, depending on one's point of view) to recuperate and consolidate power.

The beginning of the Portuguese crisis appeared deceptive in many ways. Revolution was not at all the intention of those who made the coup d'état of April 25, 1974. Yet revolution was what Portugal experienced: A major restructuring of government and society occurred, a set of values for distributive justice was established, and the former elite was replaced by a new group. As the forces of revolutionary change emerged, so did those of counterrevolution. Violence and the threat of violence were integral to both processes. The conflict remained below the threshold of large-scale armed struggle and internal war, although popular uprisings against the communists in the northern provinces and the threat of using armed force at the center in Lisbon during the long summer of 1975 blocked the momentum of revolution.

In some respects the turmoil of those years is not surprising. The heritage of half a century of repression weighed heavily on Portugal. The regime established by Dr. Oliveira Salazar after the military coup of 1926 and perpetuated after Salazar's death in 1970 by Marcello Caetano had succeeded in denying political participation to the majority of the people. By doing so its leaders had deprived almost three generations of their civil rights and the opportunity to exercise democratic responsibilities. The break with the past was profound: The old oligarchy was destroyed, massive state intervention in the economy became the norm, the great landed estates were expropriated, workers' pay and power increased dramatically, citizens organized themselves in neighborhood commissions, unions, and political parties and could no longer be ignored either by the government or by capitalist employers. The Portuguese revolutionary movement thus brought about real changes, created real victims, and challenged real assets.

The problems that faced Portugal's political leaders were not merely theoretical. All of them, including the Central Committee of the Portuguese Communist party, were faced with the necessity of responding to fast-moving events. In most countries of the Western world the political struggle was presented as something of a morality play. Dour Moscow-oriented communists entrenched in unions, the press, and local administrations—positions that they had seized in the confusion following the collapse of the Caetano regime—were portrayed as hell-bent on establishing a dictatorship of the left in alliance with radical military officers. There was something to the image—more than middle-aged intellectuals elsewhere in Europe were at first prepared to admit, although less than young radicals, who considered Portugal the beginning of a European revolution, hoped for. The threat was deemed sufficient to force middle-class socialists into the streets of Lisbon and Oporto in defense of civil liberties, to mobilize the formidable influence of the Catholic church, and to drive the small and medium peasantry of the north to demonstrate against the direction of politics in the capital and in the south. In truth the situation was much more complicated, as were the roles played by the Portuguese Communist party and the armed forces.

What happened in Portugal during that period of confusion and why? What broad lessons can be drawn from the Portuguese example? What, if anything, does the behavior of the Portuguese communists demonstrate about communist strategies in contemporary Europe?

2.

The essential element in analyzing the Portuguese revolution is so obvious that it is difficult to explain why its significance has often been overlooked: No mass movement brought down the old regime, and the participation of the clandestine political parties of the left was negligible. The army, not the communists or other leftists, toppled the dictatorship. The coup of April 25, 1974, was carried out by a small group of junior officers, all of whom were influenced by their extensive experiences in the colonial wars. Most of them believed that the military should play a major role in the political process. The actions of the many factions that represented the Portuguese military constituted the central and the unique element in the Portuguese situation, and little can be understood without taking its role into account. To be sure, popular mobilization was important in Portugal. The multitudes that took to the streets of Portugal's two largest cities, Lisbon and Oporto, in the hours and weeks that followed the coup made irreversible the army's action. But revolutionary mobilization followed the coup; it did not cause it.

Because the Portuguese military had long been regarded as among the most reactionary in Europe, the political views of the Armed Forces Movement (Movimento das Forças Armadas), or MFA, were as surprising as the coup that it launched. The Armed Forces Movement originated in response to professional grievances and concerns with status and privilege. Western observers therefore tended to consider it a conservative force. But the problem only in part reflected mounting pressures released by a coterie of captains who were angry about promotions, pay, and low esteem. Dissention within the officer corps was a reflection of a much deeper malaise that intensified with the increasing scale, diversity, and organizational disarray of the Portuguese armed forces that in turn were consequences of the seemingly endless military commitment in Africa. Of a population of a little over eight million in 1974, one in four men of military age was in the armed forces.[1] The army alone contained at least 170,000 men, of which 135,000 were in Africa. The air force had 16,000 men, the navy 18,000, the units of the Republican Guard (GNR) 10,000, and the paramilitary security police (PSP) 15,000. The armed forces represented (at a low estimate) a proportion per thousand of the population (30.83) exceeded only by Israel (40.09) and North and South Vietnam (31.66 and 55.36) and was five times that of the United Kingdom and three times that of the United States and Spain. The military budget represented seven percent of GNP, more than that of the United States. And that percentage was probably based on gross underestimations. With an annual per capita income of barely more than 1,000 dollars, Portugal spent on military expenditures a minimum per capita of 63.27 dollars, despite abysmal pay for officers and after deductions for uniforms, food, and other services and token pay for the troops.

The army contained almost no professional units. Its soldiers were for the most part illiterate, badly trained, and at times undisciplined. The officer corps was composed of an aged group of generals, a segregated elite of staff officers exclusively devoted to administration and relieved of combat duty, and a diminished cohort of junior- and middle-rank officers (captains and majors)—men in their thirties and early forties who had spent most of their professional lives overseas. The bitterness of the junior officers in the field was aggravated by class friction. Recruitment targets changed after 1958, when the government decided to grant free tuition and a salary to cadets. By the mid-seventies that pattern of recruitment had produced a marked social cleavage in the professional officer corps (the QP, or *Quadra* parmanente) at the rank of lieutenant colonel. Since the fighting began in Angola, there had been a rapid falloff in the number of candidates at the military academy, and by 1974 only one-fifth of the places were filled. The result was a chronic shortage in the middle ranks and the almost complete absence of professional subalterns to face growing insurgency.

In an attempt to relieve shortages in the professional ranks during the sixties, some conscripted officers (so-called *milicianos*) were allowed to enter the military academy and to join the QP on graduation. But that track was one of irritation, for the officers who followed it found that their seniority in the QP was computed from the moment of graduating from the academy and that their previous years of service were discounted. The government's decree of June 1973 was intended to rectify that injustice. It provided for an accelerated two-semester course for milicianos at the academy (as opposed to four years for cadets) and permitted previous service to be counted toward seniority. The measure applied retroactively to former milicianos in the QP.

Far from resolving difficulties, the decree split the QP into warring factions. From that bitter dissention in the junior ranks of the army's officer corps the Armed Forces Movement emerged. To the established authorities such disenchantment signaled danger. Ironically, instead of taking immediate action to counter or to neutralize divisiveness in the officer corps, the Caetano regime inadvertently helped to politicize the situation. In June 1973 the government encouraged the most extreme opponents of compromise in the colonies to meet in Oporto. There a "congress of combatants" assembled amid much publicity to shout the Salazarist slogans of a "pluricontinental Portugal." Four hundred combat officers petitioned the government as part of a protest organized by Colonel Firmino Miguel, Lieutenant Colonel Ramalho Eanes, and Captain Vasco Lourenço, who were to emerge as key figures after the coup. The government invitation manifested its inability to accept what soldiers on the ground had long ago realized—that the colonial wars could not be won.

Initially the MFA was composed exclusively of captains and majors of the QP. Although some of them had been milicianos, the MFA did not include men in their twenties who were still milicianos. Later some trusted senior officers were coopted, and others were informed about developments. The MFA was a small, compact group characterized by strong personal interrelationships. It numbered fewer than two hundred out of a middle-rank corps of approximately 1,600. Although members served in most units, the MFA was especially strong in Guinea and Mozambique. After December 1, 1973, the organization was held together by a fifteen-man coordinating committee that was subdivided into a military committee charged with the detailed planning of the uprising and a political committee that formulated the program for the postcoup situation.

For a determined minority within the army a protest that originated in concern over hierarchy provided cover for political objectives. Major Melo Antunes, an artillery officer who had a long record of opposition to the regime and had at first dismissed the captains' protest movement as being "a reactionary cooperative in defense of privilege," was to play a key role as a member of the political committee of the MFA by drawing up its program. Colonel Vasco Gonçalves, another member of the political committee, had been involved in an aborted putsch a decade previously. His actions on that occasion paralleled those of the Communist party. The leading member of the military planning group, Mozambique-born Major Otelo Saraiva de Carvalho, was much influenced by theories associated with the guerrilla movement in Guinea where he had dealt with psychological warfare. The movement as a whole, however, consisted of officers who subscribed to divergent political views. Their coalescence was less the result of a uniform conspiratorial objective than it was of a convergence of resentments, the loss of a sense of purpose, and emotional and intellectual estrangement. Notwithstanding conventional wisdom, the task of the young Portuguese military dissidents had to be a liberalizing and liberating one. The intransigence of the Portuguese regime and its commitment to the colonial wars made these objectives inevitable.

3.

The MFA program, which provided the institutional framework for the first postcoup year, created a situation in which political parties emerged, sought public support, and engaged in paraelectoral struggle. A year had been designated as the period needed to plan for constituent assembly elections, and perhaps another year would have to elapse before a parliament and a president could be elected under terms to be drawn up by the constituent assembly. The plan was courageous. But it provided no ground rules, and for the new parties it posed a leap into a void.

Although no one under seventy had ever voted in a free election, local organizations, known as democratic electoral commissions (CDE), did exist throughout Portugal. They had been used principally as forums for criticism and debate, for the opposition always withdrew from the contests staged by

Salazar's regime, regarding the electoral system as a fraud. The CDE was comprised of coalitions of "antifascist forces," mainly middle-class liberals, social democrats, Catholic radicals, independent Marxists, and communists. Those grassroots alliances were very important in April and May of 1974. Their activities created the false picture of a massive communist phoenix. In fact many groups did emerge from the cover of the CDE. Among them the Portuguese Communist party (PCP) formed a small, highly-organized minority.

The Portuguese Communist party was founded in 1921. Initially the communists generated little support among the working class, which was strongly influenced by anarcho-syndicalism until the 1930s. But after 1941, under the leadership of Alvaro Cunhal, the party was reorganized on traditional lines. Small cells became the basic unit, and various levels consisting of intermediate district and regional leaderships linked the cells into a hierarchical entity. Cunhal, a man of middle-class origins who had studied law in Lisbon, joined the party in 1931 at the age of seventeen. In 1934 he organized the Federation of Young Communists in the Lisbon area and attended the sixth congress of communist youth in Moscow. He went into clandestine work when he returned to Portugal and became a member of the Central Committee of the party in 1936. He was the Portuguese communist delegate in Madrid at the outbreak of the Spanish Civil War.[2]

The party had been forced underground from the beginning of the Salazar dictatorship, and the long decades of clandestinity profoundly affected the Portuguese communists' psyches and behavior. The PCP bore the brunt of repression. Cunhal spent thirteen years behind bars in Portugal and another fourteen years in exile in Eastern Europe and Moscow. The party's loyalty to Moscow and its apparent sensitivity to developments in Prague reflected the fact that its activities had been directed from Czechoslovakia for three decades. After Fidel Castro, Cunhal was the second communist leader to endorse Soviet intervention in Prague in 1968, adopting a position antagonistic to that assumed by his Iberian counterpart, Santiago Carrillo. In fact at the moment when Carrillo initiated his criticism of Moscow, Cunhal chose to reaffirm his loyalty to the Soviet party.

In 1970 Cunhal set forth the party's strategy in his book *O Radicalismo pequeno burquês de fachada socialista (Petty Bourgeois Radicalism with a Socialist Face)*. It was a violent attack on "pseudorevolutionary verbalists" and "petty bourgeois radicals." It was also a stout defense of the party's definition of the "present stage," that of a "democratic and national" revolution: "Democratic" in that it would espouse civil liberties and act in concert with social democrats and others against the monopolies and latifundiarios; "national" in that it would pursue a neutralist "antiimperialist" foreign policy.

The PCP possessed a strong base in the Alentejo, the grain-producing lands south of the Tagus River—a region of great landed estates—where the party was strongly implanted among the anticlerical, landless rural laborers. The Alentejo has a long history of communist militancy, and Cunhal knows the region well. He is the author of one of the few detailed analyses of the social and economic structures of the Portuguese countryside, *A questão agraria em Portugal (The Agrarian Question in Portugal)*. In the constituent election after the coup, the PCP received its largest shares of the vote in the Alentejan districts of Beja, Evora, and Setúbal: 39.0, 37.1, and 37.8 percent, respectively.[3]

The PCP generated strong support within the labor movement. After the incapacitation of Salazar in 1968 and during the early years of the Caetano regime, liberalization of the rules governing election to positions within the corporative syndicate structure allowed communists to play leading roles in union committees. In 1970 the communist-influenced unions joined in a coordinating organization, *Intersyndical.*

Before the coup, the communists were strongly entrenched in the metallurgical unions and were increasingly influential among lower middle-class, white-collar workers, especially the bank workers' unions in Lisbon and Oporto. (The communist minister of labor in the first provisional government after the coup was a leader of the bank workers' union from Oporto.)

In early 1974 it was estimated that not more than 2,000 members of the party were in Portugal, but it is not known how many members of the clandestine organization emerged at that time. It is evident, however, that a rapid expansion followed legalization, and by 1976 the communists claimed a membership of over 100,000 out of a total population of about 8.5 million.[4]

With a solid core of support in the unions and in the rural south, the party's strategy called for alliances with the owners of small- and medium-sized businesses. Although stressed by Cunhal in 1970, those alliances gained significance after 1973 when the PCP drew the logical conclusion from the fact that the mobilization of those social groups against the popular unity government of President Salvador Allende in Chile had been a critical element in his downfall. They concluded that the success or failure of the Portuguese revolution depended on the nominal members of the petty bourgeoisie.

In 1969 the communists established an electoral front with independents and radical Catholics. In 1973 the socialists and communists joined together to form the semilegal Portuguese Democratic Movement (MDP/CDE). After the coup, as the other groups left the CDE to form their own parties and political organizations, many communists stayed in the CDE and used it as a cover from which to control municipal and parish administrations.

An important and vocal segment of the Portuguese left, however, was outside all alliances. Unlike their disparaging attitudes toward the socialists and social democrats, the communists took seriously the challenge to their predominance posed by several ultraleftist groups that emerged in the early 1970s. It was against those radical leftists that Cunhal vented most of his ire. Since the twentieth congress of the Communist party of the Soviet Union in 1956, the debates and divergencies in the international communist movement had reverberated in Portugal. In 1970 ideological schism gave rise to a Marxist-Leninist left in Portugal that regarded the PCP as "revisionist" and either looked nostalgically to the Stalin era for guidance or looked to Mao for inspiration. Although small in numbers and fragmented into numerous factions, those groups exercised considerable influence before and after the coup, especially in student, union, and military circles.

In the first months after the coup d'état of 1974, the Portuguese communists placed themselves firmly in the center of the political spectrum, and Cunhal, as a member of the first provisional government, followed a line of studied moderation. The communist minister of labor resisted workers' demands and ensured that the minimum wage was as low as possible. At the Communist party's congress in October 1974, the first held legally in Portugal, the PCP dropped the phrase "the dictatorship of the proletariat" from its manifesto. It was the first West European communist party to do so. (*Congresso Extraordinario do PCP em 20/10/74;* Lisbon; Edicoes Avanti, 1974, p. 46.) Despite, or perhaps because of, their apparent rejection of one of the tenets of Marxism-Leninism, the Portuguese communists reinforced their defensive positions against criticism (which was not slow in coming) from "pseudorevolutionary leftists" and "petty bourgeois radicals."

But like most things in Portugal during that cataclysmic period, appearances were deceptive. The "centrist" position of the communists differed in content from that espoused by

General Spínola, the provisional president. As the fundamental divergence between Spínola and the PCP over the direction of domestic and colonial policies became more apparent, the PCP and the members of the MFA, who were also opposed to Spínola's policies on decolonization, were thrust into collaborating with one another. It was a tactical alliance that caused misgivings on both sides. The young officers epitomized the "petty bourgeois radicals" that Cunhal had denounced so vociferously, and the communists were tolerated more for their apparent willingness to follow the MFA's leadership and for their discipline and reliability than for their vision of Portuguese society. What united them was their opposition to the same antagonists, not their agreement about the same objective.

The alliance with the MFA (later, with so-called progressive elements of the MFA) became the central tenet of Cunhal's tactics. And Cunhal's rationale for the alliance had less to do with the social dynamics of Portugal than with the "lessons" of Chile. He was determined to avoid creating a Chilean situation. The emergence of a radical element within the military offered the possibility of forging alliances that could neutralize one of the potential sources of a counter-revolution.

4.

But as alliances were being forged on one front, collaboration was disintegrating on another. As Cunhal strengthened his relationships with the military, communist actions were alienating powerful elements of the Portuguese left that had previously collaborated with the communists in the anti-fascist struggle. Specifically and dramatically, the communists were alienating the rapidly expanding Socialist party under the leadership of Mário Soares.[5]

When Mário Soares returned from Paris and Alvaro Cunhal

returned from Prague in April 1974, they posed together smiling, holding between them a red carnation. But in January 1975, when the communists took to the streets in massive demonstrations in support of union legislation that would in effect perpetuate their bureaucratic control over the organized working class, the split between the communists and the socialists became visible for all to see. The MFA Politbureau, then known as the Committee of Twenty, publicly endorsed the communists' position. But the Catholic hierarchy, breaking their long political silence, condemned the proposal for a centralized union structure and called for political pluralism. The socialists and popular democrats in the cabinet succeeded in amending the provisions of the legislation in such a manner that free elections for local union officials and committees were guaranteed. The socialists feared that the proposed centralized union structure that would in turn confirm the role of the communist-dominated Intersyndical at the apex of power would arrest the major inroads that they were making among the communist workers who were disenchanted with the party's ambivalent attitude toward wage claims and labor militancy during the first year of the revolution. The sharpening ideological debate thus reflected a growing struggle to control vital bureaucratic machinery, growing regional polarization, and escalating class and personal antagonisms.

The public dispute between the communists and the socialists that erupted in January had been simmering for some time, and it paralleled and to some extent intersected with major divergencies within the military. The showdown that pushed Spínola out of the presidency had brought into public view the power that the PCP and the MFA could exercise when they acted together. On September 26, 1974, when the crisis became apparent, the Communist party had moved efficiently and effectively to organize a blockade of Lisbon (under cover of the MDP/CDE), thus preventing the thousands of protesters, expected for the demonstration in support of General Spínola, from assembling. Pickets were set in motion, and barricades were erected with the connivance and the support of COPCON, which functioned as the MFA's command structure under Otelo Saraiva de Carvalho. It circumvented the traditional military hierarchy and the politically "unreliable" elements still ensconced within it. In March 1975 COPCON once again coordinated the defense of the revolution, and again vigilantes were mobilized. Both occasions were used to weed out and incarcerate purported enemies, including major figures of the old regime and the financial and industrial oligarchy and (in March) several military officers who had been leading members of the MFA since its formation. Groups of soldiers and armed civilians who conducted the roundups often carried blank arrest warrants issued by COPCON headquarters personnel. By April 1975, one year after the coup that opened the doors of the dictatorship's jails, there were more political prisoners than there had been on the eve of Caetano's downfall.

As early as September 1974, and most especially after March 1975, it was clear that whatever the army might have wished or the leaders of the MFA might have intended, the intrusion of political and party divisions into the military was unavoidable. With the right and center effectively neutralized, the struggle for power began in earnest within the left and inside the MFA. That struggle was almost inevitable, for by institutionalizing itself after the March 11 putsch attempt, the MFA had made its revolutionary council and assembly a parallel executive and legislature.

With the backing of the communists in March 1975, the MFA assembly imposed a series of far-reaching measures, the most critical of which was the nationalization of banks and insurance companies. Because of interlocking relationships among the Portuguese oligarchy and its control of major sectors of the economy, the nationalization of the banks transferred to the state the most important sector of privately-owned Portuguese industry. Because the banks also owned or held mortgages on virtually every Portuguese newspaper, one result was that by assuming control of the banks, the state also assumed financial control of much of the communications media—all the Lisbon morning dailies, two Oporto morning dailies, three of the four Lisbon evening dailies, and a group of weekly magazines and newspapers.

At the time of nationalizations, the revolutionary council signaled that it would soon promulgate a major expropriation—probably all estates over 500 hectares—a measure that would destroy the base of the great latifundiários of the south. The nationalizations and the expropriation of the latifundiários struck at the two principal bases of the old regime and placed Portugal among the most radical of European states, few of which had dared touch the banks or engage in large-scale land expropriation without clear commitments to pay compensation.

The second series of measures that the military radicals sought to push forward was a major restructuring of the military establishment. The MFA assembly was expanded to 240 members, consisting of regular officers representing the three services and, for the first time, sergeants and enlisted men. (Sergeants and enlisted men had participated in the organs of the MFA in Africa.) Sergeants and enlisted men were in the minority, but the principle of representation was extended to the three service assemblies and to the committees that emerged at the unit level in barracks throughout the country.

The most publicized move of the revolutionary council was its directive requiring the political parties to sign a pact with the Armed Forces Movement. The pact, signed on April 11, 1975, assured military supremacy for at least three years, relegated the provisional government to a subordinate position in the new hierarchy of power, and gave to the MFA assembly a coequal voice with any future national assembly in electing a president.[6] The political parties had to acquiesce in order not to jeopardize the constituent assembly elections scheduled for April 25, 1975.

5.

As it turned out, the pact between the MFA and the political parties was not as one-sided as it first appeared to be: Elections scheduled for April 1975, the first anniversary of the coup, were in fact held. That in itself was a major victory for the political parties—a concession that the military radicals afterward regretted. The radicals should have recognized that whatever the result of the poll, it would represent a challenge to military supremacy because for the first time since the April coup, there would exist an alternative source of legitimacy.

The timetable for holding constituent assembly elections one year after the coup and national parliamentary elections one year beyond that had been an integral part of the original MFA program, and abandoning it would have meant not only disregarding the plan but affronting the public, which, after fifty years of manipulated electoral contests and a restricted franchise, was eager to participate. Nevertheless, leading officers did little to disguise their contempt for "bourgeois" electoral politics. Lieutenant Ramiro Correia, a naval officer who had become a leading figure in the fifth division of the general staff, charged with responsibility for information and propaganda, likened the contest to a "football pool." And Admiral Rosa Coutinho, former high commissioner in Angola and the executive officer of the revolutionary council in 1975, attempted to persuade people to cast blank ballots. Coutinho hoped that should such an appeal be successful, the result might be used as an argument to support a political role for the MFA that would allow it to dispense with the traditional forms of political parties. The tactic, based on opinion polls commissioned by the MFA, showed that as many as fifty percent of the electorate were undecided about whom they would support. Ironically, before the elections, much of the foreign press, obsessed with the power of the communists, also dismissed the elections as being of minor significance.

They were wrong. The elections proved to be of enormous importance almost as soon as the results were in. In one of the highest turnouts ever recorded in a national election (91.7 percent), the Portuguese Socialist party led by Mário Soares took 37.9 percent of the vote; the Popular Democrats, 26.4 percent; Alvaro Cunhal's Communist party took a mere 12.5 percent, the PCP's sister party, the Portuguese Democratic Movement (MDP/CDS), received a mere 4.1 percent, and the right-wing CDS got 7.6 percent. The blank votes numbered no more than 7.0 percent of the total votes cast.

The election returns had more than political significance because they delineated a marked regional polarization. Communist support was almost exclusively concentrated in the south, especially in the industrial towns along the south bank of the Tagus estuary opposite Lisbon, and in the Alentejo. The party's highest percentages of the vote came from the districts of Setúbal (37.8 percent), Beja (39.0 percent), and Évora (37.1 percent). In the north the Popular Democrats (PPD) and the Social Democratic center dominated the returns. The PPD received its highest percentage of the vote in the districts of Vila Real (46.0 percent), Bragança (43.1 percent), and Viseu (43.0 percent).

The elections underscored the profound differences in social and economic organization between the north and the south and the striking contrasts between the ways of life in the two regions.[7] The size of the average farm holding in the north is a little over two hectares (1 hectar equals 2.47 acres), but landownership is almost universal. The influence of the Catholic church is strong, and religiosity is fervent. Attach-

ment to tradition and family and a strong suspicion of innovation are general. Agriculture is intensive and diverse. Rain-
fall is abundant, and there is access to ancient irrigation systems. In the south, on the plains and low plateau of the
Alentejo, agriculture is monocultural (cereals or olives) and
landownership highly concentrated (the average size of a
farm in the south is almost 40 hectares). A large percentage
of the labor force is composed of farm workers, most in
precarious seasonal employment. The Mediterranean climate
is characterized by long, hot, dry summers. The influence of
the church is negligible, often nonexistent. Class consciousness is strong among the landless laborers who formed the
backbone of the clandestine PCP. It was from the Alentejo
that the PCP chose its folk heroes and official martyrs as
soon as it emerged as a legal party in 1974.

The Socialist party emerged from the election as the
national alternative, having compiled respectable percentages
in both the north and the south. The socialists did best of all
in the central regions of the country and in the major urban
centers. In Lisbon they won 46.1 percent of the vote, in
Oporto, 42.5 percent, in Coimbra, 43.3 percent, and in
Santarém, 42.9 percent. That achievement reflected an important social phenomenon. The socialists were first choice in
the more modern, open area of Portugal: in the coastal plain
between the two major cities of Oporto and Lisbon and up
the river valleys to Coimbra and Santarém. Their support was
concentrated in regions that contained good communications
facilities and tended to be at least partly industrialized. Of
course, the industrial coastal strip merges into the more
clearly defined regions to the north and the south. Almost all
nonagricultural workers in the north have some access to
land, and the factories in the region north of Oporto, up
toward Braga, are often small paternal enterprises. Unlike the
north, where most emigrants leave the land to work in the
factories of France and Germany, southern migration tends

to be internal; hence strong Alentejan influences extend into the industrial towns of the Lisbon-Setúbal area.

Important similarities existed between the regions of PPD and PCP strength. The districts of Braganca and Vila Real, like those of Beja and Êvora, suffered the highest rates of infant mortality. They had the highest percentage of the work force engaged in agriculture (over 70 percent). Each district had a high illiteracy rate (over 40 percent). They were backward and in many respects highly traditional, isolated rural communities. But in two critical respects they diverged: over religion and landownership. Those fundamental issues were the catalysts in the struggle that was about to begin.

Thus the coincidence between the seizure of power by radical military officers and their communist backers in March and the holding of elections in April that resulted in victory for moderation was of great importance. The election returns demonstrated graphically that the base of support for the revolution was narrow indeed. The returns provided a geography for counterrevolution, a geography that the enemies of the communists inside and outside Portugal would soon take advantage of.

6.

Over the succeeding eight months the fate of the revolution was settled. Despite the left's apparently formidable assets in March 1975—control of the administration, unions, army, communications media, and the political initiative—by the end of November 1975, the left was disunited, weakened, and on the defensive. Its power was broken. Why?

The answer lies in four aspects of those turbulent months. First, the all-important alliance with the military radicals failed. The MFA leadership split into various factions, all ostensibly "on the left" but each having evolved a different view of tactics and objectives. Military discipline collapsed, disintegrating more quickly among leftist units than among centrist and rightist units. Second, the decolonization process that had helped to cement the MFA's solidarity while it was engaged in opposing General Spínola became a major irritant and a point of friction after March 1975 as the situation in Angola proved increasingly intractable and as outsiders intervened in the colony at will. Moreover, several hundreds of thousands of angry refugees poured into Portugal from Africa throughout the summer, exacerbating tensions. Third, the economic situation in Portugal became increasingly precarious, allowing outsiders leverage that they had lacked before. Throughout the summer of 1975, many Western government officials informed Lisbon that economic assistance was dependent on good political behavior. Fourth and perhaps most significant, the communists made several major blunders. They misread the balance of forces and hence the power of their enemies. They misjudged the psychological impact of some of their actions, hence throwing potential allies into the embrace of their opponents. Finally (although it is difficult to prove), the Portuguese communists grossly overestimated the support that they would receive from the Soviet Union.

The tactical problems facing the PCP leadership in the spring and summer of 1975 were considerable. They confronted a new situation after March, one that appeared to possess "revolutionary potential." Until then their policies had been based on defeating the great landowners and the monopolists. By March 1975 both of those "enemies" had been put to flight. In the Alentejo some 1.2 million hectares had been expropriated, frequently at the initiative of the workers but sometimes by default, as workers assumed control in the place of absentee owners. In any event, land seizures occurred on a massive scale and with minimal resistance. The nationalization of industry was also accomplished with ease, suggesting that the PCP played the role of follower rather than of initiator. But with the destruction of the power of the monopolies and the latifundiários, it was not surprising that in July 1975, when they revised Cunhal's *For a Democratic and National Revolution* (written in 1974), his editors stressed the fact that "the present historical stage of the revolution in our country seems to be more correctly defined as a superior stage [than that implicit in the title of Cunhal's book], that of socialist revolution."[8]

The problem with the "new stage" was that it inevitably revealed the ambivalent attitude of the communists toward their would-be allies, the small- and medium-sized farmers of the center and the north and the small shopkeepers and property owners in the towns. Indeed Cunhal had declared in his *Radicalismo Pequeno Burgûes*, reissued in Portugal in August 1974, that "the allies of the proletariat for the socialist revolution are not the same as those for the democratic and national revolution. In the first, the proletariat carries out the fundamental attack on the monopolies and latifundiários allied with that part of the bourgeoisie (the petit bourgeoisie and sectors of the middle class) interested in the anti-monopolistic fight. The socialist revolution," he continued, "is directed against the bourgeoisie in its totality and for this reason, some of the allies of the proletariat in the first stage (sectors of the urban middle class, sectors of the rural peasantry, and some elements of the petit bourgeoisie) cease to be allies during the socialist revolution."[9] Cunhal was nothing if not blunt.

The would-be victims, however, had keen perceptions of their vulnerability. The land seizures in the south and some highly publicized seizures elsewhere in the country had thoroughly alarmed the peasantry and scared them into collaborating with one another. Indeed, the owners of small- and medium-sized property proved much more formidable opponents than the great landowners and industrialists. Cunhal noted a year later that there had been "without doubt deficiencies and errors" in the party's activity over those months, primarily in "underestimating the importance of these classes."[10] He spoke from bitter experience, for it was precisely the small landowners who mobilized in August 1975 to burn and sack at least forty-eight of the party's offices in central and northern Portugal, virtually expelling the party from those regions and underscoring the fact that they had the power to blockade and isolate Lisbon from the north and center of the country.

The errors committed by the communists only hastened polarization along social and economic lines. The attack on the socialist newspaper *República* became an international cause celebre. The attempt to monopolize the mass media proved to be counterproductive for the communists. *República* had a long and honorable record of antifascism; it had been sustained through great adversity by 3,500 small shareholders; and it was edited by a well-known antifascist and socialist, Raul Rego. No damage that *República* might have done to the communists could have matched the damage that the communists inflicted on themselves by suppressing the newspaper. The attack on and takeover of the Catholic church's radio station in Lisbon also produced major negative repercussions, especially among the highly religious peasantry of the north. And as if to solidify the image of Stalinist high-handedness, Cunhal gave his famous interview to Oriana Falacci. "If you believe that the constituent assembly will be transformed into a parliament, you are very much mistaken," he said. "In Portugal there will be no parliament."[11]

The communists overestimated the tenacity of their friends and underestimated that of their enemies. In the political arena the socialists showed a much greater capacity to mobilize, even to take to the streets, than the communists had anticipated. Mário Soares was tougher than even his friends had expected. As Cunhal recognized later, the communists "badly evaluated the situation in the armed forces and were overoptimistic as to the outcome of the internal conflicts within the military." The group associated with Prime Minister Colonel Vasco Gonçalves became increasingly isolated as the summer wore on. Close to the PCP, the Gonçalvistas had established formidable bases of power. They had dominated the office of the prime minister and the fifth division of the general staff, the coordinating agency for propaganda and indoctrination that was responsible for the "cultural dynamization" program both within the armed forces and throughout the country. The ministry of "social communication," like the labor ministry, had been directed by military men close to the PCP. After March the Gonçalvistas had dominated the commission established to dismantle the secret police—a key position because of the access that it afforded to voluminous secret police files. And under the direction of Gonçalvist Commander Almada Contreiras, an intelligence and counterintelligence agency— the SCDI—had been established.

But by mid-summer the initiative passed to a second group of leftists within the MFA. Associated with the name of Major Melo Antunes, that faction considered the armed forces an essential instrument in the revolutionary process. But they objected to the vanguard role usurped by the Gonçalvists. They believed that a broader base of social support than that provided by the PCP was essential if the MFA was not to place itself in opposition to the majority of the population. Collaboration with the political parties was deemed necessary if an orderly and peaceful transition to socialism was to be achieved. Melo Antunes, a Gramscian Marxist, was the main political articulator for the group that became associated with his name. It was a broad group that had elicited support in the central and southern military regions commanded by Colonel Pezerant and Colonel Charais, early members of the MFA who were close to Melo Antunes.

To the left of both Melo Antunes and the PCP-influenced Gonçalvists stood a populist radical group with fuzzy ideological views and military support. Associated with Otelo de Carvalho, it dominated the command structure of COPCON and several of the key regiments in the Lisbon area, especially the light artillery and the military police. Opposed to political parties, including the PCP, the military populists stood for a vaguely defined "people's power." The power of the populists was undermined by the indiscipline that populism wrought in the ranks. COPCON became no more than a coordinating agency. The growth of political passions at the unit level undermined its effectiveness so that the troops under its nominal command disaggregated into their component parts. The most radical units tended to become the most chaotic, and communist attempts to subvert the more disciplined units, especially the commandos, failed miserably when the tough and popular commando colonel won over his troops in the consequent showdown.

It was a fourth group in the army, little noticed at the time, that was most active behind the scenes as the summer drew to a close. Known at times as the operationals, the group was composed of officers who represented the professional interests of the officer corps—a current of opinion, of course, that had been a powerful element in the original captain's movement. A leading figure in the group was Colonel Ramalho Eanes, the future president of Portugal.

Several factors beyond the PCP's control help to explain the communists' behavior during that critical period. The party expanded very rapidly after its legalization in the spring of 1974. From a rump clandestine organization directed by a leadership that lived in exile, it grew to over 100,000 by the summer of 1975. Few of the newcomers had received the ideological indoctrination or had accumulated the experience within party organizations that would have tempered them into a reliable and disciplined force. Many of the rank and file were to the left of the party leadership, and tensions developed between "new" and "old" communists. According to Cunhal's retrospective criticism, the new communists were highly sectarian, intolerant, and indiscreet, hindering them from making friends and influencing people. The rapidly moving political situation in Portugal thus caught the PCP in a state of suspension, no longer a sleek clandestine organization but not yet a mass party.

Second, the large and noisy factions of the far left continued to agitate during these months, and events, such as the nationalization of the banks, the land seizures, the takeover of *República* and the Lisbon Catholic radio station, often moved faster under grass-roots pressure than the Central Committee of the PCP might have wished. Cunhal was right in believing that the staying power of the far leftist factions was limited, but toward the end of the summer, despite his constant criticism of those "verbalists," the PCP entered into a "revolutionary front" with the extreme left and was so linked when the November showdown took place.

The demands that "international" solidarity placed on the Portuguese communists may explain this misalliance. But it is impossible to be certain. Nevertheless, there can be no doubt that as early as August 1975 Cunhal was urging caution on the Central Committee of the PCP (see the "full" text of his intervention at the Central Committee meeting of August 10, 1975, in *Documentos Políticos do Partido Communista Portûques,* Maio/Novembro 1975, Edições Avante, 1976, pp. 129-165). Yet in October he led the PCP into its reckless front with the previously despised far left factionalists—an action that further alienated many Portuguese and helped to consolidate a very broad-based coalition of forces against the communists. The PCP has never hidden its belief that the Soviet Union is the "sun," to use Cunhal's word, of the communist movement. And it is at least worth noting that the behavior of the PCP between August and November 1975 provided a convenient smokescreen that concealed the beginning of large-scale Soviet and Cuban intervention in Angola. The communists abandoned their new "allies" when the confrontation occurred in November.

The center and the democratic right acted with great skill and restraint, far beyond what the communists might have expected from the continuing high jinks of the exiled General Spínola. As far as one can tell, the anticommunist military in Portugal was scrupulous in maintaining distance between itself and those dedicated to the return of the old regime. Moreover, on several occasions when large-scale violence might have been precipitated that could have discredited and split the anticommunist alliance formed among socialists, noncommunist leftists, and moderates in the military and civilian and church leaders in central and northern Portugal, caution and restraint prevailed. Perhaps the most dangerous moment occurred when large numbers of Alentejan workers besieged the constituent assembly and members of the government in the national assembly building in Lisbon. The commandos wanted to clear out the crowd, but they were held back by the president, General Costa Gomes, who, despite his equivocal behavior on many other matters, was not prepared to preside over plunging Portugal into civil war. The caution and the defensive strategy of the noncommunist military paid off when officerless, radical soldiers in the paratroop corps led the "left" uprising that provided the excuse for the anticommunist alliance under the command of Colonel Eanes to crush them on November 25, 1975.

Finally, it must be noted that the confused situation in the country allowed for effective action by agents provocateurs. Little information has yet to appear about that aspect of the Portuguese situation, but there can be no doubt that foreign intelligence operatives from the NATO countries were very active in Portugal between June and November 1975. The sudden emergence (and sudden disappearance) of a "revolutionary" movement within the ranks, for instance, is remarkably similar in form and impact to the sergeants' "movement" in Brazil in 1964 that helped to precipitate a coup by conservative generals and politicians. In Portugal, as might have been anticipated, the movement produced a similar sobering effect on the Portuguese officer corps—even leftist officers were affected. It is perhaps only accidental that the two leading officials in the United States embassy at that time, Frank Carlucci, the ambassador, and Herbert Okum, the deputy chief of mission, were both "old Brazil hands."

In any event, it was the isolation of the PCP among the populace, together with the isolation of the Gonçalvists within the military, that made possible the formation of a temporary alliance of anticommunist forces after August 1975.[12] On November 25, 1975, the alliance delivered the coup de grâce to the dream of revolution so avidly espoused a few months before by Alvaro Cunhal and his allies.

7.

After November 1975 the revolutionary moment passed. The compromise acceded to by the political parties during the height of the radical military's influence was undone, and a constitutional regime was established. Despite the strong socialist phraseology of the constitution, the regime that was institutionalized in 1976 was not substantially different from the Western mainstream. A first constitutional government was formed under the leadership of Mário Soares, whose Socialist party retained its plurality in the April 1976 national elections. General Ramalho Eanes, the military mastermind of November 25, was elected president of the republic by an overwhelming majority in June. But political party rule proved rocky indeed. By 1978 President Eanes was forced to summon nonparty figures to form governments when the political parties proved incapable of either forming coalitions or of governing alone. And those nonparty governments failed too, with the result that national elections were again scheduled for late 1979.

Despite the experiences of 1975, the PCP retained a strong hold on its faithful. In the April 1976 national assembly elections the party gained 14.6 percent of the vote (as opposed to 12.5 percent in 1975, although at that time the MDP had fielded candidates and attracted 4 percent of the vote). The lowest communist turnout was recorded in the presidential election, when the communist candidate received only 365,371 votes, or 7.2 percent of the votes cast. Nevertheless, the communists did well in the municipal elections of December 1976, holding onto their proportion of the vote in face of a sharp rise in abstentions (34.9 percent of the electorate abstained in December 1976 as opposed to a mere 8.2 percent in April 1975).[13]

The loyalty of the PCP's electorate is significant: Despite the fact that the proportional electoral share of the democratic parties has remained relatively uniform, the number of votes cast has steadily fallen. And the inability of the democratic parties to form stable governments and deal with the chronic economic and social problems of Portugal has not aided their popularity.

The Communist party has taken its setbacks to heart and used the period since its ouster from power to retrench and consolidate. Cunhal has never been convinced that Portugal's social and economic structures could support liberal democracy. Not enough time has elapsed to validate his prognostication, although he may well be an optimist if he thinks that the failure of Portuguese democracy would work to the advantage of the communists. Much more likely may be a recurrence of the polarization and interregional violence that marred the summer of 1975.

NOTES

1. Figures on comparative military expenditures were taken from *World Military Expenditures and Arms Trade, 1963-1973* (U. S. Arms Control and Disarmament Agency, Publication 74, G.P.O., Washington, D.C., 1975) and *The Military Balance* (International Institute for Strategic Studies, London, 1973, 1974, 1975). For details of the origins of the MFA, see Avelino Rodrigues, Cesario Borga, and Mario Cardoso, *O Movimento dos Capitães e o 25 de Abril* (Lisbon, 1974) and George Grayson, "Portugal and the Armed Forces Movement," *Orbis,* XIX (Summer 1975), vol. 1, pp. 335-378.

2. For useful background on the PCP, see Arnold Hottinger, "The Rise of Portugal's Communists," *Problems of Communism* XXIV (July-August 1975); Eusebio Mujal-León, "The PCP and the Portuguese Revolution," *Problems of Communism* XXVI (January-February 1977); Eusebio Mujal-León, "Communism and Revolution in Portugal," *Eurocommunism and Detente,* ed. Rudolf L. Tökés (New York, 1979); and *A Report on West European Communist Parties, Prepared by the Foreign Affairs and National Defense Division of the Congressional Research Service* (Library of Congress), submitted by Senator Edward W. Brooke to the Committee on Appropriations, U. S. Senate, June 1977, committee print.

3. All electoral returns cited throughout are from Nuno Vitorino and Jorge Gaspar, *As Eleições de 25 Abril: Geografia e imagen dos Partidos* (Lisbon, 1976).

4. Alvaro Cunhal claimed a party membership of 115,000 in November 1976; see Alvaro Cunhal, *A Revolução Portuguesa o Passado e o Futura* (Lisbon, 1976), p. 402. U.S. intelligence sources put the figure at close to 50,000: *CIA Factbook,* p. 107, cited in *A Report on West European Communist Parties,* cited above.

5. A good account of this period can be found in *Insight on Portugal: The Year of the Captains,* by the Insight Team of the (London) Sunday Times (London, 1975). Also see Kenneth Maxwell, "The Thorns of the Portuguese Revolution," *Foreign Affairs* (January 1976).

6. The full texts of this and other documents of the period can be found in *Textos Historicos da Revolução* (organized and with an introduction by Orlando Neves, 3 volumes, Lisbon, 1974, 1975, 1976).

7. See especially E. di Freitas, J. F. de Almeida as M. V. Cabral, *Modalidades de penetração do capitalismo na agricultura: Estructuras agrárias em Portugal continental 1950-1970* (Lisbon, 1976); and Massimo Livi Bacci, *A Century of Portuguese Fertility* (Princeton, 1971).

8. Alvaro Cunhal, *Pela Revolucao Democratica e Nacional* (Lisbon, July 23, 1975). See especially pp. 7-10.

9. Alvaro Cunhal, *Radicalismo Pequeno Burqûes da Facada Socialista* (Lisbon, 1974), p. 82.

10. *A Revolução Portuguesa: O Passado e o Futuro* (Lisbon, 1976), p. 383.

11. *L'Europeo* (Milan, June 15, 1975).

12. For a good account of the so-called resistance, see José Gomes Mota, *A Resistência* (Lisbon, 1976).

13. These conclusions are drawn from the PCP's analysis of the elections, *Dossier Eleicóes* (Lisbon, 1977) and Cunhal's blunt self-criticism in *A Revolução Portuguesa,* especially p. 382, et seg.

Appendix 1. *Communist Electoral Strength, 1975-1976*
Percentages by District

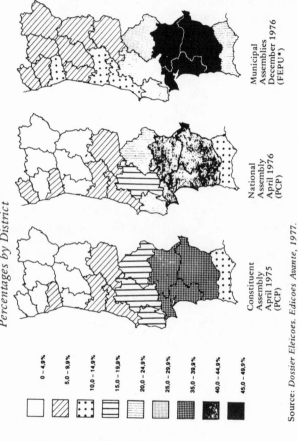

Constituent Assembly April 1975 (PCP)

National Assembly April 1976 (PCP)

Municipal Assemblies December 1976 (FEPU*)

0 – 4,9%

5,0 – 9,9%

10,0 – 14,9%

15,0 – 19,9%

20,0 – 24,9%

25,0 – 29,9%

35,0 – 39,9%

40,0 – 44,9%

45,0 – 49,9%

Source: *Dossier Eleicoes. Edicoes Avante, 1977.*

*United Peoples Electoral Front

Appendix 2

Election Results

Party	April 1975 Constitutional Assembly		April 1976 National Assembly		June 1976 Presidential			December 1976 Municipal		
	% of Vote	Deputies	% of Vote	Deputies	Cand.	Vote	%	Party	% of Vote	Deputies
PS (Partido Socialista)	17.9	116	35.0	107	Eanes	2,967,414	61.5	PS	33.2	691
PPD (Partido Popular Democrática)	26.4	80	24.0	73	Otelo	769,192	16.5	PSD (Partido Social Demócrata) formerly PPD	24.3	623
PCP (Partido Communista Português)	12.5	30	14.6	40	Azevedo	692,382	14.4			
CDS (Centro Democrático Social)	7.6	16	15.9	40	Pato (PCP)	365,374	7.6	FEPU (Frente Electoral Povo Unido: includes PCP, MDP/CDF, FSP)	17.7	267
MDP (Movimento Democrático Português)	4.1	5	-	-				CDS	16.6	117
								CDUP (Grupos de Dinamicao Unidade Popular)	2.5	5
Voter participation	91.7		83.3				75.4		64.5	

Source: Eusebio M. Mujal-León, "Communism and Revolution in Portugal," *Eurocommunism and Detente* (edited by Rudolf L. Tőkés, N.Y.U. Press, New York, 1979).

Appendix 3

POLITICAL PROFILE OF THE CENTRAL COMMITTEE OF THE PORTUGUESE COMMUNIST PARTY, 1975

Status	Total Number of Years in Party	Mean	Total Number of Years on Central Committee	Mean	Total Number of Years in Hiding	Mean	Total Number of Years as Prisoner	Mean
22 Full Members (*efectivos*)	730	33.2	395[1]	19.8	584	26.6	249.2	11.3
12 Alternate Members (*suplentes*)[2]	213	17.8	33.1	2.8	154	12.8	51.0	4.3
All Members (*efectivos* and *suplentes*)	943	27.7	428.1	12.6	738	21.7	300.2[3]	8.8

[1] This total figure, and the average that accompanies it, does not include information on long-time Central Committee members Americo Leal and Blanqui Teixeira.

[2] It has been reported that there are actually 14 alternate Central Committee members. If this is the case, *Diario de Noticias* failed to publish data on two members.

[3] In speeches before the October 1974 congress, party leaders often referred to the full and alternate members of the Central Committee having spent a total of 308 years in prison. The difference between that figure and the one presented here may be explained by the possible lack of data on two alternate members.

Source: Compiled from data published in *Diario de Noticias*, October 21, 1974, p. 12.

Source: George W. Grayson, "Portugal and the Armed Forces Movement," *Orbis*, vol. XIX, Summer 1975, no. 2, pp. 335-378.

Bernard E. Brown

AFTERWORD: IDEOLOGICAL FERMENT AND FOUNDATIONS

That the communist parties of Western Europe have changed, especially in the past three decades, is apparent to all the contributors to this volume. Of all the communist parties surveyed, only the Portuguese party remains close to the model of hard-core Leninism, openly contemptuous of parliamentary democracy and other "bourgeois" forms of liberty. But even the PCP was forced to adapt itself to new circumstances after the passage of the "revolutionary moment" in 1975. There is disagreement over the extent and the depth of the change among the coauthors of this volume; but no one contests the fact that the communist parties here examined have evolved. Nor should such a conclusion occasion any surprise. The communist parties of Italy, Spain, and France (to take the three parties of Western Europe most often referred to as Eurocommunist) seek to win the support of the working class and as large a percentage as possible of the general electorate. In competing with other political parties, the communists must pitch their appeals to societies that are themselves undergoing rapid change. All Western societies have been transformed since World War II; it is unthinkable that political parties—including communist political parties—could remain indifferent to and unaffected by that underlying social transformation.

Many of the coauthors of this volume have alluded to the nature of the ongoing transformation of West European society. Since World War II, there has been a substantial increase in productivity and in the standard of living of the employed working class. There have also been significant expansions of the salaried middle class and in the number of intellectuals, professionals, and people engaged in providing services; an explosive growth of scientific knowledge and of the universities whose function is to advance and transmit that knowledge; and a great increase in social mobility. In addition, an almost universal ownership of television sets enables political leaders to enjoy direct access to the electorate. Any political party that ignores those trends or fails to adapt its doctrine to the society affected by those trends will condemn itself to unpopularity and powerlessness.

To return to the central preoccupation of the conference in which the coauthors participated, has the evolution of the European communist parties affected their "ideological foundations"? On the basis of the contributions to this volume, we may identify at least *three* major respects in which European communist parties have changed significantly.

First, the Soviet model has been called into question and in some cases flatly rejected. Spanish and Italian communists talk openly of Stalinist perversions; and some even revive the Trotskyist argument (without acknowledging its author) that a bureaucratic stratum in the Soviet Union blocks the movement toward socialism and democracy. Even the French communists, whose criticism of the Soviet model has been rather mild, affirm that they would not simply transpose the Soviet system to France. Jean Elleinstein has gone so far as to call the Soviet Union an "antimodel," whereas Georges Marchais loyally continues to appraise the results of the Soviet experience as "globally positive"; but even Marchais has joined in the criticism of the Soviet Union, especially its treatment of dissenters. Virtually every aspect of Soviet reality has come under fire from one or another of the European communist parties—the grimness of daily life, the inability to satisfy consumer needs, the powerlessness of the workers and trade unions, and, above all, the lack of elementary freedom (to criticize the leadership, to express discontent, to travel abroad, and to emigrate). No orthodox communist party ever breathed a word of criticism of the Soviet Union or questioned its socialist character before the death of Stalin.

Second, the European communist parties—again, in varying degrees—have also dissociated themselves from specific foreign policy decisions of the Soviet Union. Spanish and Italian communists have even occasionally delivered themselves of favorable comments about NATO, openly speculating that socialist experimentation might be favored if Western Europe continued to be shielded from the direct intrusion of the Soviet Union and its armed forces. Bringing up the rear, as usual, are the French communists, who alone endorsed the Soviet invasion and occupation of Afghanistan in December 1979. But the French communists "disapproved" of Soviet intervention in Czechoslovakia in 1968, reaffirming their criticism even as they rallied to the support of Russian policy in Afghanistan.

Third, all Western communist parties (with the possible exception of the Portuguese party, among those surveyed in this volume) have proclaimed their attachments to parliamentary democracy, freedom of criticism, and pluralism of political parties. It is true that the Soviet Union also puts itself forward as a "real" democracy (in contrast to fake bourgeois democracy) and claims to guarantee democratic civil liberties. It is also true that some East European regimes (for example, East Germany, Bulgaria, and Poland) boast pluralistic party systems—by which they mean the front parties created or tolerated by ruling communist parties as a means of appealing to peasants and Catholics in particular. But most West European communists make it clear that they dissent from the Russian view of democracy, liberty, and pluralism and affirm that they will avoid the mistakes and authoritarian practices of the Soviet Union. Again, some caution is required in dealing with these arguments. Georges Marchais, for example, has actually cited the East German, Bulgarian, and Polish regimes as valid examples of a "pluralistic" party system. Nonetheless, it is striking that Carrillo, Berlinguer, and even Marchais have attributed so much importance, at least on a theoretical level, to traditional democratic liberties previously denounced as merely formal or fraudulent.

A rough measure of the extent of the above changes—referred to by most of the coauthors as Eurocommunism—is offered by comparing "Eurocommunism" with the phenomenon of "popular democracy" just after World War II. At that time communist leaders throughout Eastern Europe asserted that socialism could be achieved by democractic means, without having to go through the transitional stage of "dictatorship of the proletariat." Much of the contemporary "Eurocommunist" discussion of democracy, liberty, and pluralism echoes the doctrinal innovation of the East European communist parties from 1945 through 1947—a resemblance that makes some noncommunists wonder today about the authenticity of the new terminology. But in the postwar theory of "popular democracy" there was never any open criticism of either the Soviet model or of Soviet foreign policy. There is a difference!

The three points of change within the European communist movement may be related to the previously-described evolution of West European society. It is not possible for Western communist parties to keep their supporters completely insulated from outside contacts. As productivity and the standard of living go up, workers become more mobile; they emulate the life styles of their middle-class compatriots. The Soviet Union has become more accessible; and for most visitors, even the ideologically committed, the pure textbook version of Soviet accomplishments does not withstand first-hand observation. Perhaps the most important breach in the wall dividing working-class and middle-class culture has been made by television, which brings political opinions and programs directly into the living room. More open societies have called forth more open political parties—including more open communist parties.

Now we reach the heart of the analytic problem. Are the changes here identified as Eurocommunism superficial or profound, stylistic or substantive, tactical or strategic? Have changes in ideology gone so deep as to strike at or in some way alter the "foundations"? On the basis of the essays in this volume, some tentative answers will be ventured.

Tocqueville once observed that the political analyst is concerned not with individuals, but with classes of individuals. Similarly, it may be suggested that Eurocommunist parties should be viewed as organized political forces in competition with other organized political forces. The measure of change within European communist parties is to be found in their relations with other parties engaged in the same process of appealing to and mobilizing an electorate and a people. In the specific circumstances of the European political battle, the chief organized competitors of the communist parties have been and remain the social democratic parties; in addition, the communist parties have always been confronted by a diffuse, fitfully-organized anarchist movement with considerable appeal to workers and intellectuals. The question may now be reformulated and further refined: Have the Eurocommunist parties, in their recent evolutions, moved any closer to either one of their historic rivals—the social democratic parties or the anarchist movement?

The answer from the communists themselves is: No, in most cases, a thundering no. The reasons given by the Eurocommunists are of critical importance in assessing the extent and the significance of recent changes. To answer criticism from hard-liners within their own parties, communist leaders say that they reject social democracy root and branch. But if the communists now accept parliamentary democracy, civil liberties, and pluralism of parties, what distinguishes them from the previously-abhorred social democrats? The explanation given by communist leaders is instructive. (1) Social democratic parties subordinate socialism to civil liberties, that is, their attitudes toward bourgeois democracy are "formal," drained of revolutionary content. Communists have a "dynamic" view of these liberties; they will use them in order to achieve socialism, whereas social democrats allow the capitalist class full freedom to sabotage their policies. (2) The leaders and militants of the social democratic parties are drawn from the middle class; hence they cannot be defenders of working-class interests. Only the communist parties are authentic expressions of the interests of the workers. (3) Above all, social democratic parties are "reformist"; they seek not to transform capitalism but to "administer" it. As a general rule, the greater the emphasis placed by communists on the importance of democratic liberties, the more vigorous are their denunciations of the social democratic parties.

Equally vigorous are denunciations by Eurocommunists of the anarchist movement, even as they appropriate some cherished anarchist notions such as workers' councils. The French Communist party in particular now puts itself forward as the party of "socialist autogestion"—meaning the control of enterprise and of society by the workers themselves. But a policy of autogestion, in the view of the French communists, makes it all the more important to guard against uncoordinated activity and the "cult of spontaneity." The workers, more than ever, need the guidance of "their" party in order to take control of their destiny. Thus Eurocommunist borrowing from the cultures of both social democracy and anarchism has not so far prepared the way for the unification of the three currents. Eurocommunist leaders and theorists, on the contrary, have stepped up attacks on their social democratic and anarchist rivals, even as they use some of the same language.

The traditional ideological landmarks of Eurocommunist parties have almost disappeared, which adds to the confusion of communist party militants, to say nothing of outside observers. Take, for example, the three towering figures through whom all European communist parties defined themselves after World War II: Marx-Lenin-Stalin. What remains of this holy trinity in the ideology of Eurocommunist parties today? Beginning with the most recent of these idols, every communist party in Europe today repudiates Stalin and Stalinism in varying degrees. All Eurocommunist parties now admit and condemn the terror and repression inherent in Stalinism. Explanations of the Stalinist phenomenon run the gamut— aberrant personality, the backwardness of Russian society, and the creation of a bureaucratic stratum that perverted socialism. There is some disagreement about whether all traces of Stalinism have been extirpated in the Soviet Union today; but all agree that Stalinism is an example to be avoided.

Can Eurocommunist parties now be described in ideological terms as "Marxist-Leninist"? Even here, the horror of Stalinism has led some communist thinkers to accept the analysis of such hated enemies as Trotskyists, anarchists, and even liberals. Once Stalinism is seen as a structure of power, the question must be raised whether the "germs" of that structure can be found in Leninism. Many Eurocommunists stoutly resist such implications. Some Eurocommunists have rediscovered Lenin's tolerance of a measure of discussion and criticism within the party and condemn Stalin for his departure from Leninist practice. Others—especially among the Italian and Spanish parties—have expressed reservations concerning at least some aspects of Leninism. Appeals to the authority of Lenin no longer yield clear answers. Many militants now wonder whether Leninism means tight control of the party by its leaders or the reverse; alliances with social democrats or ideological war on social democrats. Nor is Marx any longer—if he ever was—a guide to party policy. In the course of dropping the phrase "dictatorship of the proletariat" from party programs, Eurocommunist parties have called into question the Marxist theory of class struggle. To argue that the state might be used to achieve progressive purposes and to plan economic development means that the state is not exclusively an instrument of class exploitation and is not merely the executive committee of the bourgeoisie.

Are Eurocommunist parties now in a state of ideological confusion, without any landmarks at all for the guidance of militants? Even though the old trinity of Marx-Lenin-Stalin has been shattered, the Eurocommunist parties remain ideologically distinct from their competitors and rivals. References to Marx and Lenin may be somewhat hazy, but central ideological concepts remain in place and are sufficiently well understood to be able to serve as guidelines for leaders, militants, and voters. The major components of this ideology are: (1) the notion of class struggle and of the hegemony of the working class in guiding the entire society toward socialism; (2) the notion that only one party—the communist party— expresses the interests of the working class and is capable of leading it; (3) the notion that the vanguard party—the *only* party of the working class—must be organized "effectively" so as to be able to defend workers' interests and achieve socialism (the principle of democratic centralism), and (4) the notion that the vanguard party, through its scientific analysis of society, has superior knowledge.

If any of the above notions were to be repudiated, then the distinctiveness of the communist parties would be threatened. As long as the underlying connection between a hegemonic working class and its only vanguard is maintained, Eurocommunist leaders can afford to indulge in any amount of criticism of Stalin and even guarded criticism of Lenin and Marx; and they can justify any political tactic, including the advocacy of an alliance with the Socialist party (as in France), or of an alliance with the Christian Democrats (as in Italy), or a break with the Socialist party (as in France since 1977). They can also either support or condemn specific Soviet foreign policy decisions, like the invasion and occupation of Afghanistan. In a sense, Eurocommunist leaders are resuscitating Lenin's flexible tactics in dealing with (and using) opponents and allies before and shortly after coming to power.

Even if it is granted that the working class is or should be hegemonic and has only one vanguard, one question cannot be avoided: What kind of society will that vanguard create once in power? Vague affirmations that the workers will somehow control their destiny or that "industrial democracy" (whose structures are never defined) will replace capitalism are requests for a blank check. The liberal (or "capitalist") societies of Western Europe are a reality, as is the Soviet Union. It has been the historical mission of social democracy to introduce progressive reforms of capitalism, or the market economy, and the historical mission of communist parties to create one-party systems on the Soviet model. Eurocommunists today condemn the "authoritarian socialism" of the Soviet Union (as it has been termed by the French communists); they reject liberalism and capitalism; they denounce social democracy; and they disdain anarchism. What remains is a historical void. Eurocommunists have a coherent ideology—but it is an ideology that boils down to participation in or seizure of *power*, without any positive indication of the kind of society to be created through the use of that power. The distance between the communist parties and both social democracy and anarchism is undiminished and as unbridgeable as ever. Eurocommunists have abandoned much of the phraseology of Marxism-Leninism-Stalinism; they have condemned in varying degrees the consequences of that ideology in the Soviet Union; but they have held fast to its internal logic. The ideology of West European communist parties has been in ferment; but the "foundations" are intact.

INDEX

NOTES ON CONTRIBUTORS

Bernard E. Brown is professor of political science at the City University of New York (Graduate School and Lehman). He received the Ph.D. from Columbia University and taught previously at SUNY (Buffalo) and Vanderbilt University. His recent publications include *Protest in Paris: Anatomy of a Revolt* and *Intellectuals and Other Traitors.*

R. V. Burks is professor of history at Wayne State University in Detroit. His principal work is entitled *The Dynamics of Communism in Eastern Europe,* Princeton, 1961; Westport, Connecticut, 1976. He is also the author of approximately forty articles dealing with European communism, Eastern Europe, and the Soviet Union. From 1961 to 1965 he was policy director at Radio Free Europe in Munich.

Franco Ferrarotti was awarded the first full chair of sociology that was established in the Italian university system in 1960 at Rome University. He has published extensively in the field of industrial urban sociology and social theory. He was professor of industrial sociology at Columbia University, New York, in 1962, fellow at the Center for Advanced Study in the Behavioral Sciences, Palo Alto, in 1964, professor at the Graduate Center of CUNY in 1971 and at Boston University in 1974, directeur d'etudes at the "Ecole des Hautes Etudes en Sciences Sociales" in Paris in 1978; chief of the Social Factors Section at the OEEC, now OECD, in Paris in 1958-1959. A member of the Italian parliament as an independent deputy, he did not stand for reelection in order to devote himself entirely to teaching and research. He has published in the United States, among other articles and essays, *Toward the Social Production of the Sacred,* San Diego, 1976; *An Alternative Sociology,* Irvington, New York, 1979. *Max Weber and the Destiny of Reason* is scheduled for publication by Sharpe, New York.

Annie Kriegel is university professor of political sociology at the University of Paris, Nanterre. Professor Kriegel has taught at the universities of Reims, Bruges, Geneva, Chicago, Harvard, Michigan, and Montreal, among others. Ancienne élève de l'Ecole Normale Supérieure, agrégée d'histoire, docteur des Lettres, she has published many books on the working class, French and international socialism and communism, and minority affairs. Among them are *Aux origines du communisme francais* (1964), *Les communistes francais* (1968), *Les Juifs et le monde moderne* (1977), *Un autre communisme?* (1977), and *Le communisme au jour le jour* (1979).

Juan J. Linz, Pelatiah Perit professor of political and social science at Yale University, is former chairman of the

Committee on Political Sociology of the International Socio-
logical Association (ISA) and the International Political
Science Association (IPSA). His publications include *Crisis,
Breakdown and Reequilibration,* an introductory volume to
The Breakdown of Democratic Regimes. He has written with
Alfred Stepan "Totalitarian and Authoritarian Regimes" in
F. Greenstein and N. Polsby, eds., *Handbook of Political Sci-
ence* and has written essays on Spanish politics and society in
collective volumes edited by E. Allardt, R. Dahl, S.
Eisenstadt, G. Hermet, S. Huntington, and C. Moore; S. M.
Lipset, V. Lorwin, and J. Price; R. Rose; and others. He has
written monographs in Spanish on business and local elites
and has written a long essay in Italian on the work of Robert
Michels. His research on the sociology of fascist movements
has been published in W. Laqueur's *Reader's Guide to Fascism* and in a collective volume in *Who Were The Fascists?*

Kenneth Maxwell is a member of the History Department
and senior fellow at the Research Institute on International
Change at Columbia University. He is also the program director of The Tinker Foundation, Inc. An expert on Latin
American and Iberian affairs, he is a graduate of St. John's
College, Cambridge, and holds a Ph.D. from Princeton University. He has received fellowships from the Ford, Rockefeller, Gulbenkian, and John Simon Guggenheim Foundations and was a research fellow at the Newberry Library
(Chicago). Between 1971 and 1975 Professor Maxwell was a
member of the Institute for Advanced Study, Princeton. The
author of *Conflicts and Conspiracies: Brazil and Portugal,*
which became a best-seller in Brazil, and the forthcoming
Revolution in Portugal and Angola, Professor Maxwell has
also contributed numerous articles to scholarly journals. His
writing on contemporary affairs has appeared in *Foreign Affairs, The New York Times, The Los Angeles Times, The New
York Review of Books, The International Herald Tribune,*
and other publications.

Eusebio M. Mujal-León is assistant professor of government at Georgetown University in Washington, D.C. He holds a Ph.D. in political science from the Massachusetts Institute of Technology and was the recipient of an international doctoral fellowship award from the Social Science Research Council. He has published numerous articles and chapters on the Spanish and Portuguese left. His forthcoming book is entitled *Communism and Political Change in Spain.*

George Schwab is professor of history at the City College of New York and a member of the doctoral faculty at the City University Graduate School. He received the Ph.D. from Columbia University and has also taught there. A member of the Executive Board of the National Committee on American Foreign Policy, Professor Schwab is the recipient of numerous grants. He has written on great power rivalry, legal and political theory, and German history. His writings on Carl Schmitt have just been published in Japanese.

Rudi Supek was professor of sociology at the University of Zagreb. He received the Ph.D. in psychology under Piaget in Paris in 1952 and the Ph.D. h.c. in sociology at Uppsala in 1977. During the war he was active in the French resistance movement and was deported to the concentration camp at Buchenwald in Germany. He was the coeditor of the review "Praxis" and the president of the Korčula Summer School. He has written many books in the field of psychology, sociology, and Marxism. His foreign publications include *Etatisme et Autogestion* (collection), Paris, 1973, *Soziologie und Sozialismus*, Freiburg, 1966, *Jugoslawien denkt anders* (with B. Bošnjak), collection, Wien, 1971, *Self-governing Socialism* (with B. Horvat and M. Marković), I-II, New York, 1975, *Beyond the Crisis,* ed. N. Birnbaum, a contribution, Cambridge, 1976, *Arbeiter Selbstverwaltung und sozialistische Demokratie,* Hannover, 1976, and *Socialismo e Autogestione,* ed. L. Basso, Milano, 1978.

G. L. Ulmen is codirector of the Chinese History Project, Columbia University. His graduate work in the sociology and history of "Asiatic" societies, with particular emphasis on China and Russia, was begun at the Far Eastern and Russian Institute at the University of Washington, Seattle, continued at Harvard University, and completed at Columbia University. His publications include *The Science of Society* and *Society and History.*

DATE DUE

11TH 45-102   PRINTED IN U.S.A.